Unless a Grain of Wheat

GLOBAL LIBRARY

The story of Christian Africa has often been told to fit the Western colonial enterprise, erroneously suggesting that Africa's version was simply the other side of the colonial political coin. In this volume, we have a refreshingly readable account – one that makes good use of oral theologizing – to illustrate how African initiated churches worked with a foreign mission, that is, the Mennonites from North America, as an example of what World Christianity must look like, especially when it comes to theological education as a grassroots collaborative venture. This is a volume that must be on the reading lists of theological institutions that seek to teach mission from a World Church perspective, but with Africa, as one of Christianity's new heartlands in view.

J. Kwabena Asamoah-Gyadu, PhD, FGA
President & Baëta-Grau Professor of African Christianity and Pentecostalism,
Trinity Theological Seminary, Legon, Ghana

This wonderful volume hosts a chorus of Mennonite and African Initiated Church voices that witness together to a rare encounter in mission history; a foreign missionary community and an indigenous faith community coming together for mutual edification in Bible study, worship, and friendship. Characterized by humility, honesty, and humor, these reflections suggest new possibilities for cross-cultural mission.

Thomas Hastings, PhD
Executive Director,
Overseas Ministries Study Center, Princeton, New Jersey, USA

In this partnership and over many years, Mennonites have remained humble, focused, resolute, authentic, determined, committed, and generous. In our collaboration together, there is no question of who is superior or inferior – resources have been shared and learning has been two-way. There is openness on both sides and there is sincerity of purpose.

The Most Rev. Daniel Okoh
General Superintendent,
Christ Holy Church International, Nigeria
International Chairman,
Organization of African Instituted Churches, Nairobi, Kenya

The long relationship between AICs and Mennonites is one of the greatest stories of Christian mission in the twentieth century.

Dana L. Robert, PhD
Truman Collins Professor of World Christianity and History of Mission
Director of the Center for Global Christianity and Mission,
Boston University School of Theology, Massachusetts, USA

This book gives insight into a significant chapter of modern church history. [It] deserves a warm welcome and careful attention.

Andrew F. Walls, PhD
Historian of Missions and World Christianity,
University of Edinburgh, Liverpool Hope University, UK
Akrofi-Christaller Institute, Akropong-Akuapem, Ghana

Unless a Grain of Wheat

*A Story of Friendship between
African Independent Churches and
North American Mennonites*

Edited by

**Thomas A. Oduro, Jonathan P. Larson,
and James R. Krabill**

GLOBAL LIBRARY

© 2021 Thomas A. Oduro, Jonathan P. Larson, and James R. Krabill

Published 2021 by Langham Global Library
An imprint of Langham Publishing
www.langhampublishing.org

Langham Publishing and its imprints are a ministry of Langham Partnership

Langham Partnership
PO Box 296, Carlisle, Cumbria, CA3 9WZ, UK
www.langham.org

ISBNs:
978-1-83973-271-3 Print
978-1-83973-573-8 ePub
978-1-83973-574-4 Mobi
978-1-83973-575-2 PDF

Thomas A. Oduro, Jonathan P. Larson, and James R. Krabill hereby assert their moral right to be identified as the Author of the General Editor's part in the Work in accordance with sections 77 and 78 of the Copyright, Designs and Patents Act 1988.

All rights reserved. No part of this publication may be reproduced, stored in a retrieval system or transmitted, in any form or by any means, electronic, mechanical, photocopying, recording or otherwise, without the prior written permission of the publisher or the Copyright Licensing Agency.

Requests to reuse content from Langham Publishing are processed through PLSclear. Please visit www.plsclear.com to complete your request.

All Scripture quotations, unless otherwise indicated, are taken from the Holy Bible, New International Version®, NIV®. Copyright ©1973, 1978, 1984, 2011 by Biblica, Inc.™ Used by permission of Zondervan.

Scripture quotations marked (ESV) are from The Holy Bible, English Standard Version® (ESV®), copyright © 2001 by Crossway, a publishing ministry of Good News Publishers. Used by permission. All rights reserved.

The Mennonite Church USA Archives has granted permission to publish Photo #s 4b, 32, 40, 46, and 47 in this volume from their Mennonite Board of Missions Photograph Collection. Ghana, 1969–1983. Box 3, Folder 44, Photo #s 18, 48, 60, 67, and 123. IV-10-7.2.

For all other photos, permission has been received from the photographers and subjects for the publication of the photos.

British Library Cataloguing-in-Publication Data
A catalogue record for this book is available from the British Library

ISBN: 978-1-83973-271-3

Cover & Book Design: projectluz.com

Langham Partnership actively supports theological dialogue and an author's right to publish but does not necessarily endorse the views and opinions set forth here or in works referenced within this publication, nor can we guarantee technical and grammatical correctness. Langham Partnership does not accept any responsibility or liability to persons or property as a consequence of the reading, use or interpretation of its published content.

Contents

Foreword xvii
    Andrew F. Walls

Preface xix
    Jonathan P. Larson

Introduction 1
    Thomas A. Oduro, Jonathan P. Larson, and James R. Krabill

Abbreviations 7

A Short History 9
    Wilbert R. Shenk

1 Tilling 23
    Preparing the Soil for Early Collaboration in Ghana and Beyond   23
        Francis A. Mills
    An Offer of Prayer   25
        Jim Shenk
    Worshiping with the Cherubim and Seraphim   28
        Lynda Hollinger-Janzen
    We Are Deepening the River of God's People in Africa   30
        Alphonse Godonou
    God-Centered Prosperity   31
        Phil Lindell Detweiler
    Love Your Grieving Neighbor as Yourself   33
        B. Harry Dyck
    Interpreting the Scriptures   35
        Julie Bender
    Pastoral Training and Pit Latrines   37
        Darrel Hostetler
    My Training Is for the Purpose of Training Others   38
        Esther Manyeyo Tawiah
    Grassroots Receptivity . . . Facilitated by a Churchman of Exceptional
    Faith and Courageous Vision   41
        David A. Shank

  Hospitality with a Flair 44
   Sherill Hostetter

  Guest Reflections: *Gilbert Ansre and Miriam Adeney* 46

2 Sowing 49

  Reading the Bible through the Lens of the Spirit 49
   Bryan Born

  Prayer Is Costly 52
   Don Rempel Boschman

  Tata Maka's Journey to Matatiele . . . and Ours 54
   Joe Sawatzky

  Breaking Down Barriers 56
   B. Harry Dyck

  Relationship Building Was Key to Our Success 58
   Ezekiel Nartey

  We Had So Much to Learn! 59
   David A. Shank

  My Impression of Mennonites 61
   Thomas A. Oduro

  Guest Reflections: *Darrell Whiteman* 63

3 Germination 67

  The Christian Tree 67
   Stan Nussbaum

  When I Was Chosen as a Preacher, I Wanted to Understand More of
  God's Word 69
   Alphonse Kobli Beugré

  Good Friday 2.0 71
   Jonathan P. Larson

  Only God Knows the Ultimate Results of Our Time and Ministry ... 72
   Marian Hostetler

  The Support Group We Created Gave Us Dignity, Despite Our
  Physical Struggles 74
   Hortense Assah

  It Is Impossible for a Man to Be Faithful to One Woman 76
   Rudy Dirks

  "Without Scriptural Foundations, How Are the Spirits Tested and
  Discerned?" 78
   Isaac Wontumi

Dissecting Material and Spiritual Realities Gave Me Blinders ... 79
Jonathan Rudy

The Sweetness of Unity in Christ ... 81
Veliswa Mbambo

I Came to Appreciate the Power of the Spoken Word ... 83
Ronald Sawatzky

Guest Reflections: *Amos Yong and Allan H. Anderson* ... 85

4 Growth ... 87

The Entire Body of Christ Carried the Woman's Pain That Day ... 87
Anna Sawatzky

I Soaked in the Memories of the Prophet in the Land ... 90
Rachel Hilty Friesen

Learning How to Pray the Jesus Way ... 92
Willard E. Roth

My Mennonite Friends Launched Me on My Life of Ministry ... 94
Humphrey Akogyeram

A Few Things I Learned about Sexuality, Childbearing, Mosaic Law, and the Role of Women in AIC Church Life ... 96
Delores H. Friesen

A Tribute to Umfundisi Hlobisile – A Model for Women in Church Leadership ... 98
Sherill Hostetter

Guest Reflections: *T. John Padwick and Martine Audéoud* ... 101

5 Pollination ... 105

So . . . When Do You People Pray? ... 105
Grace Hostetter

Singing in Harmony with Bishop Motswaosele ... 108
Jim Bertsche

We Have Learned Together about Worship, Marriage, Prophecy, and Burnt Offerings ... 110
Morena Rankopo

In Honor of Isaac Dlamini – My Partner, Colleague, Language Teacher, and Best Friend ... 112
Darrel Hostetter

Mennonite Affirmation of Us Ended Our Feeling of Aloneness ... 115
Isaac Moshoeshoe

I Learned the Meeting Would Happen . . . Whatever Time It Actually Began ... 117
Garry Janzen

    Friendship Flowered between Us as We Prayed for Each Other 119
        Joseph Motswaosele
    A Powerful Healing Experience at Nima Temple 121
        Stan Friesen
    "These Are No Ordinary Clothes, but *Special* Clothes for Divine Work" ... 124
        Sandi McLaughlin and Elinor Miller
    They Came to Work *with* Us 127
        Thompson Mpongwana Adonis
    Guest Reflections: *Tanya Riches, Dana Robert, Jehu J. Hanciles* 130

6 Weeding 133
    Real Work Begins When the Task Is Given over in Prayer 133
        Rod Hollinger-Janzen
    Life Lessons from the "God Will Provide Barber Shop" 134
        Julie Bender
    The Challenge of Multiple – and Sometimes Conflicting – Stories 136
        R. Bruce Yoder
    Learning Discipleship and Self-Restraint 138
        Enole Ditsheko
    Teacher-Learner: Who Is Who? 141
        Irene Weaver with interviewer Lynda Hollinger-Janzen
    What Are We to Do with the Healing Stories of Jesus in the Gospels? .. 142
        Stan Friesen
    Guest Reflections: *Todd M. Johnson and Casely Essamuah* 147

7 Watering 149
    Sounds of Singing Soaked the Wooden Ceiling Beams, Wafting a
    Sweet Aroma 149
        Nathan Dirks
    Those Mennonites Who Came to Find Us Here Surprised Us 151
        Mokweni Thusang, Mashobo Baitsemole, Raletebele Kgangetsile,
        Kgosietsile Balefile, Raseleng Phalalo, Raditshipa Pope,
        Rasumako Dipapiso, Kegopotseng Thusang, Keganne Gabanatlhong,
        and Mosuwadibo Pope, with interviewer Jonathan P. Larson
    Standin' in the Need of Prayer 153
        James R. Krabill
    Bible Study Has Increased Our Confidence and Our Standing with Other
    Christian Churches 155
        Reuben Mgodeli

Leaning on the Cross 157
    Steve Wiebe-Johnson

I Shared a Long Journey of Discovery with Rev. Philip Mothetho,
Friend and Brother 160
    Tim Bertsche

There Was Nothing That Separated Our Spirits 162
    Albert Maphasa Setumo

Guest Reflections: *Daniel Okoh and James Kwesi Anquandah* ... 163

8 Harvest 169

Rejoicing that a Ghanaian Praise Song is Blessing North American
Mennonites 169
    Alice Roth

Like in Marriage, There Is a Profound Mystery That You Can't Explain ... 171
    Modeste Lévry Beugré

Spirit-Filled Faith . . . Where the Rubber Hits the Road 173
    Rene Hostetter

It Was Hard for the Mennonites We Met to Do the Dance Moves,
but They Wanted to Try 175
    Hlobisile Nxumalo

Sacred Oil, Rustle of Robes 176
    Jonathan P. Larson

Studying the History of the Church Opened My Eyes 179
    Michel Alokpo

The Silent, Invisible, and Mysterious Ways That God's Kingdom Grows ... 180
    Sharon Dirks

It Takes a Village to Bless a Child 183
    Jeanette Krabill

Guest Reflections: *Nicta Lubaale* 186

Partnerships Map 191
Additional Resources 193
Editors Biographies 203
Subject Index 205
People Index 215

List of Photographs

Photo 1: A church in Eastern Nigeria pleads in prayer for a family in need of healing. 13

Photo 2: Apostle Kalesanwu welcomes Ed and Irene Weaver to the Church of the Lord (Aladura) in Monrovia, Liberia 16

Photo 3: The Benin community health team embark on a visit to a project: Daniel Goldschmidt Nussbaumer, Saturnin Afaton, Rebecca Assani, and Lynda Hollinger-Janzen 18

Photo 4: Frank A. Mills in prayer and counseling ministry 25

Photo 5: Infant dedication 27

Photo 6: Worshipping with the Sacred Cherubim & Seraphim Society in Birmingham, England 29

Photo 7: Former students and then professors at the Benin Bible Institute: Bonaventure Akowanou, Antoine Codjo, Alphonse Godonou, and François Bangbade 30

Photo 8: Worship, Bible study, and fellowship in Pietermaritzburg, South Africa 32

Photo 9: Taking a break from a study session during a village visit. 34

Photo 10: The Good News Training Institute student body of church leaders 36

Photo 11: Bible training for practical, tentmaking village ministry. 38

Photo 12: "Julie and I became like sisters." Esther Tawiah. 40

Photo 13: Harry Henry delivers a message on God's mission as David Shank translates for an English-speaking audience 43

Photo 14: Alfred and Makeh Msibi served as host parents to the Darrel and Sherrill Hostetter family. 45

Photo 15: Don Rempel Boschman and Bishop Bolokwe worked together at training church pastors 53

Photo 16: Tea time with pastors!. 57

Photo 17: Ezekiel Nartey conducting a lay leaders Bible study in a local congregation. 58

Photo 18: Wilma and David Shank in Harrist worship 61

Photo 19: Thomas A. Oduro offering an opening prayer in an AIC worship service 62

Photo 20: Lesotho's Black Wattle tree 68

Photo 21: Alphonse with James Krabill and son Matthew on a village Bible study visit 70

Photo 22: Group Bible study session with Marian and Frank A. Udoh. . . . 73

Photo 23: "The Group of Disabled Persons gave us dignity, despite our physical struggles." Hortense Assah 75

Photo 24: A session of the "Married Couples' Fellowship" in Botswana. . . 77

Photo 25: "Without the Scriptures, how are the spirits to be tested?" Isaac Wontumi. 79

Photo 26: Babeh Nxumalo, in prayer and dance, conducting a healing ceremony. 80

Photo 27: Veliswa Mbambo, "Mama Dwele" – a student at Bethany Bible School in Mthatha, South Africa. 83

Photo 28: The power and joy of women in worship. 89

Photo 29: Benjamin Moilwa recounts to Rachel the history of the Spiritual Healing Church in Botswana. 91

Photo 30: Faculty at Good News Training Institute: Willard Roth, Daniel Tei Kwabla, James Anquandah, and Kwesi Ellis 92

Photo 31: Humphrey teaches both on the Good News campus as well as in local congregations. 96

Photo 32: Women and children play some of the most important roles in AICs 97

Photo 33: Umfundisi Hlobisile has used drama and testimonies to train congregations about prevention of AIDS. 100

Photo 34: Desmond Tutu with Grace and Charles Hostetter. Mennonites served as bridge builders between AICs and mainline church bodies 108

Photo 35: Archbishop and Mrs. Israel Motswaosele befriended a host of Mennonites in Botswana, here with Jim and Jenny Bertsche .. 109

Photo 36: Darrel with Rev. Maseko and Rev. Isaac in Swaziland maize field 114

Photo 37: Shared work was the lifeblood of the program as here between Brian Reimer and Isaac Moshoeshoe 116

Photo 38: AIC leaders also ministered in North America. Here, Garry and Diane Janzen host Golwelwang Paul and Onkabetse Mogomela in Saskatchewan, Canada 118

Photo 39: Side by side in endeavor, friendship in Botswana grew from mutual prayer. Here, Joseph and brother, Israel Motswaosele with Garry Janzen 120

Photo 40: Collaboration in leading worship at Nima Temple, Accra, Ghana 122

Photo 41: Dedication prayer for Sandi and Elinor by Joseph Motswaosele of the Spiritual Healing Church.............. 126

Photo 42: Adonis with Anna and Joe Sawatzky: "They came to work with us." 129

Photo 43: Rod with Benin Bible Institute board members: the founding board – Michel Dossou, Henry Harry, Abel Dossou, Pierre Togbe, and Samson Assani; Augustin Ahoga, board chair 134

Photo 44: Celebrative, joyous fellowship following worship, Ghana-style! 135

Photo 45: Listening to partners is key to successful relationships 136

Photo 46: Studying the Gospel of Mark with the Church of the Messiah, Ghana 141

Photo 47: Prophet Doh with other leaders of the White Cross Society 144

Photo 48: The night when sounds of Setswana singing soaked the wooden ceiling beams 150

Photo 49: Prayers, praise, and fellowship with the Abidjan chapter of the Sacred Cherubim & Seraphim Society................. 154

Photo 50: Reuben Mgodeli chatting with Wiseman S. Gumenke and Joe and Anna Sawatzky at Bethany Bible School 156

Photo 51: Richard Djorogo, Head Preacher and Cross-Staff Carrier in the Abidjan Anono Harrist congregation 159

Photo 52: Prayer and Bible study in the New Morian Apostolic Church in Zion of Rev. Philip Mothetho, Botswana................ 161

Photo 53: "I grew in appreciation of worship springing from everyday triumphs and tragedies, victories and defeats, ever praising and petitioning God all encompassing." Alice Roth.......... 170

Photo 54: Modeste Lévry Beugré was the first Harrist Church leader to invite Mennonites to live among the Dida people of southcentral Côte d'Ivoire 172

Photo 55: Vibrant, Spirit-filled prayer and song among the Zionists in Swaziland 174

Photo 56: Ritual cleansing before ordination 178

Photo 57: "The Benin Bible Institute [is] a remarkable model for how different religious communities can peaceably live and work together." Michel Alokpo 179

Photo 58: Matshedisco's life demonstrated the silent and mysterious ways God's kingdom grows 182

Photo 59: Baby Dedication Day in the Dida Harrist Church of Tata, Côte d'Ivoire... 185

Foreword

This book gives insight into a significant chapter of modern church history. It is now widely recognized that during the twentieth century, a major shift occurred in the center of gravity of Christianity. For several centuries, Christianity had been a Western religion – the religion of the peoples of Europe and their descendants elsewhere. During the twentieth century, Christianity began to recede in Europe and to flourish in other parts of the world, notably in sub-Saharan Africa. By the end of the century, the majority of professing Christians were Africans, Asians, and Latin Americans.

A vital contributor to this development was the missionary movement from the West, which may be thought of as the detonator of the explosion. But most African Christians heard the gospel from other African Christians, and the effects of the explosion reached far beyond the churches that arose directly from the work of Western missionaries. The translation of the Bible into African languages led to African readings of Scripture, some of which drew attention to Bible passages that had not been stressed in traditional Western biblical teaching but resonated in African contexts. Sometimes African Christians found in the Bible authority for customs that were important in local society but were outside the experience of Western Christians.

This book performs a valuable service by illuminating the patterns of worship and devotion of these churches, their vigorous evangelistic activity, and their ways of bringing Christian understanding into the realities of life and society in Africa. For Christians nurtured in traditions that have developed elsewhere, this book is full of riches.

There is much personal testimony here, so perhaps I may be permitted to add my own. I went to Africa as a Western Christian academic in 1957 when there were few scholarly studies of the new churches – then often called by misleading terms such as "separatist," "nativistic," or "millennial." One of the few was Bengt Sundkler's *Bantu Prophets in South Africa*, first published in 1948, which identified two main types of churches, "Ethiopian" and "Zionist." In the very different setting of Sierra Leone, I met and had fellowship with Christians whose churches had resemblances with the South African "Zionist" model, but had equally clear differences from it.

In 1963, I moved to the department of religion at the then new University of Nigeria Nsukka. Our department set out to make a survey of all the churches in what was then called Nigeria's Eastern Region. We were astonished at the number and rate of growth of new churches which were unrelated to the denominational churches originating from Western missions, and we particularly noted the spectacular growth of such churches in and around the town of Uyo. With my New Zealand colleague Dr. Harold Turner, already the author of the ground-breaking, two-volume work *African Independent Church*, I began to visit the area and soon realized the historical importance of what in 1927 was called the Spirit Movement in that region of the country.

A few missionaries – one in particular – had seen the Spirit Movement as a revival, but most had regarded it as deviant and dangerous. Many churches had resulted and grown up without Western mission direction. In the midst of these churches, we met a solitary missionary couple, American Mennonites Ed and Irene Weaver. They had resisted the temptation to introduce a new denomination. The "Fellowship of African Independent Churches" that they fostered was at the service of all, but directed none.

For our research and understanding, this development was a turning point. For the rest of his life, Harold Turner produced illuminating studies of the development that these churches represented. The Weavers went on with their quiet pioneering in ecumenical relations elsewhere in Nigeria and then in Ghana and Botswana. The Mennonite Board of Missions, based in Elkhart, Indiana, under the sage guidance of Wilbert Shenk and his successors, continued to foster the vital work of fellowship with the new churches and building bridges with older Christian communities whose reading of Scripture and experience of the faith had been shaped by other influences. The fruits of that understanding and activity are displayed throughout the pages which follow. This book deserves a warm welcome and careful attention.

Andrew F. Walls
Edinburgh, 9th July 2020
Historian of Missions and World Christianity,
University of Edinburgh, Liverpool Hope University, UK,
and Akrofi-Christaller Institute, Ghana

Preface

A distinguished Afrikaner theologian with wire-rimmed glasses and a shock of white hair sat facing me at supper the first night of a conference on partnership with African Independent Churches. The gates of Nelson Mandela's prison had yet to swing open, and Mennonites were still *personae non gratae* in apartheid South Africa. Little wonder, then, that I should be studied so warily as a suspect guest.

When table chatter finally eased the question came. Clearing his throat, the professor put it to me, "So, you're a Mennonite?" as though addressing some endangered species. I groped for a coherent response, mumbling something about "trying my best to be one."

Then the conversation took a wholly unexpected turn. "I have traveled all over Southern Africa," he said, "and heard speak often of Mennonite workers, though never had the pleasure of actually meeting one. What's more, though you seem to have left footprints everywhere, I have yet to see any signboard, church, or institutional name with the label 'Mennonite' attached to it. It's extraordinary. You must be the last people on earth who still believe the saying of Jesus, 'Unless a grain of wheat fall in the ground and die, it remains alone, but if it dies, it bears much fruit'" (John 12:24).

I remember thinking at the time that I wished his generous thought was entirely true of me or my colleagues. But his striking observation threw a shaft of light on to something quite rare in the practice of mission, or even church history: self-giving to kingdom pursuits without regard for sectarian credit or advantage. And that from this point of departure, there flows a bracing freedom.

What is more, the willingness to run those risks of loss was matched by the indigenous faith communities Mennonites encountered in various corners of Africa. In almost every case, individuals of prophetic bent and leaders within these movements faced off the misgivings of the time, the suspicions about more Western aggrandizement, by saying that trustworthy friends had been sent by the inspiration of the Holy Spirit with whom honest partnership was yet possible. They, too, cast some seed in the ground in faith that something exquisite and bountiful might result.

The generous insight of an Afrikaner scholar, with that compelling gospel phrase of Jesus, aptly catches what lies at the heart of the stories that follow both for North American Mennonites and for the members of African Independent Churches.

"Unless a grain of wheat fall in the ground and die . . ."

Jonathan P. Larson

Introduction

Thomas A. Oduro, Jonathan P. Larson, and James R. Krabill

In 2019, Mennonites and African Independent Churches (AICs) celebrated sixty years of building relationships and cultivating partnerships with each other for ministry. The story began in the late 1950s when the Mennonite Board of Missions (MBM) received a letter of invitation to visit a group of African independent, unaffiliated congregations in eastern Nigeria who had heard *The Mennonite Hour* – an MBM internationally transmitted radio broadcast – and were interested in learning more about Mennonites.

MBM workers Ed and Irene Weaver were appointed in 1959 to begin a ministry with these churches and soon discovered scores of other similar churches scattered throughout Nigeria and all along the coast of West Africa in Dahomey (now Benin), Togo, Ghana, Côte d'Ivoire, Liberia, and Sierra Leone.

For six decades now, Mennonites have nurtured relationships with and explored ways to walk alongside these and other participants in independent African movements on their faith journey between the ancient traditions of their ancestors and the newer claims of Christ on their lives. The story of these relationships is a most fascinating pilgrimage in partnership, lined with potential land mines and pitfalls, but in the end largely fruitful and mutually rewarding to the many and varied parties involved.

To mark this important milestone, we as an editorial team have solicited and assembled the reflections of over thirty AIC colleagues and forty-some North American Mennonite workers concerning the significance and impact of these long-standing relationships. It is our hope that these reflections – along with several contributions from various outside observers of African church life in the fields of missiology, church history, education, women's studies, and worship trends – make a contribution to this milestone of celebration and to the wider audience of persons interested in global church developments.[1]

---

1. A sampler of this collection was published by James R. Krabill, "Six Decades in the Making: A Story of Friendship and Ministry Partnership between African-Initiated Churches and North American Mennonites," *Anabaptist Witness* 5, no. 2 (October 2018): 85–104.

The volume begins with an historical overview by missiologist Wilbert R. Shenk on how Mennonite-AIC relationships took root and expanded in some ten sub-Saharan countries. However the primary objective of this collection of reflections is not to present an exhaustive history of the initiative. Neither is it to recount every activity or project that has been undertaken in every location where Mennonites and AICs partnered together. Rather, we are more interested in soliciting material from both African and North American colleagues that can "cast light on the nature, texture, and significance of the experience," which is how we described the project to potential contributors when asking them to submit essays of five hundred to seven hundred words that are "personal accounts of events, experiences, conversations or discoveries arising from the encounter between Mennonites and AICs."

Many of the reflections in this collection tilt toward highlighting positive rather than negative or challenging features of the relationships that developed. In reality, fostering respectful partnerships across cultural divides is not easy work. The sixty years of relationship building have seen their fair share of *faux pas*, misunderstandings, missteps, and miscalculations. But these challenges are the nature and risk of venturing down uncharted paths with no clear roadmap to guide the journey.

Dana L. Robert, mission historian at Boston University, is one of the outside observers invited to offer "guest reflections" in this volume. Robert has followed the Mennonite-AIC encounter over many years. In her contribution, she highlights one of the unforeseen outcomes and unanswered questions arising from this partnership relationship:

> Even as the Mennonites avoided founding their own churches, Christianity was growing rapidly throughout the continent. In solidarity with their friends and partners, some African Christians wished to be called "Mennonites." One of the questions raised by this splendid history of faithfulness is at what point does dying to "self" require giving up the "rights" even to one's own name? What if one's friends wish to call themselves Mennonites? And what if the meaning of "Mennonite" changes because it has been adopted by "others"? Perhaps the Mennonite-AIC relationship has changed not only the AICs, but the very definition of what it means to be a Mennonite.[2]

---

2. See page 131 below.

Aware of these realities and many others, we offered open-ended topics from which the potential contributors could choose in reflecting on their intercultural encounters and experiences. Possible themes for their essays included the following:

- personal growth, healing, and transformation
- clearer vision of leadership and of service and its demands
- fresh insight into the Scriptures
- new understanding of tradition, culture, and history
- reworking of theology or spiritual priorities
- vivid awareness of the Holy Spirit's power and work
- new ministry, worship practices, or customs
- deepened mission calling and discipleship
- discovery of new kinship
- challenges to received wisdom, values, or suppositions

Several contributors submitted two or more essays, so the total number exceeds the full list of contributors. The essays are arranged in chapters by themes using eight categories of agricultural activity inspired by the title of the collection: tilling, sowing, germination, growth, pollination, weeding, watering, and harvesting. At the end of each thematic section, you will find guest reflections from outside observers who graciously accepted to assess the AIC-Mennonite partner relationships described here and place them in the broader context of mission history and Majority World church growth and realities.

Two final sections of the book – an Additional Resources listing of relevant books, articles, unpublished manuscripts, and dissertations and an Index of key people, places, programs, and projects referenced in this volume – will assist you if you desire a fuller account of the AIC-Mennonite relationships that have developed over these many years.

It is important to note that the acronym "AIC" has been used in scholarly writings to variously represent African *Independent* Churches, African *Initiated* Churches, African *Indigenous* Churches, African *Instituted* Churches, and more recently at the suggestion of Jehu Hanciles, African *Immigrant* Churches. For the sake of keeping in line with the historicity of the AICs – the ones with whom North American Mennonites developed friendships for more than sixty years – we are choosing, whenever we as editors reference them, to call them African *Independent* Churches, or more simply AICs.

In closing we must note that no one can live long in Africa without developing a lively sense of indebtedness to elders, both living and "late."

That indebtedness also applies to spiritual and scholarly predecessors whose heirs we are, whether in quest of spiritual wholeness in our communities, of understanding and insight, or in the tasks and roles entrusted to our hands. Following is a partial ancestry, listed alphabetically by family name, whose bequest has made this book and the work it represents possible:

Thomas Agyare	Solomon Owusu Krow
John "Jonas" Ahui	Emmanuel Martey
James E. N. Amoah	Augustus B. Marwieh
E. L. Annang	Marlin and Ruthann Miller
James Anquandah	Francis A. Mills
Gilbert Ansre	Samuel and Emily Mohono
Asante Antwi	Israel Motswaosele
James Kingsley Akwasi Appiah	Benoît Légré N'Guessan
Samson Assani	Emmanuel Nsiah
Christian G. Baëta	Sam Prempeh
Jim Bertsche	Willard and Alice Roth
Alphonse Kobli Beugré	David and Wilma Shank
Modeste Lévry Beugré	Wilbert Shenk
Florence Araba Kyere Charway	Erwin Luther and Lorraine Spruth
Joseph Attah Coleman	Emmanuel Martey Tetteh
Isaac Dlamini	Pierre Togbé
Abel Dossou	Harold W. Turner
Michel Dossou	Andrew F. Walls
Kwesi B. Ellis	Ed and Irene Weaver
Paul Fynn	Isaac Wontumi
Erma Grove	Albert Kwesi Yamoah
Adrian Hastings	Charles Yaw Yeboah-Korie
Harry Henry	John Howard Yoder
Robert Kraay	Ron Yoder

We are particularly grateful as well for generous contributions to the contents of this book from Africans, North Americans, and scholars around the world, and for the assistance of Rachel Hilty Friesen whose scrutiny burnished the text, and for the deft work of Marcella Hershberger who fashioned an index and Cynthia Friesen Coyle who designed a map illustrating ministry locations in Africa.

In Africa today, changes are happening so rapidly that it is difficult, nearly impossible, to keep up. What these changes mean for the future of the church on the continent is not certain. But what is clear is that new and fresh global partnership relationships will be required. It is our hope that the lessons of earlier endeavors will contribute to correcting past mistakes and strengthening the body of Christ as it grows both on African soil and – with increased assistance from African sisters and brothers – in the parched and thirsty land we call North America.

Abbreviations

Africa Inter-Mennonite Mission (AIMM)

African Federal Church Council (AFCC)

African Independent Churches (AICs)

African Spiritual Churches (ASCs)

All-Africa Council of Christian Churches (AACCC)

Benin Bible Institute (BBI)

Bethany Bible School (BBS)

Botswana Christian Aids Project (BOCAIP)

Church as a Community of Healing and Peacemaking (ECGAP)

Council for African Instituted Churches (CAIC)

Evangelical Center of Formation in Communications for Africa (CEFCA)

Faculté de Théologie Evangélique de l'Alliance Chrétienne (FATEAC)

Faith Bible School (FBS)

Ghana Christian Council (GCC)

Good News Theological Seminary (GNTS)

Good News Training Institute (GNTI)

Inter-confessional Protestant Council (ICPC)

Mennonite Board of Missions (MBM)

Mennonite Central Committee (MCC)

Mennonite Mission Network (MMN)

Mission-founded Churches (MICs)

Organization of African Instituted Churches (OAIC)

Pentecostal Association of Ghana (PAG)

Theological Education by Extension (TEE)

Theological Education Fund (TEF) of the WCC

United Churches Bible College (UCBC)

Université de l'Alliance Chrétienne d'Abidjan (UACA)

Western Initiated Churches (WICs)

A Short History

Wilbert R. Shenk
Senior Professor of Mission History and Contemporary Culture
Fuller School of Intercultural Studies

In 1959, few people in Europe and North America had heard the term "separatist churches." Anthropologists had studied the exotic Cargo cults in the South Pacific and the Peyote religion practiced among Native Americans. But mission scholars saw no reason to devote time to the study of nativistic, syncretistic, or other movements reacting to Christianity. Such phenomena were generally not recognized as being of direct relevance to Christian missions. In this brief reflection, I will describe in broad strokes some important steps in the first phase of what was to become an initiative that continues to the present in Africa.

Research Begins

In the 1920s, the *International Review of Missions* carried two reports on separatist church movements in Africa: "The Prophet Movement in the Congo" by P. H. J. Lerrigo on Kimbanguism[1] and from South Africa, "The Separatist Church Movement" by C. T. Loram.[2] In 1936, Karl Aldén reported on the continuing development of Kimbanguism in "The Prophet Movement in the Congo" and raised questions about how to relate to this movement.[3] The following year, R. H. W. Shepherd published a survey titled "The Separatist Churches of South Africa" in which he highlighted the continuing struggle to

---

1. P. H. J. Lerrigo, "The Prophet Movement in the Congo," *International Review of Missions* 11 (1922): 270–77.

2. C. T. Loram, "The Separatist Church Movement," *International Review of Missions* 15 (1926): 476–82. About the same time, in 1925, an inquiry was conducted by the Union Government's Native Churches Enquiry Commission, and their findings were reported in Allen Lea, *The Native Separatist Church Movement in South Africa* (Cape Town: Juta, 1927).

3. Karl Aldén, "The Prophet Movement in the Congo," *International Review of Missions* 25 (1936): 347–53.

understand these movements.⁴ Twenty years later, J. W. C. Dougall reported on "African Separatist Churches" as a continent-wide phenomenon and called for careful consideration of these movements.⁵

Wherever these movements cropped up in Africa, they were almost sure to be either ignored or dismissed as exotic and unworthy of serious study. The full extent of these indigenous initiatives and their locations remained largely undocumented. Most missionaries and missiologists failed to appreciate their significance. Fortunately, other scholars – anthropologists, historians, and sociologists – had been researching these new religious phenomena in various parts of the world.⁶

Bengt Sundkler's study titled *Bantu Prophets in South Africa*, first published in 1948, was a major step forward. This book includes a twenty-one-page appendix: "A List of Native Separatist Churches as on August 1, 1945" naming 845 churches.⁷ Sundkler added a note reporting that in May 1947, after work on the book was completed, another list was sent to him identifying an additional 123 churches that had been not incorporated in his list. The *International Review of Missions* reviewed this book.⁸ But the path-breaking significance of Sundkler's book became apparent with the publication of the revised edition in 1961.⁹ In that version, Sundkler added a substantial new chapter – "Developments, 1945–60" – indicating his own change of stance toward these movements: they were Christward movements, not bridges back to pre-Christian religion.¹⁰

---

4. R. H. W. Shepherd, "The Separatist Churches of South Africa," *International Review of Missions* 26, no. 4 (1937): 453–63.

5. J. W. C. Dougall, "African Separatist Churches," *International Review of Missions* 45, no. 3 (1956): 257–66.

6. See Gottfried Oosterwal, *Modern Messianic Movements* (Elkhart, IN: Institute of Mennonite Studies, 1973), 49–55, which includes extensive notes and references to scholarly writings available by 1970. Most of this scholarship was produced after 1950 primarily by anthropologists and sociologists.

7. Bengt Sundkler, *Bantu Prophets in South Africa* (London: Lutterworth, 1948; reprint Cambridge, UK: James Clark, 2004).

8. See *International Review of Missions* 58, no. 2 (1949): 230–33. Strangely, Efraim Andersson's *Messianic Popular Movements in the Lower Congo* (Uppsala: Almqvist and Wiksells, 1958) was not reviewed. But see Harold W. Fehderau, "Review of *Messianic Popular Movements in the Lower Congo,*" *Practical Anthropology* 7, no. 6 (Nov.–Dec. 1960): 279–83.

9. Bengt Sundkler, *Bantu Prophets in South Africa* (London: Routledge, 1961).

10. The revised edition of *Bantu Prophets in South Africa* (London: Routledge, 1961) also included a "Special Bibliography" of forty-four items, primarily articles, published between 1902 and 1961, about these movements. Again, Andersson's book *Messianic Popular Movements in the Lower Congo* was not mentioned.

Starting Over

When Mennonite missionaries Edwin and Irene Weaver disembarked at Lagos, Nigeria in November 1959, they had never heard of "independency," as it was then called.[11] Neither did they know their new assignment would put them in one of the "hot spots" of religious innovation in Africa, i.e., southeastern Nigeria. Their sponsoring mission agency was equally unaware of these circumstances.[12] But it would quickly become clear to the Weavers that their twenty years of service in India had not prepared them for what they would encounter in Nigeria.[13]

The conflicting messages the Weavers received as they attempted to become acquainted with mission and church leaders in the region intensified their confusion. The missionaries and local leaders of the mission-established churches whom they consulted refused to relate to the "independent" groups. Indeed, relations were fraught with conflict and ill will. The missionaries working in southeastern Nigeria spoke with one voice: "You are not needed here. Find another place to work!" By contrast, the "independent" churches were clamoring for assistance. This was as puzzling as it was discouraging.

After several months of struggle, the Weavers realized they had to "die" to the patterns, methods, and knowledge they had depended on in their previous missionary work. The conventional methods and approaches would have only reinforced the status quo and had to be resolutely abandoned. Yet it was becoming clear that the situation in which the Weavers were commissioned to work in southeastern Nigeria was a God-given assignment. Lacking a blueprint to follow, they had to depend on the Spirit to disclose new paths of ministry.

Confirmation of this new venture came when the Weavers providentially encountered Harold W. Turner at a guesthouse in Lagos in 1961. They quickly discovered their mutual interest in these new African religious movements. Turner, a lecturer in Old Testament at Fourah Bay College, Sierra Leone, first encountered this phenomenon on Lumley Beach, Sierra Leone, in 1957. His

---

11. Terminology has evolved. "Separatist" could be construed as a pejorative term, implying these churches had broken away from the mission-founded churches, but this was not true for many of these churches. In the 1960s, these movements were referred to as African Independent Churches, then as African Indigenous Churches, and since the 1990s, as African Initiated or Instituted Churches.

12. The Weaver's story is sketched briefly in my essay "Go Slow Through Uyo," in *Fullness of Life for All*, eds. I. Daneel, C. Van Engen, and H. Vroom (Amsterdam, New York: Rodopi, 2008), 329–40.

13. See Edwin Weaver and Irene Weaver, *The Uyo Story* (Elkhart, IN: Mennonite Board of Missions, 1970), which gives an account of their experience of finding their way in this new situation.

intrigue with what he observed led to a major research project that focused on one of these groups, the Church of the Lord (Aladura). He was then four years into this study, which would be published in two volumes as *African Independent Church* in 1967.[14]

Other initiatives were under way. The study department of the World Council of Churches' Commission on World Mission and Evangelism convened a consultation at Mindolo, Zambia, in 1962. Harold Turner and Edwin Weaver were invited to participate.[15] About the same time a continent-wide research project was being launched by Anglican missionary researcher David B. Barrett, based in Nairobi, Kenya. The results of this macro-study were published in 1968 and entitled *Schism and Renewal in Africa: An Analysis of Six Thousand Contemporary Religious Movements*.[16] The trigger for this large-scale study was the secession of sixteen thousand members from the Western Kenya Diocese of the Anglican Church in 1957.[17]

A Strategy Emerges

The Weavers brought a particular gift to this ministry; they were passionate about relating to AICs at the grassroots and devoted their energies to improvising training programs for newly literate leaders who wanted to study the Bible. At the same time, they worked to build bridges of understanding and relationship between the older churches and the AICs. Much of the "bad blood" between the various church groups stemmed from mutual ignorance. All were guilty of spreading negative and misleading information about other groups. Bringing people together to *listen* to each other was a necessary first step in fostering constructive relations. During the period 1963–1965, relations began to improve as a result of regular meetings of the Inter-Church Study Group comprised of leaders from the full spectrum of churches. Here people learned to know one another, nurturing respect and friendship.

---

14. Harold W. Turner, *African Independent Church* (Oxford: Clarendon, 1967).

15. Weaver was unable to attend, but Turner made a substantial contribution based on his extensive research and theoretical and methodological innovations in the study of these phenomena. See conference report titled *African Independent Church Movements*, ed. Victor E. W. Hayward (London: WCC Department of Missionary Studies, 1963).

16. David B. Barrett, *Schism and Renewal in Africa: An Analysis of Six Thousand Contemporary Religious Movements* (Nairobi: Oxford University Press, 1968).

17. Barrett, *Schism and Renewal in Africa*, Preface, xvii.

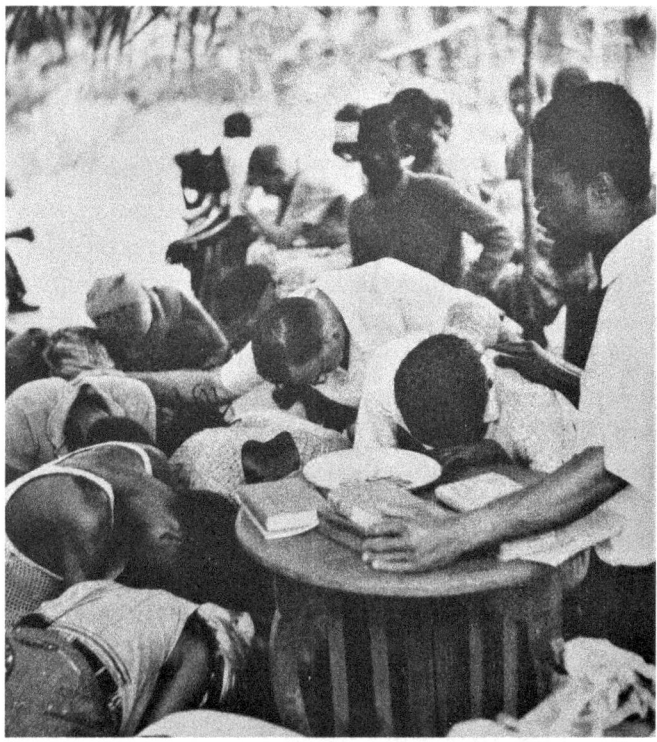

**Photo 1: A church in Eastern Nigeria pleads in
prayer for a family in need of healing**

In addition, an extensive survey of churches in southeastern Nigeria was conducted in order to learn about and know the churches and leaders. A Bible school for leaders who had only a basic education was established, and scholarships were awarded to individuals who had adequate academic background to do theological study at higher levels. But the Nigerian Civil War from 1966–1969 disrupted the work the Weavers had started in Nigeria, and all foreign workers were forced to leave the country.

Nevertheless, Mennonite engagement in Nigeria had one more phase. Harold Turner had listened for several years to the leader of the Church of the Lord (Aladura) dream about establishing a seminary where leaders might be trained. What was lacking was qualified faculty. Turner urged Mennonites to respond to this opportunity. In 1970, B. Charles and Grace Hostetter began a six-year stint assisting the Church of the Lord (Aladura) to establish their seminary in Lagos, Nigeria. The Theological Education Fund of WCC provided financial support for operating costs.

Seed Sown in Central Africa

The largest African Initiated Church on the African continent is the fruit of the ministry of Simon Kimbangu. He was refused ordination by the Baptist Mission because of his lack of education. Nonetheless, convinced he was called of God to preach and heal, he began his public ministry in 1921. Between March and September of that year, Kimbangu made an enormous impact through his ministry of preaching, healing, and deliverance. In September, the Belgian colonial government arrested and imprisoned Kimbangu on the grounds of inciting civil unrest, and he was held in prison until his death in 1951. It served the purposes of the colonial authorities to keep the focus on Kimbangu and The Church of Jesus Christ by portraying Simon Kimbangu as a threat to public order into the 1950s.

Efraim Andersson's *Messianic Popular Movements in the Lower Congo* published in 1958 helped mitigate this hostility through careful scholarly analysis of these movements, of which Kimbanguism was only one. Harold Fehderau, a Mennonite Brethren Bible translator in the Congo, not only wrote an appreciative review of Andersson's study but later published several articles on Kimbangu and his ministry.[18]

During the academic year 1962–1963, James E. Bertsche, a Mennonite missionary with the Congo Inland Mission, wrote a 355-page master's thesis in anthropology entitled "Kimbanguism: A Separatist Movement" at the Graduate School of Northwestern University. The tenor of Bertsche's conclusion was respectful, insightful, and empathetic:

> There is in the history and nature of this offspring of the encounter between Christian missions and Bakongo culture much food for thought for the missionary and not a few lessons that he would do well to learn. In view of the fact that the movement has from its earliest days grown and flourished precisely in areas which have been evangelized by both Catholic and Protestant missions, there is the clear implication that while the Bakongo have found the Christian faith, as such, to be meaningful, there has been a failure on the part of Christian missions to effectively penetrate and appreciate the cultural and religious needs of their people

---

18. Fehderau, "Review." Harold Fehderau, "Concerning a Culturally Relevant Witness in Congo," *Practical Anthropology* 8, no. 2 (March–April, 1961): 71–76; "Enthusiastic Christianity in an African Church," *Practical Anthropology* 8, no. 6 (Nov.–Dec. 1961): 279–80, 282; and "Kimbanguism: Prophetic Christianity in Congo," *Practical Anthropology* 9, no. 4 (July–Aug. 1962): 156–78.

and a failure to significantly adapt the Christian message to these same needs. It seems obvious that the Kimbanguist Church today is attempting to do what Christian missions have not done, i.e., to interpret and adapt the Christian faith to the cultural needs and realities of the Congolese people.[19]

Subsequently in a substantial article titled "Kimbanguism: A Challenge to Missionary Statesmanship," Bertsche presented the missiological implications of his anthropological study.[20] His sympathies were clearly with the Africans who had struggled to achieve a *contextually appropriate* understanding of the gospel and thus overcome the inadequacies of what the missionaries, in spite of their sincere efforts, had offered.

The efforts of Fehderau and Bertsche did not translate into positive interest on the part of Congolese Mennonites in relating to AICs. Over time, however, attitudes changed. The process by which Kimbanguists and Mennonites "discovered" each other started in Europe. In 1966, the director of the Belgian Fellowship of Reconciliation contacted David and Wilma Shank, then serving in Belgium, and asked them to host two Kimbanguist leaders who were returning to Congo from a meeting of the International Fellowship of Reconciliation in Denmark. The Belgian Protestant Churches declined to receive these pacifist Kimbanguists whom they regarded as "sectarians." The Shanks helped facilitate further Mennonite contacts that led to the placement of Mennonite Central Committee and Eirene – European service agency – volunteers in Kimbanguist schools and with the church's experimental farm over a period of years. In 1971, Kuntima Diangienda, a senior leader of the church, invited David Shank to attend the Golden Jubilee of the Kimbanguist Church, which drew four hundred thousand people to their holy city, Nkamba, Congo.[21]

---

19. James E. Bertsche, "Kimbanguism: A Separatist Movement" (Master's thesis, Graduate School of Northwestern University, Evanston, IL, 1963), 340.

20. James E. Bertsche, "Kimbanguism: A Challenge to Missionary Statesmanship," *Practical Anthropology* 13, no. 1 (Jan.–Feb. 1966): 13–33. We can only conjecture as to why Bertsche made no overt use of his thesis subsequently. Perhaps it was because "Kimbanguism" remained controversial in the eyes of most Protestants into the 1970s. However, his study clearly informed his later executive leadership of Congo Inland Mission / Africa Inter-Mennonite Mission.

21. David A. Shank, *Mission from the Margins*, ed. James R. Krabill (Elkhart, IN: Institute of Mennonite Studies, 2010), 50–51.

The Vision Spreads in West Africa

Unable to get a visa to enter Nigeria on their return to West Africa in 1969, Ed and Irene Weaver made Accra, Ghana, their base. For the next eight years the Weavers played a "John the Baptist" role, sharing the vision and passion that emerged during their short six years in Nigeria with colleagues, first in other West African and then in southern African countries. Wherever they went, the Weavers planted the seed of a vision of what could happen when Christians of all stripes meet together to study the Scriptures, listen to one another's history, and discuss distinctive convictions and theological visions. Everyone must approach the study of the Scriptures as learners, they said, open to gaining insight as people share out of their particular experiences.

Photo 2: Apostle Kalesanwu (third from right) welcomes Ed and Irene Weaver to the Church of the Lord (Aladura) in Monrovia, Liberia

In West Africa, the Weavers made contact with AICs in Liberia, Côte d'Ivoire, Ghana, and Benin.[22] In each of these countries, programs emerged. No two programs were alike, but all found their focus in Bible study and training leaders. In Ghana and Benin, multiple AICs joined together in sponsoring and

---

22. These explorations and program developments up to 1974 are reported in Edwin Weaver and Irene Weaver, *From Kuku Hill: Among Indigenous Churches in West Africa* (Elkhart, IN: Institute of Mennonite Studies, 1975).

participating in organized Bible study. The Good News Theological Seminary (GNTS) in Accra today[23] is the outgrowth of the Good News Training Institute (GNTI) organized in 1971.[24] Ed Weaver met Harry Henry, a Protestant leader from Benin, at the All-Africa Conference of Churches in Abidjan in 1969. Ed and Irene then visited Benin in early 1970. Bible study seminars were held several times in the following years. But a Marxist faction seized control of the country, and for nearly a decade no further contacts were feasible.

In 1983, David and Wilma Shank renewed contact with churches in Benin. The country's Interconfessional Protestant Council (ICPC) proposed that a seminar for church leaders be held in December of that year. The success of this seminar resulted in an annual five-day seminar organized around themes selected by the ICPC. Although the seminars continued as an annual event, the AICs increasingly felt the need for a pastoral training program. Eventually, Benin Bible Institute was established. Mennonite workers Dr. Daniel and Marianne Goldschmidt-Nussbaumer from France and Rodney and Lynda Hollinger-Janzen from Canada and the USA respectively located in Benin. A medical program serving people who did not have access to healthcare was developed, now known as Bethesda Hospital. Rodney Hollinger-Janzen taught in the Benin Bible Institute. Some Protestant churches supported this effort to provide theological education for AICs.[25] The theme running through all of these ministries in Benin was, and still is, *partnership*.[26]

The initiative in Liberia was cut short by the civil war that started in 1989. Mennonite workers Peter and Betty Hamm and Steve and Dorothy Wiebe-Johnson withdrew as war broke out.[27]

---

23. This AIC training institution has transitioned through three names since its founding – first known as the Good News Training Institute (GNTI), 1971–1996; then Good News Theological College and Seminary (GNTCS), 1996–2017; and since 2017, simply as Good News Theological Seminary (GNTS). Except in cases where it is necessary to identify early historical nomenclature, we will in this publication identify the institution simply as Good News or make use of the most recent iteration: Good News Theological Seminary (GNTS).

24. From the beginning, various Protestant groups participated in staffing the Good News Training Institute. The Lutherans provided staff for GNTI on a continuing basis.

25. Rodney Hollinger-Janzen, "A Biblical Teaching Program by the Interconfessional Protestant Council of Benin with Mennonite Cooperation," in *Ministry in Partnership with African Independent Churches*, ed. David A. Shank (Elkhart, IN: Mennonite Board of Missions, 1991), 161–70.

26. Nancy Frey and Lynda Hollinger-Janzen, *3-D Gospel in Benin: Beninese Churches Invite Mennonites to Holistic Partnership*, in the *Missio Dei* series, vol. 23, ed. James R. Krabill (Elkhart, IN: Mennonite Mission Network, 2015).

27. Stephen Wiebe-Johnson, "Background to Mennonite Board of Missions Involvement in Liberia," in *Ministry in Partnership with African Independent Churches*, ed. David A. Shank (Elkhart, IN: Mennonite Board of Missions, 1991), 106–11.

Photo 3: The Benin community health team embark on a visit to a project (back left to front right): Daniel Goldschmidt Nussbaumer, Saturnin Afaton, Rebecca Assani, and Lynda Hollinger-Janzen

Although Ed Weaver made a preliminary investigation in Côte d'Ivoire in 1969, he was limited by his lack of the French language. Marlin Miller, director of a Mennonite student center in Paris that served primarily Africans, met Ivoirian students from the Harrist Church who expressed interest in continuing relationship. Subsequently, he visited Côte d'Ivoire several times to get acquainted with the Harrist leadership. In 1972, Mennonite Board of Missions decided to respond to this opportunity. David and Wilma Shank and James and Jeanette Krabill invested several years in preparatory study in Aberdeen, Scotland, and Paris, France, before moving to Côte d'Ivoire in 1978 in response to the call from the head of the Harrist Church, John Ahui, to "help me water the tree."[28] The two couples worked in Bible teaching and leadership training with Harrists for over a decade and continue relationships with Harrist churches as of this writing in Côte d'Ivoire and Paris, France.[29]

---

28. D. A. Shank, "Mission from the Margins," in *Ministry in Partnership with African Independent Churches*, ed. David A. Shank (Elkhart, IN: Mennonite Board of Missions, 1991), 55–82, summarizes these developments.

29. See two chapters by James R. Krabill, "Ministry among the Dida Harrists of Côte d'Ivoire: A Case Study," in *Ministry of Mission to African Independent Churches*, ed. David A. Shank (Elkhart, IN: Mennonite Board of Missions, 1987), 33–55; and "Hymn Collecting among

The Vision Moves South

In 1968, Mennonite program agencies agreed to explore possible opportunities in Southern Africa. Two veteran Mennonite mission workers in Africa – Donald Jacobs, East Africa, and James Bertsche, Congo – were appointed to lead this effort. Their exploratory trip took place in April 1970 during which they visited Swaziland, Lesotho, Botswana, and Zimbabwe. With full awareness that apartheid cast a pall over the entire region, the team recommended that Mennonite agencies find ways of serving there nonetheless: "We finish this investigation, analysis, and report with the clear conviction that we must begin to participate in life south of the Zambesi. May God give courage and wisdom . . . infinite patience, and compassion as we roll up our sleeves and take up the challenge for Jesus Christ and His kingdom."[30]

Specific action recommendations were few. The Mennonite Central Committee had already placed teachers in Botswana in 1968. In 1971, the Eastern Mennonite Missions sent a missionary couple and the Mennonite Central Committee three teachers to Swaziland. Africa Inter-Mennonite Mission (AIMM) planned to send workers to Lesotho the following year. However, the question of placing workers in the Republic of South Africa proved perplexing. In view of a meeting planned for the following year, James Juhnke prepared a series of study papers. At the Maseru Consultation, 30 April–1 May 1972, Juhnke urged Mennonite agencies to "grasp the nettle" and send people to South Africa.[31]

There were developments on other fronts. The AIMM executive secretary proposed to his board that "given the vigor of the Swaziland independent churches and the expressed desire of at least one Swazi church leader for a structured training program for independent church leadership in that country, we recommend that someone be invited to visit Swaziland to attempt to determine the receptivity of these leaders to dialogue."[32]

Eventually, Edwin and Irene Weaver were enlisted to help work out a strategy for Mennonite agencies to work with AICs in Southern Africa. The

---

the Dida Harrists," in *Ministry in Partnership with African Independent Churches*, ed. David A. Shank (Elkhart, IN: Mennonite Board of Missions, 1991), 220–38.

30. Don Jacobs and James Bertsche, Foreword, *Southern Africa Study* (N.p., 1970), iii.

31. James Juhnke prepared nine papers for the consultation, reproduced in Vern Preheim, ed., *A Collection of Writings by Mennonites on Southern Africa* (N.p., 1972), 53.

32. Jim Bertsche, *CIM/AIMM: A Story of Vision, Commitment and Grace* (Elkhart, IN: AIMM, 1998), 446.

Weavers were based in Gaborone, Botswana, from January 1975 to May 1977.[33] But there was no grand strategic blueprint. The culture of each country was unique – shaped by its history, ethnic groups, languages, natural resources, economy, and political system.

Through experience, a cluster of guiding principles emerged and have shaped Mennonite response to AICs. These include the following:

1. Mennonite agencies go only where they are invited into a working relationship with AICs.
2. Having heard AIC leaders in West, Central, and Southern Africa call for assistance in equipping their people to understand the Bible more adequately, Mennonites regard their main contribution to be encouraging and enabling study of the Scriptures.
3. Mennonite workers will focus on equipping church leaders through training appropriate to the background of the leaders and the needs of their churches.
4. Workers will facilitate constructive inter-church relations, both among AICs and between AICs and the traditional denominations.
5. Mennonite agencies will avoid providing subsidies for capital projects or supporting operating budgets for churches or institutions.
6. It is not the goal of Mennonite agencies to establish Mennonite churches alongside AICs. If such churches should emerge, it will be the result of local initiative, not the foreign agency.

Conclusion

The experiences that Mennonites have had with African Initiated Churches over the past sixty years can be summarized in a general observation: Wherever Mennonites have encountered AICs, they have been received with open hands and warm hearts. AICs were eager to share out of their experiences and ready to learn from others. They wanted to be treated with respect as fellow disciples of Jesus Christ. Journeying together since 1960 has been a mutually enriching experience.

The contributions to this volume document a journey for which no map was available. Perhaps a better way of describing these experiences is to see

---

33. Bertsche narrates this founding phase and subsequent development, *CIM/AIMM*, 469–590.

them as wanderings on uncharted paths. The reflections found in the following pages are rich in insight into what it means to engage in a multi-cultural ministry. There have been failures and disappointments but also successes and achievements. Looking back on what has been attempted, one is filled with gratitude for the opportunity to be a part of this faith venture.

1

Tilling

The givens of a prospective field are rarely all conducive. The lay of the land is sometimes broken, sometimes knotted, sometimes strewn with stumps and stones. In order to deliver its promise, it must be cleared and leveled as it is brought under the plow. The accounts that follow give some idea of the demanding work AICs, Mennonites, and others undertook in pursuit of as yet uncertain prospects: overcoming wounds of the past, clearing obstacles, and challenging conventional practices in preparing a field that might yield some future reward. As these narratives show, even that beginning comes as collaboration and proceeds as shared endeavor.

Preparing the Soil for Early Collaboration in Ghana and Beyond
Francis A. Mills

Edwin Weaver came to Ghana in late 1969 having left Nigeria during the civil war. When he arrived, he consulted with Solomon Krow, bishop of the Nima Temple Church of the Lord (Aladura) and expressed his desire to begin a Bible study group of AIC leaders. Krow in turn led him to my manse at Korle Gonno, a suburb of Accra, and introduced him to me. We discussed the feasibility of this notion and planned on how to organize the AIC leaders. Later, I invited my brother-in-law, Paul Fynn, pastor of the Evangelical Lutheran Church in Ghana, to catch this vision and to participate. I advised Weaver to accompany me to visit AIC leaders one on one, which we did. I served as his secretary in this effort.

In 1970, we went from one pastor to another listening to their stories and challenges. I invited Joseph Coleman and S. P. Freeman to join the team to mobilize other AIC leaders to bring to fruition this shared vision. During the visitations, we realized that most of the leaders' stories were about disagreements with, and suspicions of, one another which resulted in divisions. To heal these divisions and eradicate the suspicions among the AIC pastors, Weaver proposed a series of seminars. Gilbert Ansre, James Anquandah, and Paul Fynn were among the speakers at these events. The Theological Education Fund (TEF) of the World Council of Churches, under the chairmanship of Desmond Tutu, provided funding support for two years.

The Good News Training Institute (GNTI) – now Good News Theological Seminary – was launched in November of 1971. Prior to that, the AIC leaders met every Tuesday at the Accra Community Center to study the Bible. I personally provided refreshments for those who attended the studies. Most of the lecturers were from Trinity College, the mainline churches, the University of Ghana, and the Evangelical Lutheran Church in Ghana. Rev. K. B. Ellis was one of the teachers at the Community Center. Paul Fynn contributed toward some expenses for the establishment of the new training institute. He also permitted Lutheran missionaries to teach at the school. Edwin and Irene Weaver, Willard and Alice Roth, Erma Grove, and many other Western missionaries benefited from Fynn's benevolence and influence.

Weaver did a good job of mobilizing lecturers and musicians from the University of Ghana to teach at the Institute. He did not face many challenges due to the assistance many AIC leaders gave him. He was a kind-hearted and nice man who preached at AIC worship services and gave everything that he had to help people. When I left him in Ghana to visit the United States, he arranged that I stay in his home there.

Weaver did not limit his ministry to the AICs in Ghana only. I traveled with him to Lomé in the Republic of Togo and Cotonou in Dahomey, now the Republic of Benin, in search of AIC leaders. We traveled in my car, an Austin Minivan. I remember that while in Cotonou, the leader of the Protestant Methodist Church of Benin pleaded with Weaver to open a Bible school for the church in Benin. Later on, we traveled with Emmanuel Tetteh to the Volta region of Ghana to meet with some leaders of the AICs. Regrettably, we did not have time to follow up on the proposed ministry in Benin and Togo due to the intensity of the work in Accra.

Mennonite mission worker Erma Grove became at one point the director (principal) of the GNTI. Being a forthright, hardworking, and nice woman, she led the GNTI for over a decade and committed her skills and life experience to raising the institute to a higher level. She visited many AIC congregations to introduce the school and sought for prospective students. Later directors of the GNTI were Lutherans, namely Robert Kraay and Erwin Spruth, a principled man with a lot of foresight. He improved the quality and size of the library and sought scholarships to train some of the lecturers at seminaries in Nigeria and the United States. Spruth developed the school to an even higher level and fulfilled one of the dreams of successive school board members by handing over leadership of the GNTI to a Ghanaian lecturer he had sponsored for education in the United States. Other notable Ghanaian collaborators with the Mennonites in establishing and managing the Good News Theological Seminary were E. L. Annang, James Amoah, Emmanuel Nsiah, Isaac Wontumi, and Herbert Amoah.

Photo 4: Frank A. Mills in prayer and counseling ministry

The Pentecostal Association of Ghana (PAG), an ecumenical association of African Independent Churches, supported the Mennonite missionaries and some leaders and scholars of the mainline churches to establish and manage the Good News Theological Seminary. Most of the students were enrolled by the leaders of the PAG. The partnership between the Mennonites and Ghanaians was mutual and purposeful.

An Offer of Prayer
Jim Shenk

It was a simple request that my young Swazi neighbor friend Amos conveyed to me in the wee hours of the morning as I struggled to stay awake in my first all-night church service. "Preacher Mambo is asking if it is OK for him to pray for your wife."

We had arrived in Swaziland several months earlier. After formal language study in town and periodic visits to this rural community in the center of the country to help the community build our house, we had moved to Gilgal. Our house was located next to the local Christian Catholic Apostolic Holy Spirit Church in Zion. As a follow-up to the Bible teaching ministry of Harold and Christine Wenger and an earlier contact with Ed and Irene Weaver, the Mennonite team in Swaziland had asked whether this church community would like a couple to live among them. The response was positive with suggestions for our involvement to include developing a water supply, a community garden, and a medical clinic.

A central part of our assignment was to develop a close relationship with this congregation. Our training and philosophical orientation encouraged us to fully immerse ourselves in the local culture and life of this community. So, we were prepared to spend many a night in these all-night celebrations filled with preaching, testimonies, choirs, and prayers for healing. Yet as I watched the dancing, singing, frenzied praying, and sometimes vigorous shaking and poking of persons being prayed for in the center of the congregation, I was not so sure I wanted to subject my wife to this. "Why does Preacher Mambo want to pray for my wife?" I whispered to Amos.

Somewhat embarrassed, he replied, "Preacher Mambo thinks she is sick because she doesn't have any children."

I remembered one of the first questions our neighbors in Gilgal asked: "Where are your children?" When we said that we did not have children, they assumed we had not heard them correctly and politely asked with whom we had left our children when we came to Africa. Married three years and no children! It was a concept that was difficult in a society where traditionally a man wanted to make sure a woman was fertile before investing in bride wealth.

It was now clear that the community assumed something was wrong with Donna. What should I say to Amos? The assumption that Donna was sick was so off base, I thought. If I said it was alright to pray for her, how would my wife feel? Agreeing would simply reinforce the local male-dominated patterns. There was no chance for me to check signals with Donna; she was seated with the women and I with the men.

Rarely had I been so conflicted. I wanted to fit in, but this didn't seem right. My embarrassment was concealed by the dim light from two pressure paraffin lanterns hanging over our heads, but suddenly I felt quite sweaty under my white robe. I leaned into Amos and whispered in his ear that Donna was not sick. We simply were too busy to have children while in college and wanted to wait until we could be settled in Swaziland, I explained.

Photo 5: Infant dedication

Amos nodded with understanding, but I sensed disappointment as he left to deliver my response to Preacher Mambo who was seated on the platform. I have often wondered about that incident and what my response really said about me. Was I worried about the potential response from my wife, or was this really about my need to be in control? Did I want the benefit of proving my manhood rather than giving God all the credit? Might our relationship with this congregation have been enhanced had Preacher Mambo prayed for Donna?

The community was indeed overjoyed when our daughter was born over a year later. Our Swazi mother and pastor's wife, Makeh Fakudze, not surprisingly named her *Lindiwe* – "the long-awaited one." When Makeh Fakudze and the women of the church asked whether they could perform a traditional "coming-out" ceremony for Lindiwe, we did not know what it would entail, but without hesitation we readily agreed!

Worshiping with the Cherubim and Seraphim
Lynda Hollinger-Janzen

In 1985, Rod and I went to England to prepare for our Mennonite Board of Missions assignment in West Africa. We planned to spend eight months studying with Harold Turner and Jack Thompson at the Centre for New Religious Movements at Selly Oak Colleges in Birmingham and then to go on to London to pursue masters' degrees in African studies (Rod) and tropical community health (me).

Rod and I believe in attending a church in the neighborhood where we live, so we tried to worship in the closest Church of England parish church to our lodgings in Birmingham. This attempt turned out to be dismal. Ten elderly women clustered in the front pews around an eagle-adorned pulpit where one of two males present presided over the service. The only other male hovered near the entrance, pointing us toward the coffee. Not wanting to be hasty in our judgment, we persisted for three weeks, trying to ignore the damp cold from the stone floor seeping through our thick-soled shoes and waiting to hear God's word. The third Sunday, however, was dedicated to paying homage to Queen Elizabeth. That was more than our Anabaptist sensibilities could handle, and we began looking for another church.

A few days later, we saw an announcement that included the address of the Birmingham congregation of The Eternal Sacred Order of the Cherubim and Seraphim. What an excellent opportunity to experience in real life what we were studying! So the next Sunday, we boarded a bus for an hour-long ride across the city. As we stepped off the bus, Rod began rummaging in his coat pockets for the map, then stopped, transfixed. We didn't need directions. The compelling reggae rhythm of "Are You Washed in the Blood of the Lamb?" drew us to the door.

We added our shoes to a pile in the foyer and stepped into a sanctuary where the throb of drums and bass guitar gripped our hearts in syncopation. White-robed bodies swayed in worship. A smiling usher welcomed us warmly into this vibrant community of praise, no questions asked.

We worshiped regularly with this Cherubim and Seraphim congregation, composed mostly of Nigerian and Jamaican immigrants. Some of them had lived in England for decades, so they were patient – to an extent that can't be expected of people who have known only one culture – with our blunders and questions. The Cherubim and Seraphim congregation prepared us well for ministry in West Africa. They also helped us through difficulties in England.

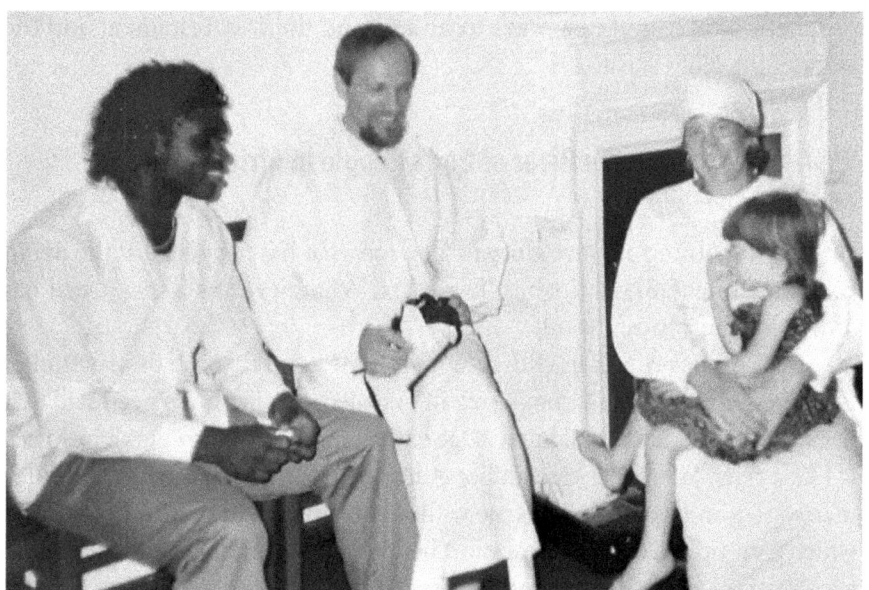

Photo 6: Worshipping with the Sacred Cherubim & Seraphim Society in Birmingham, England

Several months after we arrived in England, I received notification that I was being denied admittance into the London School of Hygiene and Tropical Medicine because of my lack of formal medical training. I was devastated. I took the letter to church with me the next Sunday, laid it on the altar, bowed down with my head to the floor, and asked for prayer. As the congregation raised their voice in a mighty roar, Prophetess Adegoke came to me with closed eyes and outstretched staff.

"Jehovah Jireh says, read Joshua 1:9: 'Have I not commanded thee? Be strong and of a good courage; be not afraid, neither be thou dismayed; for the LORD thy God is with thee, whithersoever thou goest.'" I left the service with a much lighter and more trusting heart. Several months later, I received another letter from London informing me that they had decided to waive the medical prerequisites due to the experience I had as a community health practitioner in the Democratic Republic of Congo. On the Sunday when I took this second letter to church, the fervor of rejoicing amped up to surpass that of our former supplication.

The Cherubim and Seraphim congregation surrounded Rod and me with a warm Christian community. They also taught this Mennonite how to dance, how to begin to abandon myself in worship of Almighty God, the power of prophetic words, and new ways to understand the Old Testament and the work of the Holy Spirit.

We Are Deepening the River of God's People in Africa
Alphonse Godonou

We can do nothing but give glory to God for what has happened at the Benin Bible Institute (BBI) in the past few years. What began as a small seed has grown into an enormous tree.

The prophet Hosea in Old Testament times said that the destruction of God's people will come through lack of knowledge. It has often been said that the spirituality and biblical knowledge of the rapidly growing church in Africa is like a river "one mile wide and one inch deep." That was true in Benin for many years and would still be true without the important ministry of the BBI which grew up as a collaborative effort between the Mennonites and the church leaders of the many denominations here in Benin.

Photo 7: Former students and then professors at the Benin Bible Institute (left to right): Bonaventure Akowanou, Antoine Codjo, Alphonse Godonou, and François Bangbade

The most important thing that Mennonites did many decades ago was refuse to found their own church and instead give themselves to training the hundreds of church leaders who were already leading here in Benin, but who had virtually no biblical formation. Today we see the result of that incredible commitment to building up the people of God across denominational boundaries.

I myself am a fruit of that important initiative, first as a student in the very first graduating class at BBI, and now for many years as the director of the systematic Bible training program. Who would have ever believed that such a thing would happen? I can only thank God for his blessings in giving me the opportunity to serve the church in this important way. We are deepening the river of God's people in Africa for many generations to come!

God-Centered Prosperity
Phil Lindell Detweiler

Every Sunday at Breakthru Church International, our home congregation here in South Africa, we proclaim the following before giving our offering:

As we give today's offering, we are believing the Lord for –

- Jobs or better jobs!
- Benefits!
- Sales and commissions!
- Settlements!
- Estates and inheritances!
- Interest and income!
- Rebates and returns!
- Checks in the mail!
- Gifts and surprises!
- Finding money!
- Bills paid off!
- Debts demolished!
- Royalties received!

It's offering time –

HALLELUJAH!!!

I have to admit that when I first encountered this offering declaration in our early days of attending Breakthru, my anti-health-and-wealth-gospel radar would immediately fire up. I would even break out in a sweat and would look around to see if there were any people around me whom I didn't want to have seeing me making such a proclamation. And I would mumble through the declaration – or not say it at all!

I have since decided for a number of reasons that my immediate appraisal of this declaration was misguided. Of course, knee-jerk reactions to such things are hazardous to us as Christians in general, and even more so as missionaries working with partners who don't share – and shouldn't have to! – all of our values, theological inclinations, and traditions.

One of the ways that Breakthru congregation has challenged me in thinking about the tithe declaration is my recognition that I, as an American Mennonite, had little belief that God could or would desire to shape my economic reality. Like many Westerners, I too often don't give the Lord much authority in my daily life over such mundane affairs. Could it be, therefore, that the tithe declaration says more about an absence of faith on my part than about my South African colleagues' belief in prosperity to save them?

Related to that realization is the recognition that I may have spiritualized salvation too much. For the Breakthru congregation – and of our other partners over the years – the Lord is not only interested in saving our souls. He is also interested in helping break us out of poverty, aiding us in succeeding in school, and making our crops grow – all of this so we can provide for our families and for God's larger family.

Photo 8: Worship, Bible study, and fellowship in Pietermaritzburg, South Africa

Traditional worldviews in Africa and elsewhere are holistic, linking the material and the spiritual. So in most ways, it makes perfect sense in Pietermaritzburg, South Africa, to connect spirituality and economics. "Is this only a contextualization of the gospel appropriate for *this* setting, rather than for *our own* setting?" we might ask ourselves. Well, I have in fact come to believe that this association of spirituality to economics is probably a more biblical worldview than my own.

Yet another challenge to my anti-prosperity-gospel radar came when I learned to differentiate between self-centered and God-centered prosperity. Indeed, I am still quite infuriated by a gospel that preaches prosperity devoid of self-sacrifice and the cross. But I have come to believe that there might well be a place in a biblical worldview for prosperity that is God-centered and self-sacrificing. Might this just be part of the gospel after all . . . and a part at which we, as Westerners, need to take a second look?

Love Your Grieving Neighbor as Yourself
B. Harry Dyck

As only the second of a string of Africa Inter-Mennonite Mission (AIMM) workers in Botswana to follow the pioneering labors of Ed and Irene Weaver, I remember feeling alternately excited at the opportunity to be involved in this venture with African Independent Churches, and doubtful at the prospect that I could impact these churches given my ignorance of their cultural and especially their religious norms. Finding myself set down in a context of considerable ethnic diversity and with my linguistic limitations, my first quandary was finding handles by which to gain admission into at least some of these suspicious, supposedly ubiquitous, and proliferating congregations – no easy task that for a rather timid foreigner like me.

But suddenly contacts and connections began to emerge like so many mushrooms after the rain. First came Freedman Rueben of the Spiritual Healing Church. Then I met Otsile Ditsheko of the Eleven Apostles Healing Spirit Church, followed by Silas Morapedi of The Head Mountain of God Holy Apostolic Church in Zion, Prophetess Madam Lekuta of St. John's Healing Church, Peter Matakule of The Holy Nazarene Church . . . and on and on. In the end, I found myself working both individually and ecumenically with no fewer than a dozen different bishops, pastors, and youth leaders teaching subjects of biblical and pastoral leadership concern.

Photo 9: Taking a break from a study session during a village visit

Obviously not all church leaders were receptive to my initiatives, especially those who feared that younger participants might attempt to incorporate new teachings, to usurp leadership, or to alter established protocols. But with time, persistence, and local support, I felt increasingly legitimated in the work AIMM had entrusted to me.

What personal memories linger for me of these relationships? After ten years of living, learning, and sharing among AICs, let me highlight three stories which capture some of my experiences and discoveries.

Story One: It was an extremely hot Sunday morning, and I in my typical North American mindset dared to come to worship for a preaching assignment without a suit jacket on. My assumption was that staying cool was to be preferred over having sweat drip profusely from my body. The lecture I received following the event, however, left no doubt in my mind that my assumption was incorrect in the context of the local culture. No jacket? An open-collared shirt? Short sleeves? These communicated that I might as well have come prepared to start a fight!

Story Two: I had been invited to accompany a bishop to an overnight conference in his home village. A new road was being built, but the project was on hold due to excessive rains. Not to worry, I was told, "Where there's a will, there's a way." The bishop assured me that he knew the road and drove accordingly, making me ponder the possibility that this ride might be my last. As the bishop put foot to floor, the car lurched about, and then B-O-O-M! B-A-N-G! R-U-M-B-L-E! I hit the dashboard, but with all of the bedding and blankets piled on my lap, I was unhurt. We stopped, inspected the car for inevitable damage, and found that our steel bumper was broken off as if cut with a serrated knife. My cultural reflection following the event was, "This need not have happened had the bishop paid attention to the road conditions." But I quickly learned that from the local cultural perspective, very different conclusions were being drawn: "This proves one's indestructibility when one is doing God's work."

Story Three: Death is universal and nondiscriminating – a two-year-old falls into a duck pond and drowns. A six-year-old touches a bare electric wire and is electrocuted. A truck barrels over a cow lying in the road and the teenager standing in the open truck bed is catapulted over the hood and killed instantly. However fruitless the search for conclusive answers, explanations, or responses to such situations, the question inevitably surfaces – where amidst the traumas of the world is that all-loving, Almighty God we have been preaching about? I learned from my African brothers and sisters that these are the times and places when *teaching* must give way to *silence* in simple and humble acts of compassion and solidarity by loving your grieving neighbor as yourself.

Interpreting the Scriptures
Julie Bender

What a delight and privilege it was teaching young aspiring African pastors in the late 1980s at Good News Training Institute – forerunner to the present Good News Theological Seminary – in Accra, Ghana! The pastoral students were eager to learn, often making great sacrifices, leaving their families and churches, to come into the city of Accra. Many of them struggled financially as their mostly rural churches had little money with which to sponsor them.

These pastors served African Independent Churches. I left the difficult scriptural passages for them to interpret, as the goal was for them to apply the Bible in relevant ways within their African culture. Passages that may seem relatively straightforward for Westerners, for example "A man shall leave his father and mother and cleave to his wife" or "A deacon shall be married to only one wife," are much more difficult to interpret in a collective society where grown children are expected to support their elderly parents, or where new believers may already be in polygamous marriages.

Photo 10: The Good News Training Institute student body of church leaders

I was quite strict, however, when promoting Christian marriage as a respectful relationship between husband and wife, free from abuse. One of my strong male students attended a practical Christian living course that I was teaching. I was impressed with how he was taking the teachings to heart and applying the principles to his own marriage. He would return from weekend visits to see his wife and report to me how happy he was to see positive changes in his marriage due to applying his new learning. He and his wife were growing closer together. A teacher could hardly wish for more!

Imagine my surprise with one of this pastor's answers on the final exam. To the statement, "Husbands beat their wives," he had chosen "H" (Helpful) versus "NH" (Not Helpful), but had scrawled in the margin, "This is common in Africa." I felt I had the kind of relationship with this pastor that made it possible to question him about his answer. I was dismayed that one of my better students, appreciative of my teaching, would err on this particular and seemingly obvious test question. To my query of why he would answer the question as "helpful," and my assertion that, surely, he had not learned this from me, he responded, "But in Africa some wives expect this as an expression of love."

I responded, "But Paul, do you believe this?" His smile in response indicated that he was teasing me, but also reminded me of how much I still needed to learn about some of the cultural challenges my students were facing in their home communities.

Pastoral Training and Pit Latrines
Darrel Hostetler

"After their training," he said, "they must still be comfortable using pit latrines." It is now many decades since Mennonite mission worker Ed Weaver said words something like these. He had a vision of training pastors in the African Independent Churches of southeast Nigeria. This vision had some clear boundaries. It needed to be (1) sound theological training, (2) on their level of understanding, (3) that included "tent-making" skills, and (4) that kept them feeling at home in the setting to which God was calling them. Welcome to the United Churches Bible College (UCBC), Uyo, Nigeria.

When the ship *The Libreville* brought us to the dock at Port Harcourt in the fall of 1963, the vision of what could happen was only in Ed's head. His prayer was that it would soon become a reality. This is the plan as it unfolded.

UCBC had two tracks for the student body. One was for those who had little formal education. Teaching in these classes was in the Ibibio language. Students with elementary training were taught in English at a somewhat more advanced level, as English was the language of most Nigerian formal education. These two tracks were crucial to enrich the gifts of AIC leaders as we found them. Money was scarce in most African Independent Churches, and without outside funds, they could not support a pastor. We questioned whether full support would have even been a good idea. This is why UCBC encouraged pastors to engage in a "tent-making" ministry, and thus a class in carpentry was offered.

UCBC served, as I recall, about ten different AICs. One of those was Mennonite Church, Nigeria. This cluster of congregations was attracted to Mennonites through "The Mennonite Hour" radio program and took the Mennonite name before Ed and Irene Weaver arrived. The fact that independent churches were working together was in itself a major accomplishment of the school. Add to that the fact that other Western Initiated Churches located in the area were supportive and supplied a teacher, which happened through the Inter-Church Study Group which Ed spearheaded to work at healing divisions between mainline Protestant groups and the AICs.

Photo 11: Bible training for practical, tentmaking village ministry

UCBC held sessions for three months, followed by a three-month break. The weekly plan was to have classes from Tuesday through Friday. The leaders traveled on Monday, went to classes for the four days, and then returned home on Saturday to serve their congregations. Both the monthly and weekly schedules were designed to have the students learn and immediately use their learning in their home settings. This schedule was carefully planned to avoid the pitfall of the students returning home with excellent training but feeling like a stranger. UCBC students were to grow in pastoral gifts and, in Ed Weaver's vision, "still be comfortable back in their home settings with pit latrines." We felt it worked.

My Training Is for the Purpose of Training Others
Esther Manyeyo Tawiah

I grew up in the Ghanaian Presbyterian Church, but loved the music in the AICs and would sneak away from the formal liturgy to attend their services. When my parents would find out about this, they were very upset and would beat me. But I was more attracted to AIC worship and eventually left the Presbyterian Church in the early 1970s and joined the Universal Prayer Fellowship.

I joined Good News Training Institute, now Good News Theological Seminary (GNTS), as a copy typist in the late 1980s. I was a member of the World Evangelism Ministry from 1984 till February 2005. I joined the college from the Universal Prayer Fellowship. This church at that time was a member of the Pentecostal Association of Ghana (PAG), later Council for African

Instituted Churches (CAIC), Ghana. I am now a member of the Immanuel Believers Ministry.

When I went to my first Good News seminar, I was fascinated by the way the teachers approached the Bible and theology. This was about the same time that two new teaching couples arrived at Good News, Ed and Lorraine Spruth from the Presbyterian Church and Phil and Julie Bender from the Mennonites.

I was asked by GNTS to play a secretarial role at the school. This gave me an opportunity to listen in on some of the discussions, to take minutes, and to prepare handouts for the various professors. Occasionally I would read through the handouts and became more and more interested in what was being presented. When professors would ask me to make twenty copies for their class, I would make twenty-one and take the extra one home to read on my own. The next day in the office I would ask different professors questions about things I had read, though they had no idea where I was coming up with all these questions! Eventually I was encouraged to take the three-year program myself, which I did.

I joined classes in 1989–1992 when the school was still meeting on the beach location. During this time, I became very close to Philip and Julie Bender. Philip taught me Old Testament, and Julie taught me shepherding and counseling. I learned a lot from sitting in their classes, and I have not regretted one bit being their student. The Benders loved to work with the indigenous churches in Ghana. They honored most of the invitations from these churches such as harvest and thanksgiving services, funerals, and naming ceremonies. I was invited to go with the Benders to do interpretation from English to local languages when they were asked to teach or preach. I speak three Ghanaian languages fluently, so one of my jobs anytime there is a joint service is to serve as an interpreter.

I was new in the faith then and peppered the Benders with all kinds of questions. Some of the names and terms in the Bible are very strange, you know, and I had no idea what they meant. The Benders often invited me into their home for meals, and when they traveled to teaching assignments outside of Accra, they would ask me to house-sit their home. I did this at least a half dozen times. I was so impressed that they would entrust their place to me. That shows you how deep our relationship had become! There was a special bond between the couple and me such that I was able to go to them at any time for clarification if I did not understand what they taught. I enjoyed going out with them because I learned many things that I did not fully understand in the classroom.

Photo 12: "Julie and I became like sisters." Esther Tawiah

Julie and I became like sisters. We sometimes went out shopping and did cooking together, Ghanaian dishes and American cookies. I spent so much time with the Benders. My passion for African indigenous women began in my association with Phil and Julie. I saw that the church I belonged to and other indigenous churches needed to study the Bible more seriously. Julie was often invited to teach church leaders as well as women. So, I have been very much involved with women in such studies for more than ten years. The purpose has been to train women to lead Bible studies in their own congregations.

After my job as a secretarial assistant at GNTS and my graduation in 1992, I took a job as the school librarian. Then I was invited to further my studies at Daystar University in Nairobi, Kenya, from 1993 to 1997. From there, I attended Bethel Seminary in Minneapolis from 1997 to 2000, and worked in the seminary library. I returned to GNTS to teach, lead women's Bible studies, and work in the library. We have a great collection of books at the seminary, around twenty-five thousand volumes, one of the best of any theological seminary in all of Ghana. My desire is to continue on and get my master's degree in library science. The accrediting agency in Ghana is requiring it.

All I can do is to offer a very big thanks to Phil and Julie Bender and to the Mennonite churches who have assisted GNTS in providing the training we need so that we as local leaders can also train others.

Grassroots Receptivity . . . Facilitated by a Churchman of Exceptional Faith and Courageous Vision
David A. Shank

West Africa's Benin – formerly Dahomey – was a particularly fruitful place for biblical nurture among AICs, especially because of the way in which Benin's leading Protestant churchman, Pastor Harry Henry, understood both the Western Initiated Churches (WICs) and the AICs.

Pastor Henry was installed by the British Wesleyan Methodist Mission as the first African president of their Dahomean Methodist Church – the oldest of the former French colony's WICs, rooted in nineteenth-century missionary church planting. Theologically trained in Paris, Henry also later presided over the Benin Interconfessional Council of Protestant Churches which was created by the country's Marxist government and included both mainline and evangelical Protestant bodies along with AICs. Rev. Henry was also an executive officer of the All-Africa Council of Christian Churches (AACCC). It was his very candid appreciation of the WICs – combined with his respect for the AICs' potential – that was so instructive for us during our 1973 exploratory trip to West Africa.

Mennonite missionary Edwin Weaver had met Pastor Henry at the AACCC meetings in Abidjan in 1968 and found him to be exceptionally open to the kind of Bible teaching ministry the Weavers had undertaken among AICs in Uyo, eastern Nigeria. So in Dahomey, Henry decided to facilitate on two occasions a weeklong Bible seminar for Dahomean AIC denominational leaders – in a style developed by Ed Weaver – with Mennonite mission worker Marlin Miller as a French-language interpreter. These seminars were part of a broader Mennonite Board of Missions inquiry into understanding the full reality of the postcolonial AIC phenomenon across West Africa and the eventual openness of these grassroots churches to biblical studies.

During our visit to West Africa with Marlin Miller in 1973, the contacts with Pastor Henry were absolutely crucial in opening doors for our future ministry among Dahomey's AICs. On a typical weekday morning, Henry first drove us past Cotonou's Methodist Church building which, he noted, "was locked up during the week like the Methodist churches in Great Britain," except for a Wednesday evening prayer meeting, the Sunday morning liturgical worship, and Sunday evening youth meeting. Henry explained how the clerical collar he wore was a required necessity for his Methodist people who had learned well how a proper British clergyman should be outfitted. The church which the missionaries bequeathed to him was a foreign entity in Dahomey, considered to be free from polygamy and African traditional spiritual realities – even though Pastor Henry confided to us that he "knew better."

Henry then took us to the Porto Novo faith community of the Cherubim and Seraphim Church. The courtyard around the gathering place was filled with small clusters of people – some having traveled long distances – squatting around wood fires with cooking pots. Inside the church building, a man was lying on a blanket on the floor, and two white-robed individuals were hovering over him in prayer. Elsewhere, a woman quite obviously in birth-pangs was being attended to. A third person seated in a corner was receiving an interpretation of a dream. Another was receiving pastoral attention, possibly for an evil spirit. It was 10:30 a.m. on a typical weekday. "This," said Pastor Henry, "is an *African* church. It is addressing the real needs of Dahomeans." This congregation didn't always have the "right Word" via the Scriptures – as was the case of the Methodist Church reality – but they were a highly effective medium of gospel communication in the local context.

It was fruitless to suggest that the Western Initiated Churches had a mission to fulfill with AICs, since these had mostly broken away from the "foreign" WICs over different attitudes and approaches toward spirits, money, charisma, conjugality, authority, and other issues. What was needed, according to Pastor Henry, was an "outsider" ministry of the word where the Spirit might work through a shared understanding of the Scriptures from a denominationally disinterested source, enabling grassroots faith realities to evolve and grow together as fruit of the one kingdom of God.

The AIC leaders Henry gathered to meet with our visiting Mennonite delegation represented a wide smattering of indigenous movements – *Eledja*, *Bodawa*, Celestial Christianity, Apostolic, Cherubim and Seraphim, *Eglise Christique Primitive*, and others – all with some biblical orientation yet with different accents, practices, charisms, and traditions. We did not ask how each group had become connected with the Bible or how they understood its authority or the authority of Christ. If one or the other of those two elements characterized their group, they were eligible for participation in a Bible seminar for study, prayer, and praise – together.

In this way and at their request, the first of my annual Bible seminars was held. It was sponsored by the Benin Interconfessional Protestant Council of

Churches and was initiated by Pastor Henry who proposed the theme of "The Shepherd and His Flock." This seminar took place in a locale of the Cotonou Methodist Church. These seminars expanded from one to seven annual events and eventually grew from twelve participants to one hundred and forty with some forty different AIC denominations taking part. With time, this initiative led to the creation of the nationally operated Benin Bible Institute, the Bethesda Hospital, a national garbage collection and disposal system, and a small loan investment program involving hundreds of entrepreneurs and families.

Photo 13: Harry Henry delivers a message on God's mission as David Shank translates for an English-speaking audience

Hospitality with a Flair
Sherill Hostetter

"I would never make it to be a Swazi woman!" I exclaimed after doing a live-in with our Swazi family in April of 1984. We had been living in Swaziland for eight months doing language study when we were adopted by an AIC Zionist pastor's family who lived in the mountains far from the main urban areas. The family knew only a couple of words of English. We took our children, ages three and five, and moved in with the Msibi family for ten days.

The Msibis taught me a lot about true hospitality. They went to a lot of work to prepare for our coming. Off the side of the latrine, they built a mud enclosure with a tin roof around an old bathtub so we could have privacy in bathing with a bucket of water. They even recycled seats out of a wrecked car to make swings for the children.

I convinced Makeh Msibi – the mother – that I wanted to be included in the work that needed to be done, so gradually she accepted me as one of the crew and would tell me things to do. The kitchen was the place of the family gathering for the warmth of the fire in the stove, so firewood needed to be cut up morning, noon, and evening. I joined the older children in chopping firewood in between the many other chores that needed to be done. Keeping the drinking water container filled was always a challenge. I decided that if the children could carry large buckets of water on their heads from the community spring to the house, then I could, too. When I succeeded with a bucket full, I then tried carrying five gallons of water at a time – though, of course, I needed my hands holding tight to help balance it. Washing all the dirty clothes by hand was another challenge. After a couple of hours of scrubbing, I was exhausted.

On the third day, Makeh informed me that she was going to join the men in harvesting the maize, and I was to cook dinner for everyone. She left one older child behind to help me with the woodstove. I looked in the cupboard and found only salt and curry powder. I had brought some chicken along in a "wonderbox" that would keep it cool for a couple of days, so at least I didn't need to go catch a chicken, kill it, and pluck the feathers before cooking it.

When the wagon returned with the maize, we all helped to bag it before it was stored in a wooden enclosure. We spent hours taking the kernels off the cobs, resulting in only a small pail of kernels and large blisters on my thumbs. After another hour of crushing the kernels in a hand cranked maize grinder, I only had enough *imphuphu* (porridge) to make one meal for everyone. What an incredible amount of work just to be able to eat!

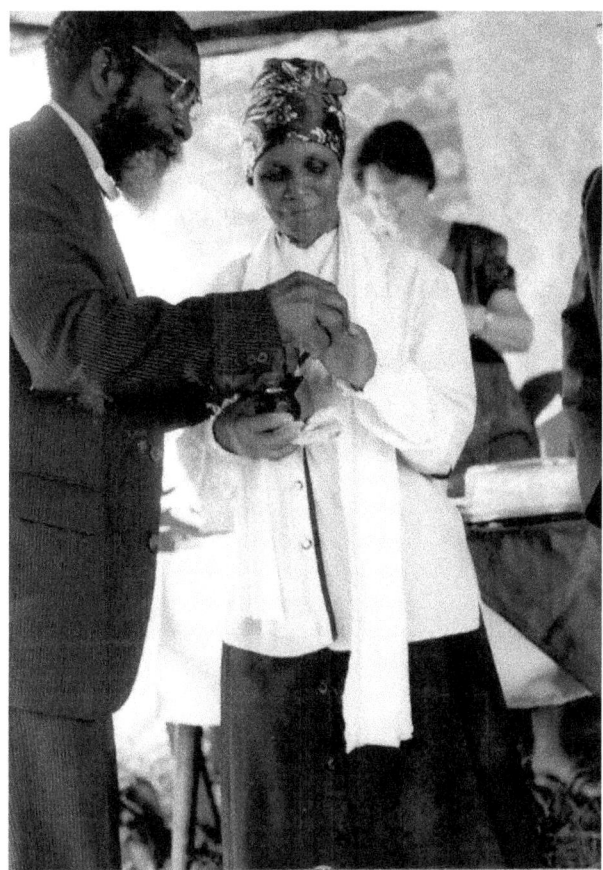

Photo 14: Alfred and Makeh Msibi served as host parents to the Darrel and Sherrill Hostetter family

The Zionist church building where the family attended was on the Msibis' property. Each evening people came from the surrounding community for a worship service. My husband, Darrel, or I were to speak with a short message each evening in Siswati. We managed to speak about five minutes or so.

Late one afternoon, our three-year-old daughter, Rene, was kicked in the stomach by the family's donkey. It knocked the breath out of her and sent her into a seizure. My husband, Darrel, got his fingers in her mouth to pull her tongue down but did not get his fingers out in time before her jaw locked. In watching it all, the Msibis were quite visibly upset. We took Rene to our room where she cried for over an hour after the seizure finished. The Msibi family disappeared into the kitchen. Later I realized that they had gathered together to intercede in prayer for Rene.

It was incredible to me how much this family was willing to give of themselves and their resources to us when they had so little. They insisted on killing their chickens to feed us. And on the evening before we were to leave, Makeh was butchering yet another chicken. When I asked about it, she winked, smiled, and said it was for the morning. As we packed our things into our vehicle, she brought us cabbages, squash, potatoes, and a nicely roasted chicken for us to take home for dinner.

As we said goodbye, Makeh told us that our visit had made her realize that white people were "just like them" and that we were "true Africans." Oh, how I wished that were true. Though I knew I struggled to be a true Swazi woman in many aspects of the local culture, Makeh's example of practicing hospitality in love has continued to challenge me no matter where my life journey has taken me.

GUEST REFLECTIONS

Gilbert Ansre, Evangelical Presbyterian Church of Ghana
While I am a lifelong Presbyterian in Ghana, I am also deeply committed to encouraging the resourcing of African Independent Churches. There is a long history of interaction between mainline mission-founded churches (MICs) and AICs. The MICs often look at the AICs as syncretistic and too close to the traditions. In return, the AICs see the MICs as too "sanitized" by Western culture and too disconnected from African realities. But in fact, all these churches need each other to discover together what it means to be the church in Africa.

The Ghana Christian Council (GCC) was deeply involved in the early days of Good News Training Institute discussions. I was deeply honored to give the inaugural address at the inauguration of Good News in 1972. I collaborated closely with Mennonite workers Willard and Alice Roth. Willard was on the GCC and was also working with AICs. He became a very important bridge between the two bodies, fostering relationships with AICs and at the same time recruiting mainline university professors to serve as Good News board members and lecturers at the training institute. I continued lecturing at Good News up until 2011.

Good News Training Institute – now Good News Theological Seminary – has played a huge role in helping AICs become more aware of the Scriptures and more engaged in conversation with the broader church family in Ghana. Mennonites played an interesting role in this growth because of their deep rural roots. During my visit in 2010 to the Mennonite-Amish community of Shipshewana, Indiana, in the United States, I met the personnel of Mennohof – a museum and visitors' center that interprets Mennonite life and history. Mennohof is located in a rural setting! I was reminded of the homespun, down-to-earth nature of the Mennonite people. This characteristic of Mennonites contributed to their capacity to relate to AICs who are for the most part themselves made up of down-to-earth, rural people.

Gilbert Ansre is a lifelong member of and leader within Evangelical Presbyterian Church of Ghana and a dedicated friend of the AIC Good News Theological Seminary since its inception in the early 1970s.

Miriam Adeney, Seattle Pacific University
When Mennonite workers first encountered indigenous African Christian movements, they adopted a listening mode. They knew the Christian faith is not the property of Westerners, no matter how rich our theological education. The churches with the longest heritages are not in Europe but in the Middle East, India, and East Africa. Mennonites know that the image of God shines through every person. So they settled in to learn.

At the same time they kept sharing Scripture, which was welcomed in African-run churches and seminaries. Scripture affirmed them all, critiqued them all, and circled continually back to Christ, the center of the cosmos. Submitting locally while reverberating with the universal word of God was the genius of these

Mennonites in Africa. Both Africans and foreign Mennonites stepped into a sadly familiar gap between Christians and unobtrusively built bridges. In so doing, they left a heritage that is an example for us all.

Miriam Adeney *is associate professor of world Christian studies, Seattle Pacific University, and author of* Kingdom without Borders: The Untold Story of Global Christianity.

2

Sowing

Once prepared, the ground, now susceptible of seed, becomes the lodging place of secret life. Shared watchfulness discloses how life is scattered in unexpected corners of reflection and practice, challenging settled wisdom. Old understandings give way to something like a new creation pattern, whether of hermeneutic, history, or custom. What was lost is found. What seemed barren is reclaimed. What appeared hopeless quivers anew with life, potential, and promise.

Reading the Bible through the Lens of the Spirit
Bryan Born

My friends in Botswana would say of a lively and spiritually insightful person that he or she is "very full of spirit, life" (*o tletse ka moya thata*). Nowhere is this truer than in the dynamic group of churches known as the African Spiritual Churches (ASCs). The high value of spiritual life among Africa's indigenous Christians has prompted in me some reflection on "the hermeneutics of the Spirit" practiced in these communities.

As one would surmise, it is their willingness and deep desire to receive and obey direction from the spiritual world that has given ASCs their name and provides one of their defining features. By embracing African spirituality, ASCs connected with the surrounding culture in ways that the mission-founded churches often missed. The ASCs reflect the traditional African outlook on the spiritual world and on community life. At their best, ASCs demonstrate a wonderful sense of community, the healing power of Jesus, and a vital longing for peace.

This focus on African spirituality has deeply impacted all areas of their Christian lives, including the way they approach the Bible. Musa Dube, a Botswana biblical scholar, has made a strong argument that ASC hermeneutics are based upon a *semoya*, or "spiritual" framework. Dube argues that when reading Scripture, ASCs members are seeking healing in its most holistic sense, which includes the need to tackle unemployment, reconcile relationships, recover from bad harvests, find lost cows, expel evil spirits, cure bodily illness, and deal with misfortune. Based on her research, Dube concluded that *semoya* hermeneutics requires one to approach the Bible with a bias toward healing of all relationships within society, especially for the suffering, poor, and marginalized.[1]

In my own research, I have spent considerable time exploring the ways in which the congregation of the Hermon Church of Sefophe village in eastern Botswana interpret and apply the Scriptures with their proclivity for seeking a holistic healing and reconciling interpretation. A good example of this interpretation is their foundational text, Psalm 133. This passage was revealed to the founder of the church, Archbishop Joel Madimabe, in a dream when praying and fasting about the name of the church. The emphasis on unity within the community – "How good and pleasant it is when brothers live together in unity!" (v. 1) – and the resulting blessing for life – "For there the LORD bestows his blessing, even life forevermore" (v. 3) – provide a hermeneutical lens through which to view all of Scripture. This is the interpretive end toward which the Spirit leads.

Hermon Church members have indicated that their favorite biblical texts are the story of Jesus and Zacchaeus in Luke 19:1–10 and the parable of the ten virgins in Matthew 25:1–13. The parable of the ten virgins is one of the archbishop's favorites, and he likes to use it to challenge his listeners to commit to God. But it is worth noting that his interpretation actually takes the passage in an interesting direction. "God is watching for the five wise virgins and the five foolish virgins," he notes. "You may find yourself waiting at the door, with the feast under way, and there will be no time to confess your weakness so that you might be interceded for and be healed. I want you to be like the five wise virgins whose lamps were not extinguished."

Instead of focusing on the eschatological return of Jesus, as is often the case with this parable, the preacher enlarges the text to encompass a concern for healing in the present context. In addition, the oil in the lamps is likened to

---

1. See Musa W. Dube, "Readings of Semoya: Batswana Women's Interpretations of Matt 15:21–28," *Semia* 73, no. 1: (1996): 111–29. Also Musa W. Dube, "What I Have Written, I Have Written (John 19:22)?" In *Interpreting the New Testament in Africa*, eds. M. Getui, T. S. Maluleke and J. Upkong (Nairobi: Acton Publishers, 2001), 145–63.

the presence of the Spirit in one's life, with the result that the message focuses on uniting with the group and walking in the power of the life-giving Spirit.

The fondness for the story of Zacchaeus is seen in a similar light. For the people of the Hermon Church, this is a story about what should happen when people turn their life over to Christ. When I asked church members if God promises to help Christians prosper financially, almost everyone answered in the negative. Prior to that question, I asked whether Western culture conflicts with their church teachings, and nearly half of the responses were variations of the idea that Western culture focuses on money, unlike their church! Further light was shed on this discussion by Archbishop Madimabe who mentioned that years before when people entered the church building, they did not just remove their shoes, they left their money at the door as well. In the Hermon Church, the story of Zacchaeus confirms that wealth pollutes and destroys life and that true Christianity – even salvation – is demonstrated by giving money away to the poor in the community. For people who are struggling financially, this text becomes one that encourages them to know that they are "children of Abraham" because they are not among those who hoard financial wealth.

One final example concerns the relationship between Old and New Testaments. Regarding the issue of Mosaic law, many have commented on the ASCs' propensity to emphasize a legalistic interpretation over a message of grace and freedom. Evidence of legalistic tendencies certainly exists within the Hermon Church, but this tendency is tempered by views that are far more nuanced than outside commentators often realize.

This point was driven home to me on a visit to the home of the archbishop in 2007, when he brought to my attention an issue that was literally right in front of us. The night before my arrival, one of his cattle had been mistakenly allowed onto the road and had been struck by a car and killed. When he was informed in the morning, the archbishop took his donkey cart out to the spot and salvaged as much of the meat as possible, bringing it home.

The carcass was now lying on the ground in one corner of the courtyard where we were visiting. He knew full well that Mosaic law prohibits the eating of something found dead as it will defile the person (see Lev 11:39–40; 22:8; Deut 14:21). But he told me God understands the need for people to live. They had been experiencing another difficult drought year, and to allow the meat to simply go to waste would be wrong. His point from this example was that Mosaic law is very important, but it must be subservient to the higher value of life and community. Even the emphasis on the Mosaic food laws is understood from this perspective. They do not follow these rules in order to "get to heaven" but in order to remain pure and preserve life and health in the present. *Semoya* hermeneutics, reading the Bible through the lens of the Spirit, must always lead to life.

Prayer Is Costly
Don Rempel Boschman

The knock on the door woke me from my sleep. I looked at my watch. It was 2:00 a.m. Who could it be at this hour? I stumbled to the door and found one of my coworkers standing there. Briefly she explained that one of the missionary children was very sick and had been airlifted during the night to the village in which I was living in order to be seen by a pediatrician.

The next morning, I went to visit some good Batswana friends in order to ask them to pray for the child. Bishop Bolokwe and his daughter were well-known throughout southern Botswana for their spiritual insight and for the effectiveness of their prayers. Almost every day people would come to visit them, asking for such healing prayer. Bishop Bolokwe, now in his eighties, had asked me to help train the pastors of his church, and thus we had become close friends.

After hearing what had happened, Bishop Bolokwe and his gifted daughter Mma Tiny agreed to pray for the child. They left the room in order to put on the clothing in which they prayed while I waited for them in their small living room. When they returned, Mma Tiny handed me a thick, soft towel. I was bewildered at first. What was the towel for? Seeing my bewilderment, Mma Tiny explained that the floor was hard, and I would need the towel to protect my knees from the cold, hard cement during the long time we would be praying.

Later as I reflected on our time of prayer, I realized I had been taught a lesson. In Bishop Bolokwe's mind, both he and his daughter could pray at length on their knees on the concrete floor, but the missionary needed a towel. In other words, Bishop Bolokwe was sure that his eighty-year-old knees were equal to the task of prayer, and his daughter was sure that her fifty-year-old knees were up to the task. But they both doubted whether the knees of the thirty-year-old missionary had developed the strength and the calluses needed to pray for any length of time.

Many Batswana Christians spend large amounts of time in prayer, and our family increasingly came to value this. In April 1995, my wife, Kathleen, injured her back. Medical treatment in June of that year made the situation much worse, and Kathleen was virtually bedridden for several months. During that time, literally hundreds of people, both in North America and Botswana, prayed for Kathleen. Many of those people had never met Kathleen but only knew of her plight.

Photo 15: Don Rempel Boschman and Bishop Bolokwe worked together at training church pastors

One group of Christians in particular was a source of strength to us. The Parana Apostolic Church is a small denomination of about one hundred members comprising two active congregations. Two of their pastors attend a Bible study I lead, and they were very concerned about Kathleen's health. They asked if they could come and pray for her on a regular basis.

Every Wednesday evening during those difficult months, about fifteen Christians, mainly university students, came to our house for an hour to sing and pray for Kathleen. A highlight for us during those services was the preaching, which focused on healing stories in the Bible. The message was always the same: God performed miracles in the Bible, and God is still performing them today. Of course we knew that, but during those bleak months our hearts needed to be constantly reminded of it.

As Kathleen continued to struggle with pain, the Parana Church decided that hers was an especially difficult case which needed the elders' intervention. At their own cost, a group of five older people boarded a bus and traveled the three hundred kilometers to our home. None of these people had ever met Kathleen, but they felt called to come and pray for her. They prayed and fasted that weekend for someone they didn't know.

Because of the Parana Church, I have learned how costly prayer can be. "I will pray for you" is a promise that is often too freely given. The members of the Parana Church gave large amounts of time to pray for us. They spent a lot of money to pray for us in person. I am sure that God would have heard them just as well had they stayed home and prayed for us for a shorter period. But their costly sacrifice was not only pleasing to God, it also lifted our spirits as very few other things could. Even missionaries need to be preached to and reminded that God can and does see and help people today.

"I'll pray for you" can be a costly phrase. But it is one that can bring great blessings, even a miracle.

Tata Maka's Journey to Matatiele . . . and Ours
Joe Sawatzky

"Pastor," he said, leading me by the hand to a corner of the small, concrete worship structure, "I want to tell you my dream." Tata Maka pulled out a small piece of paper and a pen and began to scribble out a scene over the support of his Bible. He was *showing* me his dream.

"I was standing on a mountain looking at other mountains," he recounted, lining out a string of triangles on the paper. "They looked like Xhosa houses," he said. Something of the scene bespoke for him the region of Matatiele, a mountainous district in South Africa north of Mthatha near Lesotho. Something of the scene was also overwhelming to Tata Mata: "'No! God! I said in my dream. 'It's too much.'" Then something happened. "One by one the mountains were taken and put into the mountain that I was standing on until there were none left. Then I looked again, and I saw that I was not standing on a mountain, but on the Bible. I wonder what it means?"

We parted ways that Sunday. I left grateful that Tata Maka had entrusted me with the gift of his dream and committed to pondering its meaning. I knew that I could not give specific directives from his dream, but thought that I might be able to shed light on it by placing it within a broader biblical context.

The next time that our family worshiped with the little church in Mandela Park, Tata Ntapo, my usual interpreter, was not present. So the task of translation fell to Tata Maka. We were both reluctant to attempt the sermon together, but seeing Tata Maka beside me was confirmation that today was the day to preach *his* dream. I asked his permission to tell it to the congregation. I retold it and then explained its significance through the story of Jesus – the Word made flesh by the power of the Spirit. "When the Spirit drove Jesus into the wilderness to be tempted, he rebuked the devil by the word of God. The Spirit points to the word, and the word points to the Spirit. If the two do not agree, God has not spoken. The Spirit and the word go together." *UMoya uhamba nelizwi* – "the Spirit goes with the word," said Tata Maka as he left that Sunday.

Some months later in our Bible school office, Tata Maka told me of where the Spirit and the word had taken him. He had been tarrying over his dream. One day on a Mthatha street, he passed an acquaintance – "not a saved person, just an ordinary man" – who chided him, "What are you doing here? Aren't you supposed to be somewhere else?" Tata Mata took this as a prophetic word and headed out immediately for Matatiele as indicated in the dream, though uncertain how he would get there with no money for transportation.

God intervened. On the way, in Mt. Frere, Tata Mata met a man also on his way to Matatiele. The man gave Tata Maka a lift and in addition offered him a welcome place to stay with relatives. There, Tata Mata's host confided in him that his father was ill. The two prayed together for the father's healing, and the host later reported in thankfulness that his father was much better. From this place of welcome in Matatiele, Tata Maka set out to preach to whoever would listen. He went from *rondavel* to *rondavel*, round Xhosa mud houses with pointed, thatched roofs. Some people received him and others refused. "I don't want Jesus," one mama told him. But a number embraced his message, and Tata Maka returned from his trip to Matatiele with joy.

Tata Maka's dream and faithful response reminds us that many years ago, "the Lord appointed seventy-two others and sent them . . . to every town and place where he was about to go" (Luke 10:1). Like Tata Maka, these messengers went without provision for their journey save what they were to receive from whoever would welcome them (10:4, 7–8). Some people did not welcome them (10:10). But those who did had their sick healed, signifying the nearness of God's kingdom (10:9). The seventy-two messengers also "returned with joy," exclaiming in wonder that the power of the Lord's name could pulse through even them (10:17). And just as it took an "unsaved" man to prompt Tata Maka on his journey, so the Samaritans – despised objects of wrath to the messengers of Jesus – helped to show the disciples the way of God's mercy (see Luke 9:51–56; 10:30–37).

In the person of Tata Maka – and I suspect also in countless others in remote corners of the world – is "no beauty or majesty to attract us to him, nothing in his appearance that we should desire him" (Isa 53:2). Nothing, that is, but the mysteriously compelling presence of the Suffering Servant to whose Spirit they are obedient. In Tata Maka's journey to Matatiele – indeed in the journey of whoever listens to Jesus (Luke 10:16) – is the word of the biblical story again made flesh. "How beautiful on the mountains are the feet of those who bring good news, who proclaim peace, who bring good tidings, who proclaim salvation, who say to Zion, 'Your God reigns!'" (Isa 52:7). Amen.

Breaking Down Barriers
B. Harry Dyck

Lois and I with our children, Heidi and Ted, had been in Francistown, Botswana, for approximately a year when Motibe, one of the local leaders who had already been involved in my Bible classes, stopped by for reasons I can no longer remember. As was customary – we had learned – almost anytime is tea time when friends come into the yard. Desirous of following local patterns and inspired by my desire to get better acquainted with Motibe, I invited him to stick around for a cup of tea. Motibe seemed a bit surprised by the invitation, yet clearly pleased by the offer. So with cups of tea in one hand and scones in the other, we chatted there under the shade of my recently constructed bamboo carport.

I remember that part of our conversation included his experiences with racism, most bitter for him since Botswana was after all the land of his forebears. But this land had become increasingly attractive to and occupied by the *Makgoa* (white people), particularly those from neighboring countries. He characterized these folks as "bosses" rather than friends or neighbors. After our half hour or so of social time, it was time to go, and as I walked Motibe out to the gate, he turned and volunteered these startling words: "This was the first time that I have ever received a drink in a white man's real teacup." I did not understand the full meaning of the "real teacup" until Motibe explained that I had served him tea not out of a *tin* cup but out of a *regular* cup used for normal table service.

Another similar incident took place when Letsatse, the first youth leader to attend my classes, invited me to do a weekend series of lessons in his home village. After our evening session, I had the option of sleeping in my Peugeot station wagon or accepting the timid but hopeful invitation that Letsatse extended me to carry my cot inside and sleep in his house. I was pleased to accept his offer.

Photo 16: Tea time with pastors!

Later as we lay in our respective accommodations – he on his floor blankets and I in my cot – we chatted about subjects of mutual interest and especially about my coming "all the way to Botswana from my familial home, so far away." But the significance of the night came in the testimonial Letsatse shared toward the end of our conversation: "You are the first white man ever to sleep in my house," he said. That is when I realized why his invitation had been extended with such tentativeness: He had feared his gift of place might be refused.

I experienced that night the delights of that proverbial "cup of cold water" in two opposite stages – first giving, and then receiving. How misguided we are to think we are the *only* or even *primary* knowers, teachers, doers, and givers! How relevant that humorous confession, usually attributed to the Amish:

Ve get so soon oldt, and yet so late schmardt.
(We get so soon old, and yet so late smart.)

With the conveyance of respect and mutuality in normal everyday life, barriers of suspicion and worse come down, doors open up, and relationships are spawned that have all the ingredients present in the prayer of Jesus for his disciples "that all of them may be one, Father, just as you are in me and I am in you" (John 17:21).

Relationship Building Was Key to Our Success
Ezekiel Nartey

When I first became connected with the Good News Training Institute (GNTI) in Ghana in the early 1980s, participation by African Independent Churches had severely dropped off to the point that Erma Grove, a Mennonite worker and then principal at Good News, was wondering whether the school could and should continue. The decision was made to promote the school by spending nearly every Sunday visiting different congregations and promoting the school's programs.

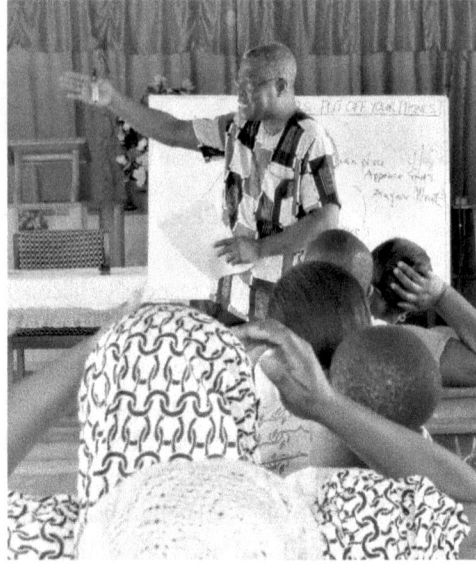

Photo 17: Ezekiel Nartey conducting a lay leaders
Bible study in a local congregation

I got to know the churches by visiting them with a variety of Mennonite and Lutheran mission workers Erma Grove, Ed and Lorraine Spruth, and later Phil and Julie Bender. What impressed me in our Sunday encounters was the sensitivity and care the workers gave to respecting these various churches and their leaders. The workers entered into the worship experiences, listened to the wide range of questions and concerns registered by the churches, and then warmly and gently encouraged the churches to take advantage of the opportunity that the Institute provided in training leaders in the Scriptures.

The visits to the churches turned the situation around. Soon after this, enrollment started to pick up, and we began to observe more support from various AIC quarters. It is so easy to get out of touch with what is going on out in the churches and to not invest the time necessary for building solid relationships with AIC church leaders. This is an ongoing challenge at Good News today as well, but I learned during this earlier period that relationship building must not be neglected if Good News is to succeed.

We Had So Much to Learn!
David A. Shank

We had responded to a request in 1973 from John Ahui, the supreme head of the Harrist Church in Côte d'Ivoire, to help him "water the tree" which the Prophet William Wadé Harris had planted in 1914 and had entrusted to him in 1928, just a year before Harris's death. Arriving in Abidjan in 1979, after research on the prophet's roots, history, thought, and ministry, my wife and I made ourselves available to John Ahui and his people.

Even as the older, largely nonliterate generation of the Harrist National Committee was suspicious of our motives due to previous negative experiences with Western mission agencies, the younger generation, organized as the Union of Harrist Youth of Côte d'Ivoire, was open to what they might learn from us. And the Dida people, with the full approval of Supreme Head John Ahui, wanted us present in the village of Yocoboué for biblical training for their youth and preachers. The James and Jeanette Krabill family, in response to that request, had established themselves there and had initiated a program of biblical study.

Simultaneously, the Harrist National Committee had known some tensions and reorganized several times. We had scarcely kept up with those transitions and the church politics behind it all. Then in the mid-1980s, we learned of a new reorganization of the executive committee with a certain Pierre Anin as its president. Despite our many Harrist contacts, we did not know of him at all. But we thought it would be a good thing for us to get into contact with him in order to let him know who we were and that we had been invited by the church's spiritual head, John Ahui, and to explain why we were there and available. For despite orality – or maybe due to it – all such information does not necessarily get passed on with clarity and as intended.

I was told that Monsieur Anin was a young intellectual, a university graduate and professional geographer who had earned advanced diplomas. He arranged for a meeting with us at one of the downtown hotels. We suspected that he chose this site for the sake of discretion, not wanting to be seen with a white man, "Monsieur David." To our surprise, he was accompanied by a preacher, Julien Akousi, the secretary of the new National Committee. Julien was the right-hand man to the head of the Order of Preachers, Pita Loba, a designated bishop-cardinal who was apparently among the elderly leaders most threatened by our presence. His presence did not augur well for our ministry of "availability." To our advantage, however, Julien Akousi had been present with Pita Loba in 1973 at the Mother Church in Petit Bassam when the Supreme Spiritual Head John Ahui had formally concluded our conversation with the invitation to, "Come and help me water the tree." Akousi had been an oral witness to that official welcome.

After the customary formalities, I explained to President Anin the reason for my request to meet with him: to explain to him clearly who we were, to tell him about our earlier invitation from Ahui, and to explain my study of the Prophet Harris. I provided documentation and emphasized our posture of availability for service in the Harrist Church. After this lengthy summary of our activities up until then, Anin asked Julien Akousi to give his reaction to my words.

Preacher Julien, representing his Spiritual Head Pita Loba, was very brief: "As far as I am concerned, you can leave tomorrow. We Harrists do not really need your services in any way whatsoever, and we will not in any way suffer from your departure."

Anin listened very carefully, hesitated a moment, and then picked up after Julien. "It's just exactly as my secretary says," he began. "Preacher Julien has put it very well. As president of the National Executive Committee, I need your work as a historian. You can be highly useful to me at this particular time in Harrist life, and I am grateful for any help and documentation you can offer us. I would hope that you might stay on in Côte d'Ivoire for the time being, and share with us whatever you have learned."

When my wife and I had returned to our apartment, we looked at each other in bewildered wonderment. We obviously had so much to learn about Côte d'Ivoire . . . a process that seemingly never ends!

We eventually decided – in consultation with our colleagues, the Krabills, and other Harrists – to accept Pierre Anin's invitation and stay on. And in the years to follow, we had many opportunities to share the Harris story, with specific documentation and a slide set, with various Harrists in our home and elsewhere. In addition, with the Krabills' lengthy Harrist teaching ministry in the Dida region, my wife and I continued to be invited to visit in Harrist villages, particularly among the Attié people, with the help and affirmation of Raoul Aby, the president of the Attié Harrists and their only ethnic member on the National Executive Committee.

Photo 18: Wilma and David Shank in Harrist worship

My Impression of Mennonites
Thomas A. Oduro

I got to know Mennonites when I enrolled at what was then the Good News Training Institute, a presecondary-level Bible college, in 1980 in Accra, Ghana. The head of the Institute at that time was Erma Grove, a middle-aged American Mennonite missionary. Madam Grove, as she was popularly called, was a committed Christian who always emphasized the study and reading of the Bible. It was her persuasion that compelled me to read through the Bible for the first time. I never thought I could read through the Bible, but Madam Grove challenged the students to read it since, according to her, she had read through the Bible several times. After reading through the Bible for the first time, I got to know a lot about the overall salvation plan of God. So I did not stop there; I bought a new Bible and read through it. Since then I have read through the Bible, just like Madam Grove, several times. I have also challenged some friends and students to read through the Bible.

My greatest impression about Mennonites, however, was their spirit of voluntarism. The Good News Theological Seminary, a metamorphosis of the Good News Training Institute, bought a ten-acre piece of land on the northeastern side of Accra in 1996. The purpose was to develop the land into a campus, but the money left in the accounts of the seminary was only enough to build a three-room classroom block. I heard that a Mennonite building team was scheduled to arrive in Accra to lay the foundation of an eight-classroom block, but I did not believe it. I did not believe that people who do not have any interest in the seminary would raise money to travel to Ghana to build for an institution they had practically no knowledge of. In those days the use of Internet and websites were not widespread, so it was difficult to have knowledge of people and institutions across oceans.

Photo 19: Thomas A. Oduro (center) offering an opening prayer in an AIC worship service

My doubt grew into speechlessness when the team did arrive. They were very happy and grateful to God that they were going to contribute to the building of the seminary. Wendell Schloneger, the leader of the team, was enthusiastic about the role of the team. As I watched them digging dirt and sweating under the merciless West African sun, I found it difficult to believe my eyes. Is it true that these people have left the comfort of their homes to work for an institution they will gain nothing from? Is it true that these people raised money from their fellow Mennonites just to come to Ghana to build, without expecting any commensuration? What kind of Christians are these people? Why are they working so happily? These were some of the questions that were running through my mind.

In the course of the Mennonites' work, the local authorities asked them to temporarily halt their activities because of some perceived litigation over the land. The building team complied with the order and prayed that the controversy would soon be over. God heard their prayer. After waiting for three days, they were asked to continue building. The joy and enthusiasm with which they resumed digging the dirt, mixing cement with sand and stone, putting the mixture into pans, and using their bare hands to carry the pans to pour the mixture into the trenches they had dug made a lasting impression on me about Mennonites' understanding of helping less privileged Christians and their commitment to do so no matter the circumstances.

Later in a conversation with the building team, I realized that they had been doing work like this quite often for many Christians and institutions around the world. I salute Mennonites!

GUEST REFLECTIONS

Darrell Whiteman, *Global Development; editor of* Missiology, *1989–2002*
As a missiological anthropologist celebrating the diversity of expressions of world Christianities, I see the African Initiated Churches as authentic examples of what Lamin Sanneh championed when he argued that, "Christianity demands to be translated" into multiple languages, worldviews, and social structures.[2] But when the form of Christianity looks very different from our own familiar, privileged position and interpretation, it is easy to brand the difference as heretical. And sometimes it is.

The development of AICs in the past century or more is an instructive example of the rise of world Christianities. Initially

---

2. See Lamin Sanneh, *Whose Religion Is Christianity? The Gospel beyond the West* (Grand Rapids, MI: Eerdmans, 2003); and *Translating the Message: The Missionary Impact on Culture*, 2nd ed. (Maryknoll, NY: Orbis, 2009).

they were called splinter groups, sects, breakaways, and separatist movements, along with other pejorative terms. They were perceived to be negative reactions to colonial Christianity propagated by Western mission organizations. And in the cases of prophet-healers like William Wadé Harris and Simon Kimbangu who initiated significant indigenous Christian movements, AICs were threats to colonial governments.

Later these churches were often called African Independent Churches, and now in some circles the term "African Initiated Churches" has become the norm, since many of these churches are not simply reactions against mission Christianity. Rather they are splendid examples of efforts to connect the gospel to the deepest parts of Africans' worldviews, needs, concerns, and aspirations. These churches are examples of radical biblical contextualization and underscore the belief that people do not have to deny their birth identity in order to affirm their second birth identity as followers of Jesus.

In my teaching on contextualization, I have often used the documentary film "Rise Up and Walk: The Life and Witness of the African Indigenous Churches" (1981) that profiles five of these churches and begins with the observation that "Africans sing and dance their theology." When I have used this film in teaching, it knocks the theological and ecclesiastical socks off my students every time that I show it. The forms of worship, church organization, spirituality, and theology are so very different from their familiar Westernized expressions and understanding that they sometimes question if these are legitimate examples of Christianity. Often students' initial responses have been to brand these churches as neopagan or syncretistic. But employing the lens of an anthropological perspective, these students eventually recognize that these African churches are legitimate examples of the ways in which Christianity is imagined, embodied, and enacted in cultural contexts different from their own.

Most mission organizations opposed these African expressions of following Jesus. So "different" was interpreted to mean misguided, wrong, and even heretical. A notable exception to this negative reaction to AICs came from North American

Mennonites. Why would Mennonites rather than Methodists, Baptists, Roman Catholics, or Presbyterians take a more positive approach to interacting with these churches? Instead of ostracizing these African Christians, why did they choose to partner with them in their training institutions? Could it have something to do with their own Mennonite history that splices into the DNA of their worldview an understanding of what it means to be persecuted and assigned to a minority status by the ecclesiastical majority? Might it be that their commitment to the doctrine of the priesthood of all believers enabled them to make room for African brothers and sisters in Christ? Has Mennonite history provided a heightened sensitivity to the other and appreciation for perspectives different from their own?

Missiological anthropologists are a rare breed, but Mennonites have produced more missiological anthropologists than any other ecclesial tradition of which I am aware. Beginning with the "dean" of missiological anthropologists, Paul Hiebert (1932–2007), and recognizing the contributions of others including Jacob Loewen (1922–2006), Robert Ramseyer (1929–2016), and Donald R. Jacobs (1929–2020), I have often wondered what is it in the Mennonite tradition that has given us so many excellent missiological anthropologists.

I believe it is the same ecclesial DNA that has spawned friendships between AICs and North American Mennonites. It is a commitment to advancing the kingdom of God instead of simply expanding one's denomination. It is an understanding and appreciation for what we anticipate in the fulfillment of Revelation 7:9, that around the throne of God there will be an enormous crowd of people from every race, tribe, people group, and language, and might I add, from a diversity of ecclesiastical traditions including AICs, Mennonites, and the rest of us followers of Jesus.

Darrell Whiteman *of Global Development is a retired professor of cultural anthropology and was dean of the E. Stanley Jones School of World Mission and Evangelism at Asbury Theological Seminary and editor of* Missiology *from 1989–2002.*

3

Germination

The seed, carrying a promise and having been broadcast on a field, does not fail in announcing its life. Come some dawn of the heart or mind, tendrils appear. Astonishment, even among people of resurrection faith, follows as insight, understanding, and friendship displace misgivings and stumbles.

The Christian Tree
Stan Nussbaum

In 2002, I was privileged to visit Lesotho eighteen years after I had finished my Bible teaching assignment there. I drove out to Kolojane Ha Thuhloane, about one and a half hours from Maseru, to visit Pastor J. K. Mallela and other members of the Bible class he had faithfully hosted for me for my entire seven-year stint with AIMM there.

My visit included a walk of two or three miles over to another village with two women who had been in the classes. As we walked, we passed many of the small black wattle trees which are one of many scenic marvels in Lesotho. I remarked about them, and Mafiniase said, "*Ee, sefate sa BoKreste.*" ("Oh yes, the Christian tree.")

"You remember that?" I asked.

"Sure. Everybody knows that *Ntate* (father) Stan taught us about the Christian tree."

This was a shock to me because I did not recall ever making a big deal about that. In fact, I may have only said it once or twice, and possibly not in a Bible class. But here I was, back in the same community two decades later, and that was *the thing* they were talking about . . . not my carefully prepared outlines and study guides, but an almost off-hand remark about something I had noticed in their world. Now I know why Jesus used parables, and if I had a do-over on my Bible teaching work with AICs, I would use a lot more of them.

Here is what these students were talking about. The black wattle tree is the harbinger of spring in Lesotho. When the long grass is still those beautiful shades of tan and rust, when it has not rained for months, when the ground is far too hard to plow, when dust is everywhere, and before other trees are starting to bud, the black wattle bursts into magnificent bloom. Glorious, profuse lemon-yellow blossoms, each about the size of a pea, appear in brilliant contrast to the blue-green foliage of the tree to display the glory of their Creator.

But how do these trees blossom before any rain comes? They know what time it is, and they know what is coming. So they act like it has already happened. In so doing they signal to the rest of the trees, the grass, the animals, and the people, "The time is fulfilled. Spring is at hand. Focus on its arrival, and welcome it with open arms."

Photo 20: Lesotho's Black Wattle tree

In other words, the black wattles are "Christian trees." They have an unseen connection to the power of life. A new state of things is arriving in them, and they are calling others to join them. In the years since I was in Lesotho, the gospel announcement in Mark 1:15 has become more and more important to me: "The time is fulfilled. . . . God's reign is beginning. Turn and welcome the news" (my paraphrase). The example of the black wattle tree has stuck in my mind as it had in theirs.

Mennonite connections with AICs have often been questioned by outsiders because of nagging issues regarding the theological positions of these churches. I even did my doctoral dissertation on "theological dialogue" with AICs. But the real question for sizing up AICs as fellow Christians may be the black wattle question, "Are they blooming?" If they are, then they must be connected to God's life and to his kingdom that is already present and not yet here. It was an honor to stand among my AIC fellow believers, signaling with them the present-future announcement that "the time is fulfilled" and "Spring is at hand."

When I Was Chosen as a Preacher, I Wanted to Understand More of God's Word
Alphonse Kobli Beugré

In my entire life, I only had the chance to attend school for half a year. But I have had a deep thirst for learning since my early childhood. As a young preacher I often dreamed of deeper study and understanding of the Bible. But as time went along with a growing family and increased responsibilities, I didn't see how that would ever happen.

On trips from the village to the city of Abidjan, I would go to Christian bookstores and pick out books that helped me understand more about the Bible. Some of them helped me know where the Bible came from and what the difference was between the Old and the New Testaments. Others gave me tools for how to read and study the Bible by doing book studies and understanding the teaching of Jesus through his stories and parables.

When the first generation of our leaders was baptized by the Prophet William Wadé Harris back in the days of my grandfather, there were still no schools in Côte d'Ivoire. No one owned books, and no had learned to read or write. Our first preachers tried to remember and carefully pass along to the faithful what the prophet had told them during his rapid travel through our region of the country. But when I was chosen as a preacher, I wanted more. I longed and prayed for a deeper understanding of God's word.

One day I read about the story of the Ethiopian eunuch. On his way home from worship in Jerusalem, the Ethiopian was reading the book of Isaiah. God sent Philip to him who asked him, "Do you understand what you are reading?"

The Ethiopian said, "How can I unless someone explains it to me?" (Acts 8:29–31). I said to myself, that's me! And I prayed that God would send me someone like Philip to help me better understand. To tell you the truth, I thought it would never happen.

Photo 21: Alphonse with James Krabill and son Matthew on a village Bible study visit

Then in the late 1970s, one of our youth leaders living in Abidjan came out to the village and told us that a group of people called "Mennonites" had inquired whether our church leaders were interested in Bible training. My uncle, Papa N'Guessan Benoît, was the head preacher and had to make a hard decision since sixty years before, our church had been tricked by white missionaries into leaving our church and joining theirs. Many people were suspicious of what might happen if the Mennonites came and we were tricked again.

But my uncle wanted the younger preachers in the church to receive training and decided to take the chance. That opened the door to a friendship with the Mennonites that has lasted many years. They came to our village of Yocoboué, lived with us, raised their children here, and taught us many things about God's word throughout the entire region where our Dida people live.

As the Dida-language literacy teacher for the Bible translation project that was just beginning, I also worked closely with Mennonite worker James Krabill (*Kragbe*) in writing down and putting into song booklets hundreds of original hymns composed by church musicians in our village. This work helped us to appreciate our language and learn to read it so we were ready when God's word finally came to us in portions and then completed New Testament books.

I had prayed that God would send me someone like Philip. That is what finally happened. I should have been more trusting that God would keep his promises. *Dieu est bon!* God is good!

Good Friday 2.0
Jonathan P. Larson

There's nothing quite like the drama of the Passion story in the company of African Christians who travel yearly by their thousands to open-air Eastertide gatherings. In fields and towns, along river banks, and sometimes at dawn by the seashore there is preaching and singing, fervent prayer, and processions as great hosts of believers reenact the drama of salvation.

Invited by a friend, Archbishop Israel Motswaosele of the Spiritual Healing Church of Botswana, to these Easter observances, I traveled to a hilltop village close by the Zimbabwe border. The faithful began to gather Wednesday evening, arriving by donkey carts, buses, and vans. Campsites appeared under the scattered thorn trees, and cooking fires flickered in the fading light. By Maundy Thursday, robed choirs were rehearsing, orders of church leaders huddled to allot responsibilities, and in the background, cattle had been slaughtered as pots of food steamed in readiness.

In the afternoon, as hymns swelled from the hopelessly tiny church building, individuals rose to read by lantern light the Gospel portions that unfold the story. On through the night the choirs came and went, the preachers and evangelists by turn stood to retell a story of table friendship, of an innocent servant, of intrigue and betrayal, of humiliation, and of unflinching obedience. While this drama stirred to life, some rose to confess waywardness. Others spoke prophetic messages while the gathered host gave answer with their anthems.

Toward Friday evening during a choir festival, I slipped away in search of some badly needed sleep. As I drifted away, I was mortified to hear my name called on the public address system. I scrambled into respectable clothing and ran back to the meeting, all the while reproaching myself with the piercing question of Jesus to his followers, "Could you not watch with me one brief hour?" Working my way to the front of the crowd, I finally made eye contact with the old bishop who was speaking.

He addressed me with a knowing twinkle. "Teacher," he said, "I have a question for you. This past week, my neighbor came to visit. He had been reflecting in gratitude upon the many years our families have lived side by side in peace. In token of his thankfulness, he brought me a sheep. But it has occurred to me that I cannot eat this sheep since it is a sacred thing. So, I have thought it best to give this sheep back to God. It has been slaughtered in the appointed way, and I have set aside the choice portions as a thank offering to heaven. Do you find anything wrong with what I am about to do?"

Standing there beneath the gaze of a thousand eyes, I was paralyzed. Had I missed a seminary course in animal sacrifice? Why did I feel so woefully unprepared to muster a credible response? Finally, I stammered that I did not believe heaven would refuse any offering of a grateful heart.

Satisfied with my groping answer, the bishop gestured that a basin containing the reserved parts be brought forward. As the crowd took up an anthem, he led the procession across the courtyard to an altar where a bed of glowing coals had already been laid. A portion from the Psalms, "I will give praise to the LORD at all times," was read in a sonorous voice. Then reaching into the basin, the bishop took the sheets of fat and laid them on the coals. There was a hissing and snapping as the flaring fire took hold, and a column of smoke boiled up into the clear night sky.

I stood there transfixed by this moment, weak in the knees and faint from the power of what I was witnessing. As my eyes followed the rising smoke to the depth of the darkness, to the distant stars, it dawned upon me that this was Good Friday! I had been called from my drowsiness to experience the drama of this rare day as I had never understood it before. I will never pass a casual Good Friday again. I am forever imprinted with its colossal passion. And I am grateful.

Only God Knows the Ultimate Results of Our Time and Ministry
Marian Hostetler

In a document I put together recounting my life story, I have two chapters on Africa. The Nigeria chapter is entitled, "Off to Africa," and the Swazi one is, "Second African Sojourn." In retrospect, I note that there is not much "mission" language in what I have written! As I think back on my West African experience, I realize I have always had a sadness within me that I did not develop any close relationships with Nigerian women. My shy, fearful child within kept me from trying the "small-small" amount of Ibibio language I did learn. And very few women in our churches had any serious command of English.

So why did I go to Nigeria? Did I have a mission there? Two things come to mind. First, I have often said that in those years of "growing" our family, when my husband, Darrel, accepted jobs in various places to teach the Bible or direct choral music, I took my job with me – "wherever." And that job was the family which in Nigeria included teaching our two daughters during their kindergarten, first, and second grade years. Second, in light of family responsibilities, the Mennonite mission board did not give me a specific assignment they did to Darrel.

However, we all felt a part of Darrel's mission, especially as we went with him on Sunday mornings to yet another congregation where he might preach and definitely serve communion. In such instances, I provided the "wine." I was also in complete agreement with the type of mission we were offering, of assisting AIC leaders in their desire to follow God, rather than going about establishing a new church name to add to the proliferation of unique church names already all around us. As requested by local leaders, I also led some women's meetings, discovering how easy it was to connect when you begin with an Old Testament story which relates quickly to their way of life.

Photo 22: Group Bible study session with Marian and Frank A. Udoh

One experience does stay firmly in my memory. After a typical Sunday service one morning, several women came to me with great smiles and began to lightly pat my stomach and breasts. I got their message very quickly. They knew that I was pregnant and were quite happy about it. I thought I had been doing such a good job of hiding that fact! As I ponder this event, it seems to me that the Spirit has revealed more meaning. People were watching me – and us as a family. They "knew" things about us that did not need words to explain. Did they learn lessons about family life? About accepting others not like ourselves? Of seeing Christ-love in action? Other women came to our compound after our son's birth and gathered around his bassinet to pray for him. And when he was deathly ill at six months, it was the church and the Bible school students who prayed him back to health. They had been so proud that Nigeria had finally given us a son and knew God would not want him to die so soon.

Why did I go to Nigeria? Because God called us there. We didn't prevent the Biafran war, or build a cathedral, or even have a building named for us. And our sojourn only lasted two years. But for me it was enriching and life-changing ... hard sometimes, yet secure in God's love. Beyond that, only God knows the ultimate purpose and results of our time and ministry there.

The Support Group We Created Gave Us Dignity, Despite Our Physical Struggles
Hortense Assah

I am so happy to contribute to this collection of stories because my friendship with Mennonite workers Rod and Lynda Hollinger-Janzen in Benin changed my life. I will never forget the Sunday in 1986 at the Hinde congregation where I attend church in Cotonou. The Hollinger-Janzens had just arrived in Benin. Lynda saw me sitting in my wheelchair in the aisle and asked if there was anything that she could do for me. I was amazed that this woman would take notice of me. I said no. She insisted. I said, "Well, you can lift me up out of my chair and place me on the bench." Before I could realize it, Rod promptly did just that. Again, I was amazed at what this foreign man would do for me.

That was the beginning of a long relationship between us. I visited them in their apartment, but discovered that they lived on the second floor. Rod came down and carried me up the stairs, placing me on a chair in their living room. I couldn't believe he would do this for me.

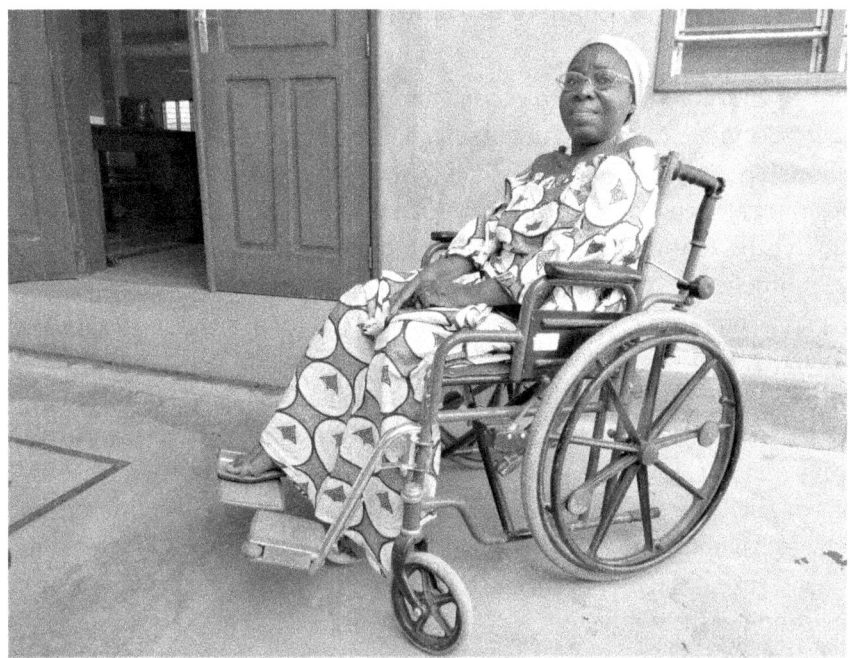

Photo 23: "The Group of Disabled Persons gave us dignity, despite our physical struggles." Hortense Assah

Eventually, we organized *Le groupe des handicapés* (the group of disabled persons). For our first "festival," we drew over fifty disabled people from all over the region. We met as often as we could, making crafts for sale. Lynda and Rod helped to sell these products in the missionary community in Benin. We also prayed together as a group, reminding ourselves that God loves us, despite our physical condition. Many of those who participated were Christians, but others who came included Muslims and traditional religion practitioners. Lynda and Rod contributed some funding for these activities, which made them possible.

Later when Mennonite worker Nancy Frey came, she continued the work of supporting our group. There is no way to describe how much this encouraged us and gave us pride and dignity, despite the physical struggles we were experiencing. My close relationship with these dear friends changed my life.

It Is Impossible for a Man to Be Faithful to One Woman
Rudy Dirks

One of the most rewarding, exciting, and unexpected interactions my wife, Sharon, and I encountered in our AIC relationships was the married couples' fellowship. As the HIV/AIDS crisis in Botswana manifested itself with HIV-positive rates hovering around one third of the adult population and weekly funerals becoming the norm, a key question forced itself upon us: "How do we most effectively minister the gospel in this context?"

In addition to HIV/AIDS education and training, teaching youth about sexuality, and relating with compassion to those who were already sick with AIDS, we began to think of prevention and the future. Our Batswana leaders expressed their concerns about the spread of HIV even in their own congregations. It was clear that a more fundamental issue was the quality of marriage relationships within the churches. If marriages could be strengthened, if marital faithfulness could be the norm, if youth learned from their parents to reserve sexual activity for marriage, then the HIV epidemic could eventually be a thing of the past.

The married couples' fellowship was an effort to move in this direction. Two things made this group particularly exciting: how it came together and the enthusiasm of the couples. At an AIC worker conference in Kenya, the sharing of the Swazi delegation about their marriage teaching inspired us to invite them to "bring the flame" to Botswana. And that's exactly what happened. The Dlaminis and two other couples from Swaziland joined with about eight AIC couples in Gaborone for a weekend retreat, and the Swazi couples taught their marriage material. It was wonderful to observe AIC couples teaching each other. By the end of the weekend, the couples from Botswana were determined to begin their own couples' fellowship.

For a period of time, the Gaborone married couples' fellowship met regularly to study biblical teaching on marriage and to discuss Setswana cultural practices and challenges for these couples. We Mennonite workers adapted biblical marriage teaching from resources we had, and the Batswana took these teachings and applied them to the Setswana cultural context. *Moruti* (teacher, pastor) Fanani Moshweshwe was the key to this integration. An older leader from St. Michael's Apostolic Church, he was steeped in Setswana culture, while also serving as a living testimony to the transforming power of Christ. He had come to know Jesus over the years and was led, in his own words, "from the darkness into the light." He was a fount of wisdom, and in the couples' fellowship meetings with younger couples, his credibility as an elder – both culturally and spiritually – opened up the other couples to sharing with a frankness that stunned us.

Photo 24: A session of the "Married Couples' Fellowship" in Botswana

No topic was left unexplored. The taboo of speaking about sexuality was discarded. Women shared openly about the ways they had been taught to give in to the sexual advances of men and their own ignorance about their bodies and sexuality. Couples spoke openly about their frustration in marriage relationships. They admitted to the implicit understanding among couples that women "knew" their husbands could not be faithful and that men in turn did not trust their wives. In one discussion, both husbands and wives agreed on one thing: "It is impossible for a man to be faithful to one woman."

Each week as Moshweshwe and I prepared the lessons together, he would explain the Setswana perspective on biblical marriage teachings such as communication, intimacy, child rearing, and gender roles. He was relentless in his passion that these couples learn everything that the Christian faith could have to say about marriage. He repeatedly said, "We have never been taught these things. We must learn them. This will strengthen our marriages."

Moshweshwe's enthusiasm in the meetings was infectious. The younger men sat in stunned silence as he shared his story of having been a domineering, self-centered husband. He said, "I was an animal." The contrast with who he was now was obvious as he praised his wife for her patience with him, assuring participant couples, "But now I feel like a newly married man again." One of the younger men later said to me, "Batswana men do not talk like this. I have never heard an African man admit his unkindness to his wife and speak with such openness and humility."

The times of fellowship with this group of couples from half a dozen different AIC congregations were a unique experience. Batswana are typically reserved. Seldom have we witnessed their openness to share personally such insights into their cultural and church practices and such a desire to grow in their Christian marriages. Later, at least one more group was formed out of this one, and a book on Christian marriage from a Setswana perspective was written with hopes of publication in Botswana.

I share this story because these couples touched our lives so profoundly and because we pray that God will continue to strengthen their marriages and their children's marriages for generations to come. I also share this as a way to honor a very unique and godly couple, the Moshweshwes, who exemplify the most excellent wisdom and love that we have experienced among AIC Christians.

"Without Scriptural Foundations, How Are the Spirits Tested and Discerned?"
Isaac Wontumi

I knew all of the early Mennonite mission workers, especially the Bible teacher Erma Grove with whom I worked very closely. My first exposure to AICs came with my involvement in the Church of the Lord (Aladura) when they came to Ghana from Nigeria in 1953. Later, on 26 February 1965, I founded The Church of Melchizedek.

In 1969, AICs began meeting together and founded the Pentecostal Association of Ghana, later renamed The Council of African Indigenous Churches. Within a few years, over six hundred denominations had joined the Council. Many of these churches held all-night wakes or prayer meetings on Wednesday nights and "calling on the Spirit meetings" every Friday evening. Around fifteen to twenty churches began gathering for these meetings at the Nima Temple of the Church of the Lord (Aladura) in Accra.

In the early days, AICs emphasized spiritual manifestations and gifts over the reading of the Scriptures. When Ed and Irene Weaver offered to do Bible studies with us during that period, they insisted that spiritual gifts need to be grounded in the Scriptures. "Anyone," they said, "can stand up and declare that 'the Spirit gave me this message,' or 'the Spirit told me to do thus and so.'

But without solid foundation in the Scriptures, how are the spirits to be tested and discerned?"

Photo 25: "Without the Scriptures, how are the spirits to be tested?" Isaac Wontumi

So the decision was made to have Bible studies together at Nima Temple on the same evenings that people were meeting anyway, Wednesdays for prayer and Fridays for "calling on the Spirit." At the beginning, Bible study was new to us in the AICs. We had so many questions about every aspect of the Christian life. What I remember about Erma Grove was how patient she was with us, taking all of our questions seriously and showing us how to find answers in the word of God.

Eventually, we organized ourselves and became the Good News Bible Institute. Professor James Kwesi Anquandah served as chairman of the group, and I served as treasurer. We would have never dreamed that this small beginning would develop into the important seminary for AICs that it has become today!

Dissecting Material and Spiritual Realities Gave Me Blinders
Jonathan Rudy

I was jolted from my slumber in the middle of the night by a stabbing pain in my abdomen. It felt like someone had shoved a knife in my midsection causing such discomfort that my groaning woke up my wife, Carolyn.

The year was 1993, and the place was rural Swaziland. Carolyn and I, along with our small boys Solomon and David, were staying with the Nxumalo family as our live-in experience in the first months of our assignment as representatives for the Mennonite Central Committee (MCC) and Eastern Mennonite Missions (EMM). We were "adopted" by *Babeh* (father) and *Makeh* (mother) Nxumalo, longtime friends of both MCC and EMM. Our little two-room house was part of a larger homestead farm that included an AIC church where my Swazi father was the pastor.

Photo 26: Babeh Nxumalo, in prayer and dance, conducting a healing ceremony

When the pain worsened, Carolyn, a nurse, determined that this was not just a transitory condition, but something that needed a doctor's attention. She woke the other members of the Nxumalo family, and they all came over to our house to see what was the matter. We did not have a car during this initial orientation and language learning period of our stay in the country, so my Swazi sister agreed to drive us to the capital city, Mbabane, to seek medical treatment. Not content to helplessly watch while I was bundled into the car, *Babeh* insisted on praying for me. He conducted a mini-healing service right then and there in the darkness as I sat on the ground in pain.

Babeh was a gentle, quiet, and humble man of faith. In later years when I would return to the homestead for a weekend and attend the little mud brick church over which he presided, I would be fascinated by things *Babeh* could see in people who approached him for healing. After the circle dance where members chanted and whirled around to collect their crosses, after *Babeh* or some other itinerant preacher "brought the word," and after a long prayer, it was the time of healing prayers. People with various sicknesses would submit themselves to *Babeh's* fearsome prayers. In a trance-like state, he would push the hay covering the floor back forming an open circle where he would lay hands on the ill person. His verbal prayer would ascend to a fever pitch. Invoking God to cast out demons, he would grasp the person between his hands, shaking, pressing, and pushing that part which may cause the malady. Sometimes he would light a match and fling it to the floor. And always he was firm with those malevolent spirits, which only he could see, causing the harm.

In my agony that night on the homestead, my Western logic screamed, "Get me to a doctor!" Yet *Babeh* continued his prayers for my healing. Finally, he released me to travel to Mbabane, where it turned out after a few weeks of Western medical misdiagnosis that I had typhoid fever. It was a long road to recovery, one in which there was much time for reflection.

As I pondered *Babeh's* insistence on prayer before the doctor visit, I was reminded that my Swazi father caught sight of things I could not see. Whereas my Western rationality sees human ailments as the product of little bugs, dysfunctional socialization, or chemical imbalances in the body, *Babeh* saw them as the consequences of spiritual problems. For me there is a very clear divide between the material and spirit domains. For him there was seamlessness between them, and spiritual power trumped material power.

I am glad for Western medicine. I do not know what would have happened if I would have stayed on the homestead and submitted to only what *Babeh* understood of healing. But I learned then that my dissection of the material and spiritual realms gives me blinders when it comes to truly seeing.

The Sweetness of Unity in Christ
Veliswa Mbambo

One day in a funeral gathering at the Church of God in Zion, my church here in South Africa, I noticed Joseph and Anna Sawatzky. I asked about them and learned that they were part of a training program, the Bethany Bible School (BBS). As I was curious, I began attending some of their conferences and workshops. In November 2009, I formally joined the school and serve now as a committee member to help in program planning, together with our Mennonite friends.

At first, to meet with white people was a scary thing to me. But as I traveled to meet in various places like Pietermaritzburg with Mennonite workers, I came to see that they were real friends and that their purpose was to strengthen the churches of South Africa. At a later gathering in Bloemfontein, I observed that the Mennonites were open to work with anyone, and that they had prepared a series of study booklets to address issues of faith. So, slowly, my fears were overcome. One of my fellow students told me, "The Mennonites are like us. We are one."

This country will be healed with such efforts. In the beginning I didn't know how to stand up and speak since I was a woman and a young person. But here we are all equal before God. Jesus preached as a young person. So we young people don't have to be shy. It used to be that women observed silence in the church, but here that has changed. We have seen from the story that at the crucifixion of Jesus, the men ran away, but that the women stayed with him. So we are approved, too.

It is true that some churches still do not permit women to speak, including my own. But through Bethany Bible School, we have found opportunity to grow in understanding and wisdom. My own archbishop and several pastors have visited BBS and now wish to join the studies. Our growing understanding has awakened interest among our leaders.

Our method is to follow the study booklets one by one and engage in discussion with our teachers, which both help us to grasp the meaning of the Scriptures. For example, we would read Paul's teaching about death, but weren't sure exactly what he meant, which made us hesitant to speak. But now in our study group, we come to see the depth of the meaning of the Scriptures and no longer fear to speak or share. In this process we feel enlivened by the Holy Spirit which we see in our teachers, and which is then imparted to us, the learners. This method of study has brought us a sense of freedom in discussing even difficult issues like baptism.

At present, five persons have been selected to train for three years at the Theological Education by Extension (TEE) College. I am one of those selected. Our further study will permit the Bethany Bible School to carry on into the future. We in the Zionist churches are especially happy that even mainline church students are included in our school. This is the sweetness of the unity mentioned in the Bible that is like oil running down the beard of Aaron, the high priest. Once the Zionists were regarded as outsiders in the church community, as incapable of leadership. So this togetherness is especially sweet.

My dream is to use my gifts to lead the church. I ask myself, "Am I able?" Through this training, I am coming to believe that I could lead. I want to be a good shepherd to the flock. The BBS will be my proving ground. From here I will be able to reach out to the larger community. God will help me.

Photo 27: Veliswa Mbambo, "Mama Dwele" – a student at Bethany Bible School in Mthatha, South Africa

I Came to Appreciate the Power of the Spoken Word
Ronald Sawatzky

Many experiences shaped my impressions of AICs, but following are two of them. The first was a humbling experience which made me reflect on my own participation in worship, and the second was an illustration of the healing effects of a caring community.

Ed and Irene Weaver came to Botswana in the mid-1970s to explore the possibility of Mennonite involvement with indigenous churches. At their encouragement, I attended the St. John's Apostolic Faith Mission in

Francistown, Botswana. I had intended to be an observer that first morning. But when I arrived, I was told that I would be giving the morning sermon.

Not having any experience in such a worship service, and not having brought my Bible to church, I was a bit panicky. The prophetess Rachel Lekuta found an English Bible for me, and I spent the next minutes feverishly trying to find a text and prepare some remarks. I finally settled on a passage from John 15, "I am the true vine." This presentation was translated into Setswana, and then each of the ministers in the service added their own comments.

Several months later I attended the same church. This time I was prepared. But I had forgotten the passage I had used previously, so chose a passage from John 14, "In my Father's house are many mansions." To my surprise when I finished, the prophetess in her remarks told the congregation that on my previous visit, I had used a passage from John 15 and that it fit with the passage I had used that morning from John 14. She then began to summarize what I had said on the first visit and tied it to what I had just said. That experience made me appreciate the power of the spoken word. I was humbled to realize that what I had said was remembered, even though only a few days after the first service, I had difficulty remembering the sermon text, let alone the remarks I had made.

A second experience followed with the St. John's congregation. By this time, I had attended worship with them on a number of occasions. During the healing portion of the service, I along with others was asked to bless those who were present. I noticed that one man at the back of the room did not come forward. When all had been blessed, the prophetess took a cup of holy water and went to the man, offering him a blessing. He put up his hands in a defensive position and moved toward her. I noticed his hands were manacled. At his movement, she threw the cup of water into his face and turned away.

Later I asked her about the incident, and she told me that he had been admitted to the mental hospital in Lobatse where he was treated and released. His family was not convinced he was back to normal, so they brought him to church. The church compound had several buildings which were used to house those who needed help. In return for this housing, residents were expected to help around the church compound in whatever way they could. Such visitors also took part in evening prayers, along with congregants from St. John's. Several months later I returned and noticed that this man took part in the service and seemed happy to be there. The prophetess told me he was soon returning to his family and that the time spent in caring and praying for him had been of great help to him. This transformation demonstrated to me the importance of a caring congregation and the power that they have to give support, healing, and encouragement to us.

GUEST REFLECTIONS

Amos Yong, Fuller Theological Seminary
The Scriptures tell us that on the day of Pentecost, the Spirit of the living God was poured out on all flesh, on those gathered from around the then known (Mediterranean) world. In this volume, we hear from just some of these voices resounding especially from contemporary sub-Saharan Africa. There are for starters Mennonite voices. Yes, these are mostly those of Caucasian missionaries from Europe and North America, but nevertheless they represent a Christian witness that has more often than not been on the margins, if not altogether neglected in mission history. But also we have a broad range of African Christian voices, those doubly if not triply marginalized. These are indigenous voices at least twice removed from the centers of African Christian circles: once with regard to their indigeneity, here because of drawing from traditional African sources, sensibilities, and perspectives that have long been dismissed as a remnant of a premodern past, and second further sidelined from a Christian perspective still too wedded to historic traditions shaped by Euro-American normativity. Our brothers and sisters in this volume help us to appreciate that the church ecumenical has colleagues literally from every tribe, people, and nation whose minority reports can free us from cultural captivity to the modern West.

Amos Yong is a Malaysian-American Pentecostal theologian, director of the Center for Missiological Research, and professor of theology and mission at Fuller Theological Seminary. Since July 2019, he has served as dean of the School of Theology and the School of Intercultural Studies at Fuller Seminary.

Allan H. Anderson, University of Birmingham, England
As an outside, somewhat casual observer, briefly reflecting on the impact of the decades-long interaction between AICs and Mennonites is a privilege. This really has been an inspirational

story. I was educated at the University of South Africa and wrote my doctoral thesis in missiology in 1992 on the relationship between African religion and Christianity, and how well AICs had negotiated the resulting tensions. Among other documents, I drew on the published experiences of Mennonites. My promotor, M.L. (Inus) Daneel, had enthused me with his lifelong dedication to AICs in Zimbabwe, his practical involvement from the 1960s onwards in theological education and ecological projects, and his insistence that AICs were Christian churches contextualizing their transformative Christian faith with African beliefs. Mennonite partnerships with AICs have followed the same principles of humble learning and practical assistance. Most importantly, Mennonites eschewed the traditional missionary methods of "planting churches" and instead sought to support existing ones with theological education and development projects. They have been trailblazers for others to follow. Through responding to real needs, Mennonites have brought greater understanding and cooperation between churches in Africa than was ever remotely possible six decades ago. Hallelujah!

Allan H. Anderson is emeritus professor of mission and Pentecostal studies, University of Birmingham, England, and author of numerous works on global Pentecostalism.

4

Growth

The early shoots having made their appearance and delicate moments patiently negotiated, opportunities requiring strength now come to hand. As confidence is established in depth, friendship takes hold with learnings, both personal and programmatic, weighing in. The real potential and demanding nature of partnered work begins to emerge.

The Entire Body of Christ Carried the Woman's Pain That Day
Anna Sawatzky

Upon arriving in Mthatha, South Africa, to work at a Bible school for leaders of AICs, we understood that our work would include a lot of travel to various churches to participate in their worship services. But as the months wore on and the invitations were not forthcoming, we began to wonder what we were doing wrong. Increased understanding of the culture helped us to realize that it was our duty to invite ourselves, which we began to do. Yet very few people accepted our offer to come and visit. Those who did wanted us only for special services and not for their regular meetings.

Various comments over time led us to believe that many churches were not actually meeting on a regular basis, but were mainly coming together for special services. At one such service, we met a pastor who was ministering to a tiny fellowship in a township outside of Mthatha – Mandela Park. We began to attend their weekly services and to work closely with this pastor. Our connection to this congregation was life-giving beyond our fondest hopes. I want to tell a few of the stories of some profound lessons I learned at this church.

I was once taking a woman pastor home from a meeting to discuss plans for an HIV/AIDS ministry. At the end of the meeting, everyone had begun to sing and dance as usual. This particular woman pastor went around praying for each woman in turn and placing her hands on their heads. As she left each woman, I saw her shake her hands as if the power had gone out from them and they needed rejuvenation.

In the car, I asked her about it. She is a healer, founder, and bishop of her church. She told me that she is sad because everyone wants to come to her for healing, but having been healed, they do not come back. She said that, as a pastor, you have to be prepared that on any given Sunday, you may be preaching only to your husband.

Soon after, we were attending our small church in Mandela Park. One Sunday, a young man showed up for the service. At the time in the worship experience when people are prayed for, he came forward and said that he had "fits" and wanted healing. Everyone gathered around and prayed for him. That man came back. Every week. Every mid-week service. We have never been at church when he wasn't there. And we have never arrived at church for a service before him.

The pastors have continued to pray for him. They have also taken him to a doctor. When it was time for his circumcision, his initiation into manhood, the pastor took him to a doctor for the physical circumcision, and then visited him during his time of seclusion to teach him what it means to be a man and a follower of Jesus.

While the nine lepers who encountered Jesus went on their way, satisfied with their healing, this man followed the example of the one who came back to give praise to God. While his healing may have been initiated in that first visit, truly it is his faith that has made him well (Luke 17:11–19).

At church on another Sunday, the visitors and those returning after an absence were asked to introduce themselves and greet the congregation. The last in the line was a young woman. She spoke quietly, and after the initial line of greeting, she cried out and fell to her knees weeping. One woman began a song, and another came over to rub her back as she lay on the floor. As her sobs died down, this mama helped her to her feet, wiped off her knees where they had hit the dirt floor, and put her gently back in her place on the wooden bench. The service continued as she recovered herself.

At the end of the service, everyone who wanted to be prayed for came forward. There was a teenage girl who was worried because her parents were fighting, a young man who wanted to accept Jesus, a teenage boy who wanted to be strong as he is "very weak," and the young woman described earlier who appeared again. Each person was prayed for in turn as the congregation sang.

We still don't know why that young woman was there, but her pain was carried by the entire body of Christ on that day.

Photo 28: The power and joy of women in worship

On yet one other occasion at church, the pastor called up our son Isaac, age six, and his own son Lilitha, age five, to stand behind the table as the offering was brought forward. When the pastor had counted the money, he told Isaac how much had been collected, and Isaac told the congregation. He then announced that Isaac was going to pray over the offering. We waited, wondering how our shy boy would handle this sudden elevation to leadership. The pastor stood patiently and silently while Isaac found his words. The pastor then thanked him and repeated to the congregation what Isaac had prayed, "God, bless everything we do."

The pastor didn't ask Isaac ahead of time to offer the prayer. He didn't question whether Isaac would be able to do it. He simply brought him forward and expected him to find the gift within himself. And Isaac did it.

I Soaked in the Memories of the Prophet in the Land
Rachel Hilty Friesen

They will know that a prophet has been among them. (Ezek 33:33)

Memories of the Prophet Mokaleng, founder of the church, were what I was seeking during a year and a half of questioning, listening, and recording as I prepared to write the history of the Spiritual Healing Church in Botswana. Members of the church who had witnessed the prophet's healing ministry in the 1950s were still around. But they were aging, and memories were on the verge of being lost. So I traveled around the country, seeking the people whose stories could fill in the gaps in the emerging picture of a great prophet, Jacob "Mokaleng" Motswaosele.

Five times I traveled to the simple home of Benjamin Moilwa, a *moruti* (minister, teacher) in the Spiritual Healing Church and the manager of a construction company in the capital city of Gaborone. Like the stories of so many others whom I had interviewed, his were frankly incredible. The matter-of-fact tone of his voice contrasted sharply with the amazing events he recounted. What was I to make of all this? On one visit, he told me the following story:

> I went to Matsiloje – the village where Prophet Mokaleng lived – as a teenager because I had a problem, but the prophet told me to stay. So, I stayed with him for ten years. I was one of about ten teenagers who worked for Mokaleng, helping him in the treatment of the sick. I saw many people healed in startling ways – bones straightened, the blind able to see. He did many miracles in front of my own eyes. Mokaleng used a variety of methods – usually prayer, but not always. He sometimes used water, salt, ashes, or mud.
>
> One crippled man was there for three weeks before he was healed. Suddenly one day the prophet told those supporting this man as he entered the church to let go of him. They feared he would fall, but suddenly he could walk, and started to sing happily. I saw such things not once but many, many times.

When interviewees communicated to me what was most important to them, they made themselves vulnerable to being treated with disbelief and skepticism. In my North American church life, I had little experience of dramatic outpourings of the Holy Spirit. In my theological studies, we sought to find argumentative, descriptive words and propositions to express the nature of God. In the AICs, I was learning that the nature of God is communicated in story, mythic language, narrative, and communal memory.

Photo 29: Benjamin Moilwa recounts to Rachel the history of the Spiritual Healing Church in Botswana

My thoughts strayed from the track of historical scholarship as I listened to Moruti Moilwa's voice and watched his eyes. I sensed that he was searching his memory for recollections of those events which had changed the course of his life. How many lives, I thought, had been changed as they put their trust in Jesus under the influence of Prophet Mokaleng's ministry?

While I waited, I searched my own heart as well. Could I open my mind and heart to manifestations of God's power and grace which seemed so foreign to my own experience? At the conclusion of the interview, I knew that I was also being changed. I turned to Mr. Moilwa. "Moruti, you have been blessed to witness these things."

So it went as I soaked in the memories told to me by others who had been part of the story – Moruti Wright, Archbishop Israel Motswaosele, Moruti Molake, Mrs. Marumo, and many more. All of these stories came together, along with other research, into a printed history, *Ditso tsa Spiritual Healing Church mo Botswana*, for the use of the congregations and members of the church.

Published in 1992 under the auspices of Mennonite Ministries in Botswana, the written account marked a quarter century of fruitful relationships between Mennonites and the Spiritual Healing Church in Botswana.

Learning How to Pray the Jesus Way
Willard E. Roth

The year is 2020 – a new decade, now five decades later as AIC personal memory rewinds. My journey began as teacher, quickly moved to learner, then slowly matured into friend – a profile patterned after our mentors Ed and Irene Weaver. Everything I ever needed to know about living among AICs I learned in the Weaver kindergarten.

As an ordained Mennonite pastor and an experienced journalist, I went to West Africa in 1968 with a well-filled tool kit. But I soon sensed, like the young man who queried Jesus about the kingdom, that I lacked one overarching thing: a disciplined prayer practice grounded in simple trust. I soon discovered that within AIC circles, prayer was not one belief among many, but a foundational way of being.

Photo 30: Faculty at Good News Training Institute (left to right): Willard Roth, Daniel Tei Kwabla, James Anquandah, and Kwesi Ellis

LESSON 1: *Thanksgiving is the core of prayer for AIC practitioners.* About 2:00 a.m. one Friday morning, five of us were leaving an all-night service in Kumasi, Ghana, for the ninety-mile journey home. Unaware of our intentions, a man took the microphone. He reported a vision that a Peugeot full of travelers was leaving that would encounter an accident, and then called the assembly to pray for their protection. Rounding a hilltop curve a couple hours later, our driver lost control. His dozing passengers found themselves down a slight embankment, unhurt but wide awake. As the tropical sun rose that morning, we drove up to Nima Temple, a Church of the Lord (Aladura) meeting house near our home in Accra. Instantly, the three Ghanaians sprang out of the car and entered the building. The two white missionaries stayed in the vehicle. Some minutes passed, and then one of our companions returned. "Why are you still here?" he inquired.

"Where should we be?" I innocently asked.

"We must be in the temple," was his perturbed reply, "offering prayers of thanksgiving for God's protection and journeying mercies."

LESSON 2: *Confession acknowledges human frailty.* King David's classic prayer for cleansing and pardon retained in Psalm 51 is prayed at least weekly in many churches with whom we regularly worshiped.

> Have mercy on me, O God,
>   according to your unfailing love;
> according to your great compassion
>   blot out my transgressions.
> Wash away all of my iniquity,
>   and cleanse me from my sin. (Ps 51:1–2)

I learned from my West African brothers and sisters, although not quickly, that admitting wrong-doing and error is prerequisite to forgiveness. Prayers of confession spoken aloud so that all within listening distance may hear seem to have greater staying power than prayers merely breathed silently to God alone.

LESSON 3: *No earthly condition limits intercession.* No human predicament is so complex that one need refrain from imploring divine intervention. AIC adherents who became our friends choose a worldview that does not quickly divide into natural and supernatural. Prayers for healing do not split medicine into herbal or hospital. In faith, either or both may well be God's answer. During an extended bout of clinical depression, for instance, I was humbled to often be the recipient of anointing with oil, along with laying on of hands, even as I swallowed drugs prescribed by Ghana's lone psychiatrist.

LESSON 4: *Prayer in the way of Jesus is work – intense and intentional.* My AIC prayer coach was Prophet Frank Mills of Faith Brotherhood Praying Circle. As I was recovering back in the United States, also as prescribed by my Ghanaian doctor, Brother Mills assured me by letter that "the congregation and myself will always keep in touch with you in spirit, and we will continue to remember you and your family in our everyday meditation." He went on to explain their prayerful diligence in preparation for Easter:

> As you well know, we are in the Lenten period, and gradually the passion of our Lord Jesus approaches. Toward this end the congregation and myself are in deep meditation with fastings and prayers – hoping, waiting, and looking above that the Lord's mercy and compassion will be upon us. I hope and trust that while our spirits join in fellowship, you and your family and all Christian brethren over there will receive Christ Jesus' blessing and grace. We are preparing to ascend onto Mount Faith on 11th April (as has been our usual practice) to mourn, suffer, die, and arise with the Lord Jesus. I invite you to tune in with us that day in spirit so that while we remain in fellowship to be witnesses of that important day when he died on the cross, we share in his glory on the resurrection day. Amen.

I went to West Africa as a teacher. After five short years as an expatriate resident in Ghana with extended visits across the region, I learned a lot more than I ever taught. But the lasting gift I cherish is the bond of spiritual friendship forged deep among those women and men who practiced prayer in what I now know to be the Jesus way.

My Mennonite Friends Launched Me on My Life of Ministry
Humphrey Akogyeram

I graduated from the Good News Training Institute in Accra, Ghana, in 1990. I first met Mennonite workers Philip and Julie Bender in 1989 when they were lecturers at Good News. They taught me for three years, and their love for peace and reconciliation attracted me to them. On the last day of my student work, they called me out from among all the other students and wanted to help in furthering my education.

Before they left Ghana in 1992, the Benders went with me to my church and met with the leaders who agreed to send me for two years to Christian Service College – now University – in Kumasi, Ghana. During these two years,

Phil and Julie supported me financially, visited my church to give reports, and took me to visit the Ghana Mennonite Church in Amasaman, north of Accra.

Through their initiative and my studies at a Mennonite seminary in the United States, a peace library was started in Ghana at Good News. The Benders spent part of their sabbatical leave at Good News as visiting lecturers, and during this period, they assisted in launching and leading eight peace and reconciliation seminars in local AIC churches in Ghana, training mediators for intervention in church conflicts, distributing literature on peace themes to local churches, and conducting a daylong seminar-workshop for Good News students. Both leaders and members showed keen interest in the peace studies. Through the seminars, people discovered new ways to work to resolve conflicts, both on the interpersonal level and on the larger societal level.

In 1992, I was encouraged to consider applying to teach at Good News. I submitted my application in July and started teaching in September. My professional history has since then included the following:

- 1992–1998 taught at Good News
- 1998–2000 Associated (now Anabaptist) Mennonite Biblical Seminary in Elkhart, Indiana, where I completed an MA in theological and biblical Studies
- 2000–2009 back at Good News
- 2009–2011 Lutheran Theological Seminary at Philadelphia (LTSP) where I completed an MA of sacred theology
- 2011–2012 returned again to Good News teaching Old Testament both on campus and in a certificate program in Accra. The program meets every Thursday. Each course runs for six weeks and envisions four such cycles with two courses each time for eight courses total. The courses include "Understanding the Old Testament I," "Understanding the Old Testament II," "Discipleship," "New Testament Survey," and "Key Bible Themes." During the 2011–2012 academic year, there were fifty registered students from about twenty denominations.

My lifelong friendship with Phil and Julie Bender has had an enormous impact on me. They have strengthened the churches in Ghana through their preaching, teaching, and counseling. I hope the seeds sown by the Benders will continue to grow and extend beyond the sphere of Ghana. May the LOVE of God be with us all!

Photo 31: Humphrey teaches both on the Good News campus as well as in local congregations

A Few Things I Learned about Sexuality, Childbearing, Mosaic Law, and the Role of Women in AIC Church Life
Delores H. Friesen

Women play an important role in the African Independent Churches, but they also experience some restrictions and expectations that only gradually became known to us. When we arrived in Nigeria, my husband, Stan, was twenty-five years old, and I was twenty-three. As we learned language, we became aware that I was referred to as his girlfriend, not his wife. Sometimes after church women would rub my womb, shake their heads, and then say, "God will do for you," or they would openly pray for us to conceive. This situation created an internal conflict, since we were using Western means to delay childbearing until we had time to learn language and adjust to the new culture and work. Later we discovered that many were worried that Stan would send me away since we had been married already for more than two years with no issue!

When we worshiped at Nima Temple in Ghana with the Church of the Lord (Aladura), Stan was asked whether I was somehow different than their women. We had noticed that every Sunday, one third or more of the women would be seated outside the sanctuary on the porches of the church, but we assumed they did so because it was cooler there, or they had small children who needed to be fed and cared for. When we learned that they were following the Mosaic code of Leviticus and believed that no menstruating woman could enter the temple, there were some earnest conversations about this restriction.

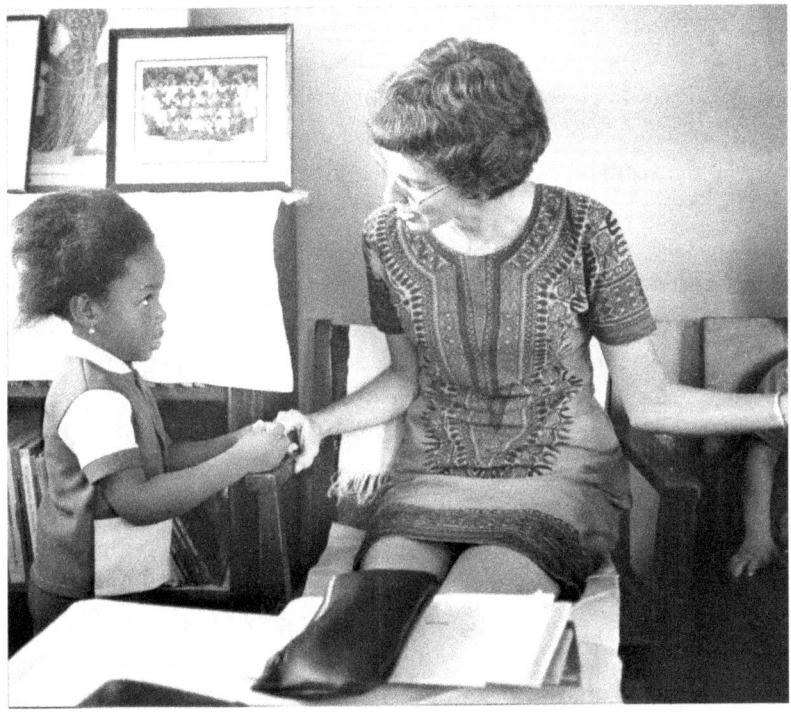

Photo 32: Women and children play some of the most important roles in AICs

I first decided to follow their belief, but since we only attended on the first Sunday of every month when Stan preached, this never coincided with my period. Then I learned that this restriction was twice as long following the birth of a girl than it was when a boy baby was born, though scientifically the lochia would be the same amount of time for either gender. I began to study the Old Testament laws of cleanliness and purity and decided that sexuality and gender might be a place where we could helpfully search the Scriptures together.

Over a period of several years, I participated in Bible studies about sexuality and the Christian home, always doing this work with an African pastor as my colleague in teaching and fielding the questions, and working in cross gender groups rather than with women alone. These lessons were published by Editions Trobisch under the title *Let Love Be Your Greatest* and were translated into at least eight languages including Twi (Ghana), Swahili (East Africa), Portuguese, German, French, Spanish, and Japanese.

When I was seven months pregnant with our son, as I drove to pick up our daughters from school, the Volkswagen I was driving was impaled on a roundabout of the multilane Ring Road by a truck which cut in too sharply. The truck pierced the roof above my head and crushed the back fender so the car was no longer drivable. I was unhurt, but our AIC friends and pastors feared that I would go into early labor, or the baby would be marked by this experience. So they showed up at our house for heartfelt prayers of thanksgiving for deliverance from harm and intercession for a safe delivery and healthy baby. When Jonathan – *Nyameche* (God's gift) – was born to us, we asked Mrs. Dagadu, a revered churchwoman who had never birthed any children of her own, to do his outdooring ceremony. She was a mother to us and many others.

One of my first experiences in Nigeria came home to me in a very personal way – a woman who is pregnant or barren needs constant, fervent prayer. But she also can be a leader of God's people if she has access to the Scriptures and their message of release and love. When I helped several women from the Holy Face Church in Nigeria learn to read, their deep desire to be able to read the Bible on their own and my few words of halting Efik-Ibibio and elementary education background helped. But often our only way to communicate was our love for Jesus and his word. Even being able to read a few words was rewarding to them, and my language learning grew exponentially. Together we were amazed at their discovery that there was more than one Mary in the Bible – the mother of Jesus was not the one who wiped his feet with her hair, and not the sister of Martha!

In our thirteen years in West Africa, we found we could worship as one in the body of Christ when we gathered around the Scriptures, claiming Jesus as Lord and seeking together in community to learn what this means. The role of the Old Testament rules, laws, worship, and prohibitions, which were so central to our AIC brothers and sisters, and the Anabaptist emphasis on Jesus and the Sermon on the Mount became a nexus of discovery and growth for them and for us.

A Tribute to Umfundisi Hlobisile – A Model for Women in Church Leadership
Sherill Hostetter

Hlobisile Nxumalo was sixteen years old when we met her in Swaziland while traveling on a bus to South Africa for an all-night AIC service. She was a lively young woman with many ambitions. When Darrel and I began the Zionist (AIC) youth conferences in Swaziland during the school breaks in May and December, Hlobisile was always there if at all possible. She was a natural leader, and others looked up to her for her wisdom and leadership in the fun activities.

Hlobi went on to graduate from the University of Swaziland with a degree in accounting, and she willingly served as the treasurer of our Faith Bible School for many years. In many ways she became like a daughter to our family. Our children enjoyed the times when Hlobi came to stay with us in our home.

Early on in the youth ministry, we decided some of the youth needed further training to become the leaders of the Zionist youth. We talked about sending some youth to the United States to the Youth Evangelism Service (YES) program of the Eastern Mennonite Board of Missions. Hlobi challenged us to run a training school right there in Swaziland instead of sending youth away because they often were the ones earning money for younger brothers and sisters to be able to attend school.

So we began a discipleship training program in our home for seven weekends. Hlobi was one of the selected young adults to be trained. But she did not want us to carry all of the cost of the food and materials, so she figured out an estimated cost for each participant. If they were not able to pay, she covered their costs from her own personal finances. That amazed us.

In Swazi culture, a single woman is considered to be a child until she marries. She is not treated as a leader even if she is in a leadership role. Many times Hlobi faced the difficulties of being an anomaly in her own culture as a leader in the church. She had opportunities to be married, but they never seemed to be right for her. Her grandfather had had thirty wives and many children. But her Zionist minister father had made the decision to be monogamous, and Hlobi was standing tall with her head held high in a culture where single women had no rights.

What a tribute to her character! When our family left Swaziland in 1994, Hlobi carried the vision and passion of the youth ministry forward. She became a mentor and a pastor to many of the youth. She built small rooms onto their family homestead so that she could care for orphans from her community and put them through school. She gave leadership to the youth conferences and discipled many of the Swazi Zionist youth. Through hard economic times, conflicts, and logistical problems, Hlobi continued to keep the potential of the youth and their spiritual journeys as a top priority for her time and investment of energy.

While we were in Swaziland, I had started an educational and testing program for AIDS through a Salvation Army Clinic and had the opportunity to train some of the AIC leaders. Hlobi has since given leadership to the

AIDS ministry of Faith Bible School – a Zionist Church Bible school which was started in cooperation with the Eastern Mennonite Board of Missions in 1976 and which evolved into a community of Zionists seeking to faithfully follow Jesus. Hlobi has also led teams of youth in using drama and testimonies to train congregations about the prevention of AIDS. When the last Anglo Mennonite Central Committee (MCC) representative left Swaziland, Hlobi became the MCC representative and received further training in conflict transformation for her role. She continues as Christ's *umfundisi* (minister/teacher) of reconciliation to her own people in Swaziland and to other southern African countries.

Photo 33: Umfundisi Hlobisile (second from left) has used drama and testimonies to train congregations about prevention of AIDS

Hlobi's courage in the face of the odds against her, her passion for Christ and seeing others come to faith, and her continuing concern for orphans and youth have challenged me. Hlobisile Nxumalo has lived the life of an *umfundisi*, even if she has never been given that title officially. Hlobi is steadfast from day to day, loving, caring, and incarnating the kingdom of God in Swaziland.

GUEST REFLECTIONS

T. John Padwick, Oxford Centre of Mission Studies
Reading through the draft of this book has brought back warm memories of fruitful interactions and friendships with the Mennonites, both personally and in connection with my own ministry within the Organization of African Instituted Churches (OAIC). It's also led me to reflect on our rather different models of ministry.

Viewed from the outside, the Mennonites were first in the field in developing and sustaining ministries with the AICs, and their countercultural roots back in North America had in part prepared them for this. The AICs they were seeking to work with had themselves been marginalized (and at times even suppressed) by colonial regimes and by the main Protestant and Catholic mission churches working under the aegis of these regimes. As this book shows, the AICs welcomed the affirmation, recognition, and friendship the Mennonites offered.

In its early years the OAIC also offered AICs acceptance and recognition, but by a different route. We sought to build on two forms of AIC initiatives, the formation of local and national AIC councils, with all of their confused history and frequent failures, and the attempt by some AICs to reach out to the Coptic and Ethiopian churches. It was in this context that in 1978, the Coptic Bishop Antonious Markos, with the support of ecumenical funding and the scholarly assistance of David B. Barrett, called an AIC conference in Cairo, which established the OAIC as a continental body.

The contrast between these two forms of ministry was marked – the low key, small scale approach of the Mennonites, "no grand strategic blueprint," to quote Wilbert Shenk in this book,[1] and what must sometimes have seemed like the wildly ambitious continental level program of the OAIC. This contrast was one of the underlying causes of an unfortunate level of

---

1. See page 20.

mistrust that developed briefly between a few key players in the two groups during the mid-eighties, myself being one of them. But this mistrust was overcome in part by three really useful continental conferences, in Abidjan in 1986, Kinshasa in 1989, and Nairobi in 1993. The first conference, hosted by David A. Shank, was primarily academic; the latter two opened their doors more widely to practitioners and AIC leaders. The Abidjan conference also created the Network on AICs and Missions, a loose network of people defined as crossing denominational boundaries to work with AICs. The Network in turn produced the *Review of AICs: A Practitioners Journal* about three times a year, initially edited by Stan Nussbaum from the INTERACT Research Centre at the Selly Oak Colleges, UK. *The Review* created a friendly forum for the exchange of ideas and reached a wide variety of practitioners, AIC leaders, and scholars.

Another factor which was more significant in reducing tensions over the longer term was that in Southern and West Africa, the AICs themselves were happy to work with both Mennonites and OAIC, and significant leaders in OAIC had themselves been interacting with Mennonites – Ntate Sam Mohono (Lesotho), Otsile Ditsheko (Botswana), and Thomas Oduro (Ghana) come to mind. (Eastern Africa doesn't appear here because the Mennonites did not have an active program with AICs in that region.) The work of the Mennonites and the OAIC frequently complemented each other – it was, for us, a fruitful liaison.

As an expatriate worker with the AICs and from a mission agency, the Anglican Church Mission Society (CMS) that had many other irons in the fire, I would initially have felt isolated and lonely in my ministry without the previous experience and continual background presence of the Mennonites. I have continued to hold them in high regard ever since.

T. John Padwick *of Oxford Centre of Mission Studies was formerly of the Organization of African Instituted Churches, Nairobi, Kenya, and is an Anglican lay minister.*

Martine Audéoud, Université de l'Alliance Chrétienne d'Abidjan
Today in sub-Saharan Africa, one can observe crises and conflicts in numerous countries. These develop very frequently due to situations that have not been appropriately dealt with to begin with. Furthermore, the often unconscious transfer of the traditional chiefhood experience to the present concept of leadership has led to an inaccurate understanding of the role of leaders in an African continent where relationships are more and more globalized.

In view of this situation and the need to reevaluate and redirect the concept of leadership, the Mennonite Mission Network (MMN) has for many years strongly supported the development of master's and doctoral programs in transformational leadership to equip African men and women for positions of responsibility from which they can foster and facilitate community transformation efforts in congruence with the agency's own mission statement: "Mennonite Mission Network exists to lead, mobilize and equip the church to participate in holistic witness to Jesus Christ in a broken world."[2]

At Faculté de Théologie Evangélique de l'Alliance Chrétienne (FATEAC) – today the Université de l'Alliance Chrétienne d'Abidjan (UACA) – and especially in the Department of Holistic Development (DHD), we are convinced that the best solution in the struggle for peace on our continent resides in a better understanding of leadership according to biblical principles and forming people to serve their communities and bring transformation in ways which witness to the authority of Christ. This agenda is particularly important for our training institution, located in a country that is over forty percent Muslim, and in a subregion that is increasingly being Islamized. Our influence has been especially felt in recent years in our nation's socioeconomic crises and civil war.

In an international colloquium organized by FATEAC in 2014 on the theme of "AICs – Challenges and Perspectives," African Independent Churches recognized the need and requested more

---

2. See Mennonite Mission Network, "Mission and vision," https://www.mennonitemission.net/about/Mission%20and%20Vision.

training for their leaders.[3] In anticipation of that need, the DHD has for the past number of years welcomed leaders from AICs who amount to one quarter of its student body, while another quarter comes from denominational churches and the remainder from professional organizations. Repeatedly, these participating AIC leaders express to DHD administrators and teaching faculty their appreciation for the quality of their learning and its effectiveness on the ground. Mennonite values of diversity, innovation, stewardship, and the need to develop communities of grace are constantly woven into the DHD curricula so that students graduate with a strong focus on peace-building, justice, and advocacy.

Finally, one should not forget the strong support that was provided by the Mennonite Mission Network some years back when our country was emerging out of a long civil war. The Church as a Community of Healing and Peacemaking (ECGAP) organization was created within the DHD with Mennonite financial backing and was able to provide trauma healing counseling, training, and material support to diverse groups of Christian churches – including many AICs – as well as to several Islamic communities throughout the most war-damaged parts of the country.

Is the work finished yet? Not at all! AICs develop faster than the training opportunities that FATEAC can provide. But FATEAC – with Mennonite support – is committed to pursuing the training of AICs leaders as long as it is needed.

Martine Audéoud is on the Faculté de Théologie Evangélique de l'Alliance Chrétienne at the Université de l'Alliance Chrétienne d'Abidjan, Abidjan, Côte d'Ivoire

---

3. See Issiaka Coulibaly and Rubin Pohor, *Les Églises et ministères d'initiative africaine: Enjeux et avenir* (Abidjan: Les Presses de la FATEAC, 2015), 156.

5

Pollination

However sturdy the developing crop, its fruitfulness depends upon pollination. Side by side in the field, even as they gain strength and flower, the plants enrich each other by pollen carried on the wind or by pollinators. Though barely noticed, this exchange sets in motion powerful processes – sometimes in the following accounts that can appear as fresh reading of Scripture, sometimes as encounters with deep culture, sometimes as demands that engender growth, sometimes in whispered prayer for each other.

So . . . When Do You People Pray?
Grace Hostetter

In the 1970s my husband, Charles, and I answered a call from the Mennonite Board of Missions to serve with an African Independent Church in Nigeria. This group wanted help to start a seminary – a Bible school in reality – for their pastors and prophets. This group, the Church of the Lord (Aladura), or "praying church," was less than fifty years old. It was started by an independent, polygamist, Nigerian prophet in response to the group's prayers and fasting after the Lord had worked through them in a time of crisis. The head of the church was called the "primate" and functioned like a pope. By the time we joined the group, the second primate had been in charge for a number of years, and the Nigerian church had been extended to many congregations in Liberia, Sierra Leone, and Ghana.

Charles went to Nigeria five weeks before the rest of the family in order to find housing and schooling for our sons. Chuck was a high school senior; Phil was in sixth grade; and Rick was in fifth grade. Little in Charles' past experience had prepared him for this unplanned venture. We had been under the impression that the school had been well-thought through and was ready to begin, but that was not what we found upon arrival. But having been the mother of eight children at home had equipped me to deal with the unexpected.

On our first Sunday in the country, we were invited to the church's large annual conference. This gathering was being held at their holy city where the mountain was considered sacred and where the first primate was buried. The service was already in progress when we arrived, but we were taken up onto the stage to be introduced. This was a large congregation of several hundred white-robed members joyously worshiping. Many years earlier, the first primate had prophesied that one day some white people would come to work with them. So we were the fulfillment of that prophecy!

In the midst of the loud drums beating, the enthusiastic singing, and the free-spirited dancing, one of the women drew me to the center of the stage to dance with her. Dancing had definitely not been included in our mission's orientation and training! I wanted to simply observe for my first time, but instead I was being asked to be involved before getting culturally oriented. I knew this was part of the church's worship practices, so I tried to be flexible and join in as best I could.

The Church of the Lord services are long, but still interesting since there is so much variety. The first part of the service is strictly worship and prayer. I found it so meaningful, and I thought that if they worshiped with us in America, they would ask, "When do you people pray?" Giving and interpreting dreams, visions, and prophecies were always a part of the service. Offerings were given by dancing to the front and depositing one's gifts of money, food, or candles. The message wasn't the most important part of the service. I found that the spirited dancing, hand clapping, and drums added to the celebration and worship.

Most Aladura church compounds had a place of worship as well as a healing house where the prophetess would pray for the sick, for pregnant women, and for depressed or troubled people. Sometimes these people would stay for a few days. The healing house had beds, but family members needed to provide the sick person's food. There was usually a prayer ground in a sandy, enclosed area where people could go to pray or rest in the sand in repentance or for punishment.

Eventually some of our support money was needed to build a house for us on the seminary compound. This meant also building the primate's house, the church, the prayer house, a classroom building for the seminary, and a student dormitory. The compound was a busy place with people coming for prayers and seeking direction or blessing. At the church, prayers were held every three hours except for the 3:00 a.m. time slot. Our students, who were primarily responsible to the primate, were often called to pray all night.

On one occasion and for some unknown reason, I seemed to be the only "prophetess" or "prophet" on the grounds. A man came to the house saying he had come for prayer and couldn't find anyone at the church or healing house. I invited him in and assured him I would be glad to pray for him. So he knelt before me with hands cupped to receive the blessing. I extended my hands over him as he would have expected and prayed for him and his request. After the prayer he arose, smiled at me, and said, "While you were praying for me, I saw a cross-shaped hole in your forehead with a bright light shining out."

And I said, "Thank you, Lord."

While in Nigeria, many of the missionary groups questioned why we would work with an AIC group. They considered such groups less than Christian. One missionary from Ohio said that Charles had his horse hitched to the wrong buggy. But as time passed, our assignment was better accepted. At a farewell for us by other missionaries in Nigeria we knew well, a Sudan Interior Mission worker said, "You have done something none of us could do. You've been teaching the Bible with them in their school. We could only help them if they *left* their church and joined ours." Some of the Church of the Lord people reflected that before we had come, they knew a lot about God and the Holy Spirit, but we helped them understand who Jesus is. What a privilege it was to study the open Bible together!

Many years after we had been in Nigeria, I learned that the primate's wife was visiting in the United States, so I called her. We had a delightful conversation. I asked about many of our students by name. Some of our students had been sent to start churches in other countries, including Germany. But for many of our best students, she answered, "He is no longer with us." This meant that these students probably started their own churches. May God continue to build his kingdom through these students wherever they are living.

When I asked about the primate's death, she said what surprised the church was that God hadn't shared it with anyone in advance. The first primate had a message from God saying who should succeed him after he died. She urged me to pray with them for God's choice for the next primate.

One of the interesting parts of our assignment was having Desmond Tutu in our home before he was well-known by others. Tutu oversaw the funds administered for our support from the World Council of Churches. When we knew he was coming, we were eager for someone to help us understand what was going on in the church we were trying to serve. We thought, "Tutu is African and will probably tell us our problem is race prejudice." But in the end, Tutu was harder on the primate than we were. Instead of talking to Tutu, the primate planned a big program to honor him with church prayers and gifts of Nigerian clothes and food. But that wasn't what Tutu had come for! We enjoyed our contacts with Bishop Tutu in Nigeria, in London, and later in Johannesburg. We always admired him for leaving the life he led in England to be part of his people's struggle in South Africa.

Photo 34: Desmond Tutu (right) with Grace and Charles Hostetter. Mennonites served as bridge builders between AICs and mainline church bodies

Singing in Harmony with Bishop Motswaosele
Jim Bertsche

The time of consultation with Bishop Motswaosele by a delegation of three AIMM workers was coming to a close. It was he who a few years earlier had opened the door for ministry among African Independent Churches of Botswana by inviting AIMM to send missionary teachers to conduct Bible classes among the leaders of the Spiritual Healing Church, originally founded by his father and of which he had become bishop upon his father's death.

The meeting had taken place in a neat chapel built on a large corner parcel in a busy neighborhood of Gaborone, the capital of the country. Dressed in his customary white shirt with a black suit and tie, Motswaosele had conversed with the delegation in a crisp, purposeful manner. It was clear that by this time he and his church were appreciative of both the approach and ministry of AIMM personnel among them and that it was their hope that this ministry might be continued.

As our time of dialogue came to a close, the bishop said he'd like to conclude our time together with prayer in his little office adjacent to the platform. As we formed a circle, the bishop reached out to either side to join hands. As we stood thus, he led us in a heartfelt, wide-ranging prayer. There were expressions of gratitude for the white-skinned collaborators who had found their way to his country and to his church. There was prayer for his colleagues in leadership that they might be able to better understand the "Book of God" which had been in their hands already for years, but parts of which they had not understood all that well. He prayed for his country and the swift changes that were overtaking it, and for the members of his own church that they might be faithful to the Lord amidst the changes. He concluded by asking the Lord's protection over his visitors in their continued travel.

Photo 35: Archbishop and Mrs. Israel Motswaosele befriended a host of Mennonites in Botswana, here with Jim and Jenny Bertsche

As the delegation was preparing for an anticipated "Amen," they became aware that instead the bishop was softly starting to sing the beautiful praise chorus, "Allelujah, Allelujah." It wasn't long until the three members of the AIMM delegation sorted themselves out musically and slipped into three different harmony parts to round out an impromptu men's quartet with Bishop Motswaosele singing the lead! As our harmonizing came to a close, we looked up to see his face wreathed in a broad smile, his eyes literally glistening in delight.

It was a golden, unforgettable moment to be cherished by the four of us. Color of skin, mother tongue, difference of race, nationality, education – none of these mattered in the least. They all dwindled into insignificance as we bonded together in the expression of our shared gratitude and praise of our common Lord and Savior.

We Have Learned Together about Worship, Marriage, Prophecy, and Burnt Offerings
Morena Rankopo

My grasp of the history of the partnership between Mennonites and the Spiritual Healing Church in Botswana is limited, but here is what I understand. During the period of struggle in the then called country of Rhodesia, there were cross-border incursions into northeast Botswana, so the base of operations of the Spiritual Healing Church was moved from the village of Matsiloje near the Rhodesian border to the town of Mahalapye. It was there that our church encountered a threesome of Mennonites who met with our elders. Our founder, Prophet Mokaleng, had prophesied that one day, white people would come to work with us. This meeting was taken to be the fulfillment of that foretelling.

What is unusual about this sharing was that it was a genuine partnership which was possible because the Mennonites were not planting their own churches here. Instead, they were partners with us. We would identify needs together and seek effective ways to address those needs. For me personally, I found that sharing to be collegial and respectful, an exchange of knowledge and skills. We have witnessed real changes in the quality of our church leaders which is evident in those in senior leadership of our church.

One example is that we now have marriage officers across the church. It used to be that only mainline churches had such authorities. The AICs were excluded from this important function. That gap was closed through training led by the Mennonites, and often in our own language, Setswana. A second example is the married couples' fellowship initiated by Sharon and Rudy Dirks. This fellowship helped us to reflect on our families of origin, on how to raise our children, and on how to build strong marriage bonds. We walked a long road in learning these things. Then in our turn, we held such workshops in other places to help others.

Third, I have been part of a Wednesday weekly class focused on understanding the Bible using study guides prepared by the Mennonites. These guides have greatly improved the quality of the teaching among our pastors, evangelists, deacons, and preachers. Their level of understanding has risen markedly, and they do not feel intimidated by anybody, which was not formerly true. Our preachers are now confident and thoughtful. Their greater ability and confidence are why the faithful have remained in our congregations.

Fourth, the establishment of the Tshepong Centre for HIV/AIDS counseling opened up discussion in our church about this crisis affecting our nation and helped us to grasp the principles necessary to address this issue, principles that apply to all aspects of our life.

For their part in their life with us, the Mennonites learned a lot about *botho*, the community dimension of life in this part of Africa that encompasses extended family, as well as the balance between modern life and our traditional, rural background. *Botho* touches on the planning of marriage, the practice of *patlo* – requesting the hand of a young woman – and the various further steps that lead to marriage. It is the world of human and family relations in the African setting.

Mennonites also learned about our practice of worship: no instruments, the clapping of hands, and, of course, our dancing. Our Mennonite partners had a challenge falling in with our rhythms. They also learned to appreciate the breadth of active participation in our gatherings and our culture of choirs.

In the experience of partnerships, often one partner has greater power than the other. But across the board in our sharing with Mennonites, we found a genuine collegiality and a principle of mutual respect that was worth noting. In our theological conversations, we had great interest in the notion of prophecy, a common practice in our churches. But Mennonites had limited experience of this phenomenon and could shed little light on our many questions. Our own elders are not able to explain these things to us or to articulate their background. As a consequence, the next generation has little grasp of this spiritual gift. As a thinker, I would be keen to understand this distinctive of our church and to know its cultural and divine sources because in our past at key moments, the prophets operated in distressed circumstances to minister God's healing to us.

On other occasions, we have ventured with our Mennonite peers into delicate theological areas such as sacrifices and burnt offerings. We have asked whether honoring our ancestors can have a place in Christian church life. Our generation wants to dialogue about these things, but that desire has sometimes met with pushback from our older leaders for whom these are no-go areas and who prefer these things to remain ambiguous.

Another difficult area for the partnership was engagement with women's groups who tend to resist systematic study of the Scripture. They continue to rely on inspiration and spontaneity in their life together. But as a result, the women are also not as confident in their grasp of Scripture, which limits their capacity to lead in public gatherings like funerals.

A great challenge of our time comes from the "fire churches" – the Pentecostal megachurches. Many of their practices are even reminiscent of our own, though we tend to be more private in their application. In other respects, we have distinctive music and dance in our worship which our young people appreciate. On the one hand, we want to modernize our rituals for this age, but on the other, we do not want to lose our identity.

We are observing a shrinking of engagement with the Mennonites now, and those who have been beyond the reach of these interactions feel cheated. I recently returned from three years abroad in Australia where I was surprised to see abandoned church buildings, the effect of a growing secularism. In light of this trend, I am especially grateful and have broad affirmation for the partnership with the Mennonites that we enjoyed for its rare candor and balance. We share with our Mennonite kin the belief that it is at the initiative of individual members that the church lives. And we are sad to see the ebbing of the benefits that came from this partnership.

In Honor of Isaac Dlamini – My Partner, Colleague, Language Teacher, and Best Friend
Darrel Hostetter

"Go preach, and you will be healed!" were the words that came to Isaac Dlamini in a dream while he was being trained as a *sangoma* (a diviner/traditional doctor).

Isaac had experienced a difficult childhood with his father living away from Swaziland working on the railway in neighboring South Africa, and his mother marrying another man who did not like Isaac. He spent most of his early years living with an uncle. The first memory for Isaac of being with his father is at the age of twelve when he ran away to find him in South Africa. While staying with his father, Isaac became deathly ill. He was taken to a hospital where the doctor discovered that both of his lungs were diseased. After Isaac had been in and out of the hospital for nine months, one lung was removed, and he was given about five years to live. For the next four years, Isaac struggled with chronic illness.

When Isaac was eighteen, a man came to request of his father that Isaac be trained as a *sangoma*. Since his grandmother had carried this role and Isaac's illness seemed to be evidence that the spirits were calling him to be a *sangoma*, Isaac's father agreed for Isaac to enter training. When Isaac heard the words in his dream, "Go preach, and you will be healed," he had no idea where this dream was coming from. But the dream and penetrating words would not leave him, so he felt compelled to leave the training, despite that doing so was considered dangerous and could result in the spirits killing him.

Shortly after Isaac returned home, he fell ill again and was in the hospital for weeks. Back at home, he had another dream encouraging him to make contact with a blind evangelist who was visiting a neighboring homestead. When Isaac visited the evangelist, he was told that he was possessed by many demons. He stayed in the evangelist's home for a month of ministry and experienced deliverance and physical healing. Isaac did not fully understand what it meant to give himself to Jesus, but he returned home and later responded to the altar call of another evangelist in his community.

As Isaac began to share his newfound faith, he met with resistance. At his father's Zionist church – an African Independent Church – the minister did not allow Isaac to teach and testify very often, so he left and joined another Zionist congregation where he was allowed to teach and preach. He tried to attend an evangelical Bible school but could not gain admission because the school officials would not accept that as a Zionist, he was a Christian. It was a path strewn with difficulties.

Getting to know Isaac and ministering with him was for me an inspiration. He was such a hospitable, humble, and fun person to be around. Rarely would anyone visit him in his watch repair shop without laughing. Isaac was criticized by some evangelicals because he was a Zionist, but on the other hand, he gained the respect of both the king of Swaziland and the leaders of the League of African Churches, a loose federation of African Independent Churches. I came to see Isaac as a Paul-like figure in his own country. When he spoke, people listened. He had both an authority and a love for his people. I remember him saying to me many times that people will change with time, so give them time and respect. He was an encouragement to me, and it seems I was also an encouragement for him.

There was always something to gain by being with Isaac. He was part of the beginning of Faith Bible School (FBS) in May 1976 which was launched to further train and teach Zionist leaders in the word of God. The school was set up not in a formal way, but partnered with churches, schools, and public administrations to hold classes and weekend seminars. Isaac became a skilled teacher. He had a way of making his classes alive and interactive. I went to many *imilindzelo*, all-night services, where he preached. Little by little, he gained the respect of elder ministers in other Zionist churches and thus was able to encourage and nurture a deepening love for the word of God.

Photo 36: Darrel with Rev. Maseko and Rev. Isaac in Swaziland maize field

I remember so well the time when the Faith Bible School committee planned a seminar in Sitegi. We had arranged ahead of time to hold a seminar at a mission school compound for the weekend. When we arrived Friday afternoon, the mission leader called some of us to his home. He told us that because we were a church group, we needed to make an additional written application to a particular committee of the church to be able to use the school compound. The chairperson of Faith Bible School asked the mission administrator what we were to do because all of those coming to the seminar were to arrive that evening with no possibility to return home that night. He told us that we were not allowed to sing, pray, teach, or worship that evening. But he said he would call the president of the church to seek direction.

We could not believe our ears. It did not seem like our fault that they had not informed us of their procedures. We wondered how this Christian brother could throw us out and not even allow us to hold our Friday night meeting. As we walked away, Isaac Dlamini suggested, "If this church leader won't allow us to have our teaching session tonight, why don't we ask him to come and speak to us instead?" So Isaac and the chairperson of the Faith Bible School turned around and invited him to teach us that evening.

At 9:00 p.m., the mission administrator returned and informed us that we would need to leave the next morning. But he obliged us by giving a fifteen-minute devotional titled "Don't Forget God!" The question that kept coming up that evening was, "How can our Christian brothers treat us like this?" But I was learning from Isaac how to respect those who don't respect you. Isaac's identity did not come from how people responded to him. Isaac both knew who his God is and who he was, and therefore he gave respect and honor to people who did not respect him.

Because of Isaac's strong leadership and respect for others, he was elected as the president of the League of African Churches. I believe it was the first election ever held for this position. Isaac had earned the respect and honor of all the leaders because of his patient, loving, respectful, and honoring ways for many years. In the last years of his life, he focused on teaching these African leaders by his life of following Jesus and by his teaching of Scripture.

Isaac died some years later in South Africa where he was in intensive care after a heart operation. When his wife came to visit him after his operation, she found he had passed away. His oxygen mask had fallen off, likely due to staff neglect. Isaac lived a life far beyond what the doctors had said he would live, and then likely died because other doctors and nurses failed to care for him in his time of need. Isaac would have, however, still respected and loved them.

I miss my best friend, partner, colleague, and language teacher. He always found a way to encourage me, help me laugh, and yet keep stretching me in my language and faith. I loved his personality and realize how much of a gift he was to me and to the many who were touched by his life and ministry. *Ngiyabusiswa nguye*! I have been blessed by Isaac.

Mennonite Affirmation of Us Ended Our Feeling of Aloneness
Isaac Moshoeshoe

My first encounter with Mennonites was when I met John and Tina Bohn. They visited us after my attendance at a meeting of African Independent Churches. It was a special experience, though at first our branches in South Africa had misgivings about working with whites. I told our members to be patient and not to fear the Mennonites. Not long after that meeting, I was elected president of the African Federal Church Council (AFCC), our cooperative body here in Lesotho. In these encounters with the Mennonites, as later with Brian and Tricia Reimer, there was mutual recognition that we were brothers and sisters. We were like family to each other, even visiting each other in our homes for *braais* (cookouts).

As a council leader, I had many occasions to work with Brian in our program of Theological Education by Extension (TEE). During our partnership, we reached out to neglected communities, spending days together. Those impoverished communities now sorely miss those opportunities. Also it was during that time that we arranged a pastoral exchange when I had the privilege of working for a time with my wife, Rebecca, in a Mennonite congregation in the state of Illinois in the United States. We learned the ways of the American church with which we share so much.

Photo 37: Shared work was the lifeblood of the program as here between Brian Reimer and Isaac Moshoeshoe

This interaction was not this way with the whites we had come to know in South Africa, with whom there were no ties of affection and where suspicion ruled the day. As one who grew up in the Free State of South Africa, I personally know the reality of apartheid. We take satisfaction in knowing what strides we made in working with the Mennonites. Their affirmation of us ended our feeling of aloneness. Many in our churches said, "Now we know we are people, too."

As for what our partners took away from the friendship, I believe they learned how much we value and honor our leaders here in Africa, and how much emphasis we place upon discipline and order in our hierarchy.

My regret is that the partnership came to an end as the number of workers dwindled. I see this as a loss. In fact, it happened so quickly, we couldn't see it coming. It was like the day I was riding with my father in his *sekorokoro* (jalopy). The bonnet (hood) of the vehicle caught the wind and flew back into the windscreen. We were blindsided and could not see where we were going. Well, even the mainline churches are laughing at us that we "chased the Mennonites away."

I Learned the Meeting Would Happen . . . Whatever Time It Actually Began
Garry Janzen

Upon arrival in Botswana in September of 1985, Diane and I, along with our daughter and soon-to-be born son were whisked off to our village live-in to learn the Setswana language. After three months in the village of Mmadinare, we moved to the city of Francistown for Mark to be born. All the while, we didn't really have a job description other than Bible teaching with African Independent Churches. Jonathan P. Larson invited us to consider youth ministry. A relatively new AIC movement was needing some help. The movement was called *Bopaganang Basha ba Semoya* – the gathering of the youth of the Holy Spirit. I said yes.

I was introduced to the youth leaders who were working together from a number of AIC groups. As I was in Francistown, I got to know this group of leaders best, and they became my friends. I have learned that Bopaganang is still going strong, and some of these leaders are still involved today. I am so encouraged that AIMM now has Melanie Quinn assigned to come alongside this ministry – twenty-five years after we were doing it. My closest colleague and best friend was Golwelwang Paul Mogomela of the Diphapo Christian Church with headquarters in Letlhakane. His father was the bishop of the church, a position which Golwelwang was also later assigned. Some years after our family's return to Canada, Golwelwang and his wife, Onkabetse, were offered the opportunity to visit us for a month. On that visit, Golwelwang and Onkabetse became known as "Paul and Betsy."

During our partnership, Golwelwang and I traveled to many villages, generating interest among AIC youth groups to come together. We would arrive in a village and meet the church leaders, then they would take us around to other churches to meet their leaders. Soon we would have a "concert" pulled together. As is common among AICs, the youth group forms a choir. For youth to come together, they come as choirs and put together an impromptu concert as a friendly competition.

I have three particular memories of the Bopaganang ministry. I remember that we would often have Sunday afternoon meetings at a scheduled time, often around 2:00 p.m. Golwelwang and I would dutifully be there at the agreed upon time. After about a half hour or so, Golwelwang would start to show disgust at the others for not showing up. Then as the afternoon progressed, he would continue to show occasional outbursts of frustration. By around 3:30 p.m., the first person would arrive, then by 4:00 a few more. By 4:30 or so, everyone was there, and we had a meeting. After a few rounds of this process, I took the courage to ask my friend why we scheduled the meeting at 2:00, yet it didn't get started until 4:30. "Well," he said, "the time is set for the foreigners, so that it appears as though there is a prompt and early starting time. For the African brothers and sisters, they know there is a meeting that afternoon, and they are committed to being there. But the starting time is irrelevant. That there will be a meeting – this is what matters." Suddenly I realized that all the disgust my brother was showing for the tardiness of the other committee members was an expression of empathy for me that nobody else was on time. Once this was clear, I could also relax into the confidence that the meeting would happen, and that it didn't really matter what time it began.

Photo 38: AIC leaders also ministered in North America. Here, Garry and Diane Janzen host Golwelwang Paul and Onkabetse Mogomela in Saskatchewan, Canada

My second memory is of the power of light. There was no electricity in the residential areas of the villages where the churches were located. Often when we would get a concert together, it began after nightfall. I remember coming into a church building that was an empty space. There would be a table and a chair at one end needed to run the concert. Then someone would light a single candle on the table. As the light filled the room and as my eyes adjusted, I was amazed at how that one candle provided sufficient light. As the evening progressed, youth choirs would arrive from all over the village. The church would fill up with people, the leader would bring the meeting to order, and the concert would begin. What a great time of fun and singing!

My third memory is of a weekend when Golwelwang and I went to Letlhakane, his home village. We did our routine of meeting people and pulling together a Saturday evening concert. But what I remember was the Sunday morning worship service. The home congregation was the Diphapo Church. But on Sunday we were asked to preach in the Spiritual Healing Church, and I do mean "we!" I was given the text to preach on, and Golwelwang served as interpreter. The Holy Spirit was so powerfully present to us. The word that the Spirit gave that day flowed clearly. The interpretation that Golwelwang rendered was dynamic and powerful. It was the most amazing time of ministering together in the Spirit. And then there was the music – the women dancing and singing their hearts out – and I could see the joy of the Lord in their eyes. It is my greatest memory of our three years of partnership in Bopaganang. What a blessing!

Friendship Flowered between Us as We Prayed for Each Other
Joseph Motswaosele

The association between the Spiritual Healing Church in Botswana and the Mennonites began in Gaborone at the instigation of my brother, Israel, who approached Ed and Irene Weaver. That connection led to a series of conversations identifying our interests in studying the Scriptures. This study took the form of pastors' workshops which eventually included training as marriage officers. At that time, marriage officers in AICs were almost unheard of. Now we have many pastors who serve the larger community in performing marriages.

Over the years, many Mennonite workers have come and gone. The focus of our sharing was the interpretation of the Bible, effective administration of the church, and leadership skills. Friendship flowered between us as we prayed for each other.

We observed that the Mennonites appreciated our church – our life of prayer, our use of holy water, our uniforms, and our baptismal practices. They also encouraged us to be a crossroads community where we care for outsiders. Mma Batho and Mma Pelo – Sandy McLaughlin and Elinor Miller, Mennonite workers – received our blessing, wore our church uniform, and helped to build the church. And Tim Bertsche led some of us on travels to Kenya and the Holy Land that broadened our understanding.

Though we are still not taken on a par with the mainline churches in our dealings with the government, our growth in effective administration has helped us in filing the annual forms required to maintain our status. We also appreciate that the Mennonites encouraged us to band together with other Spiritual Churches (AICs). Eventually, we joined the Organization of African Instituted Churches (OAIC), and we participate in its local committee.

Photo 39: Side by side in endeavor, friendship in Botswana grew from mutual prayer. Here, Joseph (right) and brother, Israel Motswaosele (center) with Garry Janzen

In general, our church has prospered greatly in recent years, both in numbers of congregations and in our ability to meet the needs of this generation. In that growth, our partnership with Mennonites has helped us greatly. We recognize that we face many challenges now especially from the "fire churches" – independent Pentecostal megachurches. But we are committed to the traditions of our founding and do not want to leave our identity or practices.

There is one area where our partnership with Mennonites missed an opportunity. We had long dreamed of a residential Bible school for our church. This school was to have been based in Mahalapye under the direction of Bishop John Tshwene. We built some classrooms and offices. But our Mennonite friends thought this school should be an effort shared with other Spiritual Churches (AICs). Since there was not a unified vision, this project never came to fruition and fell by the wayside. It would have been a lasting legacy of our partnership.

We regret that in recent years, the strength of Mennonite involvement with us has been fading. We would have wished for that partnership to be as robust as it formerly was.

A Powerful Healing Experience at Nima Temple
Stan Friesen

Ed and Irene Weaver first contacted Ghana's Bishop Solomon Krow of the Church of the Lord (Aladura), and in 1968–1969, they began their Good News Bible classes in his congregation at Nima Temple, Accra. I learned to know Bishop Krow well, and during the years of our sojourn during the 1970s in Accra, he invited me to take a regular preaching appointment once a month at Nima Temple. I felt privileged over the years to become well acquainted with members of his congregation.

Nima Temple is located on the edge of one of the largest impoverished areas of Accra. During the Ghanaian independence era and the rapid urban expansion, Nima was one of the few areas of the city where the poor had relatively easy access to the major business hub of the city. Those who had recently arrived from a neighboring African country or Muslims from northern Ghana frequently settled in Nima. One of the private minibuses, the tro-tros, had a sign, "To hell and back." It plied between the center of Nima and High Street along which government offices and international businesses were located.

The other striking feature of Nima Temple was that it was located adjacent to one of the largest open sewers. The burning of incense was not only a vital part of the liturgy but essential to the worship environment within the sanctuary. Another outstanding feature of Nima Temple was that in an area with few well-built or clean white buildings, Nima Temple was solidly constructed, and its simple design, white-washed exterior, and polished terrazzo floor made it a beacon of beauty in this struggling neighborhood and an attractive invitation to worship for rich and poor alike.

Photo 40: Collaboration in leading worship at Nima Temple, Accra, Ghana

One Wednesday night as our Bible study was concluding, a distraught young woman who had been sitting at the back of the room came forward, knelt, and requested prayer. She vividly described how an evil spirit was threatening to take her life and was gripping her around her neck. The deacons – each dressed in a simple white robe with a red collar and carrying a polished steel rod, a symbol of their office – with Rev. Krow and the Church Mother, a deaconess, gathered around the woman as she knelt. As they laid their hands on her a chorus of vigorous simultaneous prayer arose to heaven. The word for prayer in Twi is *mpaebɔ* – "We implore you, Lord." The suffix *bɔ* is also used of the vigor with which one plays soccer.

After a protracted period of spirited prayer, the young woman arose with tears in her eyes and confessed that the evil spirit had not left her, and it still had a strong hold about her neck. Bishop Krow was present that evening, and he joined the prayer band for another session of vigorous prayer supported by the Bible class members. At the conclusion, the woman confessed once more that the spirit had not released her. Bishop Krow graciously reached out to the Church Mother and then spoke to the young woman, "This is the house of God, and this is where you are safe under the protecting hand of God. The Church Mother will find a place for you with her in the Healing Home of the Temple behind the sanctuary."

The Healing Home was a single row of four rooms, at the end of which the Church Mother had a small, one bedroom apartment from which she cared for the Temple and was available for prayer and counsel. Church members frequently used these rooms for spiritual retreats and times of fasting and prayer. "Rest tonight in the shelter of the Church Mother's room and presence," Bishop Krow continued, "knowing the loving prayers of God's people surround you. In God's grace, mercy, and time you will surely find your release and freedom. God's time is best. Be diligent and wait on the Lord."

About a week later, a radiant young woman and the Church Mother reported back to the Bible class the events of the week. The following morning after the prayers, the young woman had joined the Church Mother in her tasks of cleaning the Temple, and for several days she participated in the early morning and evening prayers of the church. A few days later, the young woman and the Church Mother became better acquainted, cleaning the church together and talking as women do while they work. The young woman confided that she had had an abortion, and the spirit of the child was calling her to be where it was. For this reason, the young woman was seriously contemplating suicide. The Church Mother quoted 1 John 1:9, "If we confess our sins, he is faithful and just and will forgive our sins and purify us from all unrighteousness." Then the Church Mother commanded the woman, "Sister, kneel down! In the powerful name of Jesus, I declare to you your sins are forgiven. Rise to newness of life!" The young woman arose and declared that the evil spirit departed and she was free.

Many years later, I recounted this story to my fellow pastor in California, Femi Fatunmbi, in the Pacific Southwest Mennonite Conference. Pastor Femi originally came from the Yoruba region of Nigeria, near Ibadan, to pastor an African immigrant congregation in Los Angeles. And to my surprise, he responded, "You cannot dismiss African beliefs in the spirit world by explaining them by your Western psychological terms. This young woman's belief that her life was threatened by an evil spirit cannot be explained by a guilt complex at having an abortion. An abortion in an African family setting carries far too many ramifications and implications for any simple explanation."

The meeting of two worldviews – African and Western – nevertheless find some common ground in the world of the New Testament and in the healing ministry of Jesus. The Bible gives us a meeting point from which the conversation and spiritual understanding of one another can find new depth.

"These Are No Ordinary Clothes, but *Special* Clothes for Divine Work"
Sandi McLaughlin and Elinor Miller[1]

In September 1987, we took up an assignment in Botswana to work with African Independent Churches. We moved in with local families in the large village of Mochudi and began worshiping with the Spiritual Healing Church (SHC). We both developed a strong sense that we should get church uniforms. We tested this idea with some of the other Mennonite workers and with a local AIC pastor and advisor, Otsile Ditsheko. This idea received much affirmation. We then met with the prophet of the SHC, Joseph Motswaosele, who was serving in Mochudi to ask if he would be willing to lead a uniform dedication service. He agreed to do this and a date was set.

We had several objectives in getting uniforms. One was to identify ourselves clearly with local independent churches. In order to do this, we incorporated several independent church distinctives in the design of our uniform – navy blue dresses; large, round white collars detached from the dresses; white head scarves; and blue and white twisted yarn rope belts. All these features are common to uniforms of the various AICs in the region. A second objective was to have uniforms which would not identify us with any *particular* church

---

1. In the years since their service assignment in Botswana, both Sandi and Elinor married and today use the names Sandra Richard Wood and Elinor Miller Shattack. In addition, we should note that in the original version of this essay, fellow Mennonite worker and administrator in southern Africa Judy Zimmerman-Herr contributed to the writing of this account.

group. The uniforms would rather give us an identity as women coming to teach among a spectrum of AICs.

On 20 March 1988, we had our uniform dedication event at the Spiritual Healing Church. We were also commissioned for work with AICs in Christian education for children and youth. That day a Mennonite group of nineteen adults and eight children joined us in a time of celebration.

Before the service, we entered a small house on the church grounds where the prophet prayed over and blessed our uniforms. Two of the visiting Mennonite women were assigned to help us put on our clothing while the congregation began singing. When we were ready, two choirs came out of the church forming two lines. The whole group together with the Mennonites formed a procession dancing us into the church with song.

When the time came for our commissioning, a small bench was placed at the front. We were asked to come forward while the prophet of the Spiritual Healing Church, Joseph Motswaosele, gave a sermon about the dedication of our uniforms and the work we were being called to do. He told the story of Samuel anointing David to be king. "The Lord calls who he wants. He looks on the inside of a person. When David came, God said, 'Be quick and anoint him; he is the one.' The work of these women is also the work of God. They have been called like David was, not because they were important, but because the Holy Spirit has sent them to do this work."

As we knelt before the congregation, the prophet said, "Let us turn to God, asking that their dresses be a uniform of Spirit. These are not ordinary clothes. These are *special* clothes for divine work." The church again resounded with singing and clapping as the prophet anointed our heads with oil. Jonathan Larson, a Mennonite Bible teacher with the AICs, also gave a sermon during the service, and the Mennonite group sang a favorite doxology. The church choirs sang six songs at various times during a service lasting three hours.

Following the event, we went to Sandi's family compound to serve lunch to around seventy people. Meat, rice, and cabbage were cooked in big pots. We had lots of help preparing and serving the food and washing up the dishes. By evening, we sat down to reflect in wonder on this unique, once-in-a-lifetime happening for two women from Ohio.

Sometime later we attended an event at the Spiritual Healing Church in Serowe. Archbishop Israel Motswaosele, Joseph's uncle, was leading this service. Suddenly, the two of us as Mennonite workers were called forward. The archbishop gave his blessing to our work in the Spiritual Healing Church. "These are my children," he said, "take care of them. I do not want to hear them crying on your account. But remember, they are working with *all* of the independent churches. Do not be jealous when they work with other churches."

Photo 41: Dedication prayer for Sandi and Elinor by Joseph Motswaosele of the Spiritual Healing Church

Furthermore he said, "They eat chicken, they eat beef, they eat goat meat, they eat sheep, but they do *not* eat pork!" We were looking straight at him while visions of eggs and bacon, sweet and sour pork, bacon lettuce and tomato sandwiches, pork chops, and ham sandwiches danced in our heads. After a split second he added, "And if they ever *did* eat pork, they won't anymore." In that moment we understood that if we were working with his church, we could not eat pork. It became clear that following this church law derived from the

Old Testament would help us build relationships of trust with independent church people.

During our work with the AICs, we traveled extensively around Botswana to various church events giving workshops, participating in special services, and frequently giving extemporaneous teachings for children in these settings. On a return from one of these trips, we stopped to get fuel. At the service station we met a minister we knew. He was looking for a ride to the capital city. We moved our luggage to the roof rack and strapped it down in order to make room for him inside the vehicle.

Four hours later when we stopped at a military road block, we discovered that a suitcase containing some of our clothes and a church uniform was missing from the overhead rack. We immediately assumed it had been stolen where we had stopped to buy cold drinks. However, the minister thought that the suitcase had "blown off." We retraced our route to file a police report, though with little hope we would ever see the suitcase again. The minister assured us we would get it back. But we were skeptical.

Upon our return to Mochudi, the people at the Spiritual Healing Church commiserated with us but steadfastly insisted that the church uniform would come back. We kept our jaded thoughts to ourselves. After six weeks we received a letter from the police saying they had the suitcase. We wondered if it might be empty as we drove two hours to retrieve it. We were astonished to find everything intact. Not a thing had been touched. On top of our other clothes was the missing blue uniform, white collar, white scarf, and rope belt. These were indeed no *ordinary* clothes.

As we look back now, we believe donning the uniforms was one of the most significant things we did in relationship building with AICs. The overwhelming response of warmth we enjoyed came because of the unexpectedness of it. Missionaries past and present have been known to bring ideas and things which local people adopt. By wearing the uniforms, we were adopting something which was theirs. It delighted them. It was a bond of common identity.

They Came to Work *with* Us
Thompson Mpongwana Adonis

In January 1982, Dr. Hennie Pretorius called us leaders of Zionist churches to the South African seminary at DeColigny. He had noticed that in South Africa, Zionists were frequently not included in the leadership of community events like funerals. "Why is that?" he asked. We replied that the leaders of mainline churches like the Anglicans go to school before ministry, but that our people never do that. Our leaders, whether educated or not, are appointed by the people of the congregation. We choose our own leaders.

It is for these reasons, we told him, that our leaders are not taken to be real ministers. Also, it is difficult for us to join those theological schools because of the expense and required qualifications for admission. For these and other reasons the schools of the Reformed Church and the Anglicans are not a good fit for us. We have to stand alone.

After that conversation, Dr. Pretorius took us to the local council of churches to explain our situation. Mennonite worker Robert Herr was present that day. He said, "Maybe we can find someone to help with training."

Soon after Jim Egli, a Mennonite mission worker in Maseru, Lesotho, was called to lead an initial workshop for Zionist church leaders. Before long, Larry Hills, another Mennonite volunteer, came to live in the town of Misty Mount, and a schedule of quarterly workshops was set in motion. Gary and Jean Isaac later followed, expanding that beginning. This option for training was pleasing to us because other local, mainline church teaching resources were suspect to us. We feared that we would be led away into the mainline churches, as happened to many. But not so with the Mennonites. We felt certain that they would not lead us elsewhere. They told us that they were not intending to plant their own churches. What is more, we observed that the Mennonites were like us. The people loved them.

The program we developed was a traveling resource. We took the training to the people to avoid unnecessary expense. In those outlying places, the training came within reach of ordinary people.

Since 1982, we have seen many interesting changes among the Zionists. It used to be that we had difficulty understanding our own Zionist preachers. Now, preaching is thoughtful and intelligible. Preaching used to be flitting around in the Scriptures. Now it is more orderly. Those who have studied and learned have also become an example to others.

So, the Mennonites gave us a chance. In the partnership with them, I personally have gained so much. They came to work with us not to do their own work, but to do God's work. As Zionists we felt stronger. The training awakened our confidence about what we could do in our own communities. Gary Isaac encouraged us by doing nothing without us. We learned that we had to do our part. For their part, the Mennonites learned about Xhosa culture and life. Their coming and going was not a hindrance since each had their own path and gift which enriched us.

Photo 42: Adonis with Anna and Joe Sawatzky: "They came to work with us."

We would have liked to have our own site for Bethany Bible School (BBS). It is not easy renting a location from others. And sometimes it is inconvenient. The Mennonites said, "To build a school is a problem. It may not be wise to incur expenses for equipment, salaries, and upkeep. It would be better to rent a place and avoid those burdens."

This situation was a discouragement to us, though if it were still possible, we would think it a great step forward. As with *Madiba*, our leader (Nelson Mandela), we can see that this legacy is secure. Those of us in the churches who are reaching that stage wonder about the future of Bethany Bible School. Once in a café, a man saw my BBS pin and asked me, "What about this school?" I would have loved to have showed him the place of Bethany Bible School. As it was, I had to content myself by describing it in words. To have its own location would give BBS visibility to all of this community, not just to the Zionists.

GUEST REFLECTIONS

Tanya Riches, *Australian Pentecostal worship scholar*
Congratulations to Thomas A. Oduro, Jonathan P. Larson, and James R. Krabill on a project that amplifies African realities and voices and charts the many transnational connections between North America and Africa. Such reflections are sure to prove highly useful for other continents, including Oceania. Increasingly in our globalizing world, urban centers are connected like never before. Due to migration and transnational trade, cities like Melbourne and Lagos share experience and realities that were previously unheard of and unimagined. Among the multiple and varied transnational flows are sharings of deep spirituality and faith. As historians note the center of Christianity as having shifted, similarly we need to pay serious attention to the efforts of Christian peoples to translate and inculturate the faith in its heartlands. The narratives in this collection – and that are yet unfolding all around us – yield rich data for the researcher. At the same time, however, it is worth recognizing that there are barriers to sharing such knowledge in the form of visa restrictions and limited movements. This printed work allows profound oral wisdom to be shared and studied by indigenous peoples all over the world and will continue to benefit long into the future.

Tanya Riches is a singer, songwriter, choir conductor, lecturer, and scholar residing in Sydney, Australia. Originally publishing her works through Hillsong Church, she authored the popular song "Jesus, What a Beautiful Name." Riches is currently a department of theology and religion senior lecturer and in masters' program oversight at Hillsong College in Sydney.

Dana Robert, *Boston University*
The long relationship between AICs and Mennonites is one of the greatest stories of Christian mission in the twentieth century. To counteract the colonialism and racism that too often infected

Western missions in Africa, the Mennonites avoided founding their own churches. Rather, they focused on Bible study training and peaceful relationships across racial and cultural boundaries. Like other postcolonial missionaries, they practiced a ministry of "presence." Yet even as the Mennonites avoided founding their own churches, Christianity was growing rapidly throughout the continent. In solidarity with their friends and partners, some African Christians wished to be called "Mennonites." One of the questions raised by this splendid history of faithfulness is at what point does dying to "self" require giving up the "rights" even to one's own name? What if one's friends wish to call themselves Mennonites? And what if the meaning of "Mennonite" changes because it has been adopted by "others"? Perhaps the Mennonite-AIC relationship has changed not only the AIC's, but the very definition of what it means to be a Mennonite.

Dana L. Robert is Truman Collins Professor of World Christianity and History of Mission, the director of the Center for Global Christianity and Mission at Boston University School of Theology, and an editorial committee member of the Dictionary of African Christian Biography *(www.dacb.org).*

Jehu J. Hanciles, Emory University
The emergence of modern African Christianity is a complex tapestry of multifarious events and developments that defy easy analysis. Undue emphasis on overtly dominant strands typically obscure the infinite capacity of the African world to absorb new influences and shape outcomes. The story is replete with paradoxes, tensions, and unpredictable plotlines. Foreign missionary endeavor is often inextricably entangled with local agency and aspirations, while the collisions instigated by powerful external forces are juxtaposed with compelling convergences and surprising alliances. The latter are less well examined in the literature.

Thus, a treatment that illuminates relationships and collaborations between North American Mennonites and members of AICs based on individual testimonies is likely to offer fresh insights. The AIC phenomenon was explosive but complicated, and the most effective Western missionaries were invariably those willing to subordinate *a priori* ideals and presumptions to African realities and priorities. This willingness was far from common, but it made for strategic alliances that often bore great fruit. By the 1970s, some AICs had begun to spread globally, permitting even wider connections and new interactions – institutional and interpersonal – with Western counterparts. How these interlocking strands contributed to the growth of African Christianity and strengthened the worldwide church is certainly a story worth telling.

Jehu J. Hanciles *is D. W. and Ruth Brooks Associate Professor of World Christianity, the director of the World Christianity Program of Emory University, and author of* Beyond Christendom *(Orbis, 2008).*

6

Weeding

Between the mystery of a seed cast in the soil and the joy of harvest, no toil is more demanding, or painful, than removing the weeds that can sap from the soil what is available for fruitfulness. It is a measure of real partnership that even threatening things may be spoken of without fear of offense. A trust is in place that partners seek each other's good. So the work of admonishing one another, whether in addressing blind spots, whether in failure of faith or need to reclaim a servant's role, all prepare a reward that will be apparent at the harvest.

Real Work Begins When the Task Is Given over in Prayer
Rod Hollinger-Janzen

Lynda and I arrived in Cotonou, Benin's largest city, in February 1987, at the invitation of the thirty denominations that composed the *Conseil Interconfessionnel Protestant du Benin* (Benin Interconfessional Protestant Council). The council established a commission to give me guidance as I began the task that they had assigned to me, creating a Bible teaching program.

We set the date for the commission's first meeting, trying to choose a time when the eight busy church leaders would all be able to attend. On the established day, I entered a dusty, empty hall. I brushed some pigeon droppings off a bench near the door and sat down to wait for the other members. After a long while, a dark silhouette appeared in the doorway, backlit by the tropical sun. It was Pastor Djako Célestin, an older pastor of the *Association Evangélique Universelle*, now the *Eglise Evangélique Universelle*. He greeted me Cotonou-style with three kisses – left cheek, right cheek, left cheek – and sat down beside me. We shared the news about our families. Then silence fell again.

Photo 43: Rod with Benin Bible Institute board members: (left photo) the founding board – (l. to r.) Michel Dossou, Henry Harry, Abel Dossou, Pierre Togbe and Samson Assani; (right photo), Augustin Ahoga, board chair

As the meeting time faded into the past, my complaints about the no-shows grew more and more frequent. After more than an hour had elapsed, Pastor Djako and I concluded that the meeting would not be held that day. I voiced my discouragement about the commission members' lack of commitment. Pastor Djako's response ended my complaining and opened my heart to an understanding that continues to challenge me several decades later: "How much have you prayed about this meeting?"

From Pastor Djako, I learned that real work begins when the task at hand is given over in prayer, so that God may infuse it with purpose, empower the people involved, and guide it to fulfillment.

Life Lessons from the "God Will Provide Barber Shop"
Julie Bender

My most delightful memories of visiting African Independent Churches are of the celebrative, joyous worship of the congregants. Opening worship was always a time of lively singing, clapping, and drumming, with bodies in full motion. Sharing and prayer times were interspersed with spontaneous songs thanking God for his wonderful goodness by providing protection in the midst of danger, healing from sickness, or the needed money for school fees. Singing was accompanied by swaying and turning with hands and handkerchiefs waving in the air. The offering was taken as members danced to the front of the sanctuary to encircle the collection bowl and deposit their money with smiles and joy exuding from their faces.

Worship services often lasted for two to three hours. Prayer was taken seriously, and all-night prayer meetings were regularly scheduled events. What a privilege it was to worship with these believers during our early 1990s teaching assignment in Accra, Ghana, at the Good News Training Institute – a school dedicated to training leaders of the AIC churches!

Photo 44: Celebrative, joyous fellowship following worship, Ghana-style!

I have often reflected on the contrast between worship with my African Christian brothers and sisters and worship experiences with North American fellow believers. If there is a difference, it seems to me that African Christians know in a profoundly deeper way that they need God's help than many North American Christians know. In North America, people aspire to be as independent as possible from God's daily assistance. Only when a problem escalates to a desperate level does one finally acknowledge the need for help from others, including God. When we live life so self-sufficiently, then gratitude and joy don't seem as prevalent as when we live life acknowledging our dependence on God's intervention. Expecting and receiving God's provisions result in a very natural, heartfelt response of gratitude to our generous, giving God.

Our African brothers and sisters demonstrated relentless trust in God with frequent verbal expressions of "God will provide." The slogan "God will provide," in fact, was commonly written on taxis or used as a business name in Ghana, as in the "God Will Provide Barber Shop."

May I, as a North American Christian, learn from my African brothers and sisters this wonderful truth of God's provision and develop a deeper faith with a wholesome dependence on God, resulting in gratitude and joy.

The Challenge of Multiple – and Sometimes Conflicting – Stories
R. Bruce Yoder

I traveled to Nigeria to visit Mennonite Church Nigeria for the first time in 2001. At a meeting with the church's executive committee, there was commentary by those present about the history of the relationship between the church and the North American Mennonite mission for which I worked. At one point in the conversation, Nigerian Bishop Frank Udoh turned to my colleague and me and said, "You missionaries, we wanted to be Mennonite, but you wanted us to be AICs."

Photo 45: Listening to partners is key to successful relationships

I had arrived in West Africa almost two years earlier and was convinced that in our work with AICs, my mission colleagues and I were doing mission right. That is, we rejected the colonial assumption that we should or could import a Western theological and denominational identity and instead worked to support and encourage AICs as they sought to faithfully embody the Christian faith in their context.

But when I was seated at the table with the executive committee, Bishop Udoh's statement caused me to pause. Certainly he was not suggesting that he preferred the mission practices of the colonial age to the enlightened postcolonial mission practice of supporting African agency by working with AICs. He must have misunderstood. In hindsight that assumption was a demonstration of my own naiveté. After all, Udoh had been working with Mennonite missionaries since before I was born.

I was able to have copies of the mission publication *The Uyo Story* reproduced and delivered to Mennonite Church Nigeria in an attempt to explain why the mission had chosen to focus on ministry with AICs. *The Uyo Story* is an account of the reasons for this approach instead of one that seeks to reproduce Western doctrines, practices, and structures. When I handed over a stack of *The Uyo Story* to the executive committee, the secretary looked at them and rolled his eyes. "We know this book," he said, "*The Uyo Myth*." The members of the executive committee laughed and nodded their heads. It was obvious they knew that story, but it was just as obvious that they did not agree with its characterization of the path that the mission had taken.

So, there were two narratives of Mennonite work with AICs in Nigeria. The story I knew as a missionary was that Edwin and Irene Weaver went to Nigeria in 1959 to assist a group of churches that wanted to become Mennonite. Once there, they found vibrant AICs and strong animosity between them and mission churches. In the new postcolonial context, the Weavers announced a new day in missions, choosing to reinforce African theological agency by capacitating AICs and working hard to create opportunities for reconciliation. This new approach was indeed a creative and laudable mission engagement during a period that saw the de-legitimization of the very concept of mission.

Mennonite Church Nigeria's story was different. Church leaders did not begin with the Weavers but with missionaries who had visited earlier and who had moved toward establishing a church modeled more closely on Western assumptions and structures and with strong organic ties to the North American Mennonite church. The mission, however, reversed direction and focused on capacitating AICs. In this telling of the story, missionaries would have preferred that Mennonite Church Nigeria be an AIC instead of a Mennonite church.

So, these were the two versions of the same engagement. Missionaries understood themselves to be decolonizing mission practice by not importing foreign faith expressions into Nigeria. The Nigerian church saw things differently. When Udoh said, "We wanted to be Mennonite, but you wanted us to be AICs," under the surface was, and this is my interpretation, "We wanted to be part of you, but you didn't want us to be part of you."

The zeal to decolonize mission engagement is such that we do not always understand how our attempts at decolonization are received by our African brothers and sisters. For me this highlights the ambiguity of our "postcolonial" or "post-Christendom" mission paradigms. We should maintain a healthy suspicion of these paradigms even as we strive for constructive options. A good dose of humility, careful listening to our partners, and ongoing conversion are essential as we strive to faithfully participate in God's mission in the world.

Learning Discipleship and Self-Restraint
Enole Ditsheko

Through the voice of an African Independent Church leader, the late Archbishop Israel Motswaosele of the Spiritual Healing Church, the Mennonites of North America began a sojourn in Botswana. I know this history only secondhand, as I was born in the early 1970s. What I can bear testimony to, however, and with authority is that I remember Buddy and Lois Dyck who were posted in Francistown, arriving in my dusty home village of Maun in 1982 to spend Good Friday and Easter celebrations at my childhood church, the Eleven Apostles Healing Spirit Church, where my uncle, the late Bishop Otsile Osimilwe Ditsheko, was among the clerics.

The picture of those white people in the midst of all of us is indelible on my mind. I was amazed at their adaptability to attending the many long services that characterize this major event in the Christian calendar of Botswana AICs. It is usually at Easter time that local churches, known as "branches" of the national denomination, all come together at the headquarters to worship. The main features of AIC worship are loud singing, clapping of hands, stomping of feet, being thrown into spiritual trances to prophesy, and laying of hands on the physically and spiritually sick. All this takes place at the same time and usually in a cramped space at a time of sweltering heat, the time of the year when the festivity almost always falls. It has been something to marvel that these Mennonites would actually spend four nights without sleep as we do in the African churches. This willingness has suggested to me that the partnership is based on a principle of respecting each other's cultural way of viewing religion and in this particular case, Christian faith.

Then shortly after that Good Friday and Easter experience, I came into contact with *Rra Diane* (father of proverbs) as Jonathan P. Larson is known among the AICs. The name *Rra Diane* (Rah Dee-AHN-neh) has its genesis in Jonathan's love of Setswana idioms, expressions, and proverbs and his use of them, much to the delight of native speakers. His proficiency in the language made Jonathan stand out from all the missionaries who ever served in Botswana because the AICs were founded by elderly people who were deeply rooted in their culture and had little formal schooling. Anyone, therefore, who did not need language interpretation to carry on conversations with them was deeply appreciated.

My journey in faith has been influenced by a simple story Jonathan told – which he probably has forgotten, as he tells so many of such tales – to a group of teenagers in 1985. Jonathan said he witnessed a dispute over ownership of a cow at the Kanye *kgotla* – traditional court – where two men claimed to be the owner. The cow was branded on both thighs. Jonathan used the story to say that if we wanted to be of God, we should have an undivided allegiance, and that it would be best not to patronize drinking holes, taverns, or saloons because others might then not clearly understand where our allegiance lies.

My highlight with the Mennonites concerned another missionary family, Tim and Laura Bertsche, who replaced the Dycks in Francistown. Their focus was on youth ministry. Although I lived six hours away from them by road, whenever I spent my school holidays at my uncle's place near Francistown, I was a regular visitor at the Bertsches' house. It was their outlook on moral discipline that got me thinking as I was in junior high school. They preached abstinence, self-control, and discipleship. I admit that I met these words for the first time from this couple, and though their three children were fairly small at the time with the last-born being a baby, I admired the manner in which this fairly young couple conducted their lives and mirrored the values they were preaching to a group of youth in Francistown. Since I happened to speak English quite well, they asked me to help them with the Setswana language. We became close friends.

It was this friendship that made them believe in me and invest in my growth. I became part of a youth group that was sponsored to attend a retreat in Manzini, Swaziland. As a bunch of young people from the African Independent (Zionist) Churches in Southern Africa, we benefited from lessons on life choices during a weeklong retreat. Out of the eight young people from Botswana, I was the one who took the trouble to jot down the lessons I picked up there and turned them into a report that I passed on to Tim Bertsche, who subsequently shared it with the team of Mennonite workers. They saw some promise in those reflections and proposed that I participate in the Mennonite Central Committee's year-long exchange program in North America that drew in young people from across the world.

That cross-cultural experience was an eye opener and entrenched in me Christian values of discipleship and self-restraint so that I knew how to commit to a female friend who later on was to became my wife. I owe this learning to the Mennonites, and I have made it clear to them that without them, I could have fallen into a trap like many of my peers.

However, a weakness of the partnership between the Mennonites and AICs has been a failure to mentor leaders who could be prepared to take over leadership once the founders and elderly bishops have passed on. While the Mennonites might have deliberately stayed away from the internal politics and leadership struggles of the AICs by providing training to the elderly leaders, these older folks have now died with whatever skills they acquired from the Mennonites. The programs had been designed, developed, and implemented largely by the missionaries with limited input by the local churches. Hence when missionaries left, there was little continuity which has resulted in a serious dependency syndrome, whereby unless we recall missionaries to train our new leadership, there would be no one left in our churches who can do so.

The sad reality of not investing in youthful people who showed potential in leadership has unwittingly led to complaints of those who would have been children or youth during the strength of the partnership but are now asking questions about leadership and accountability. For example, I remember that when Jonathan witnessed the ordination of my uncle in 1986, he had words of wisdom to share in the full hearing of all who attended that occasion: "Ditsheko, you are a steward of God's flock, not a master. You are a servant, not Lord. You must lead through humility and accountability." The sorry state across much of the African church now is that some leaders perceive themselves as next to Christ and beyond accountability; neither can they be challenged or accept feedback.

But the church of the twenty-first century is surely a different one from that of the 1970s, 1980s, and 1990s. While it used to be the *moruti* (church minister) who was the paragon of knowledge, today's church is full of university graduates in various disciplines. It is made up of professionals and leaders in their own right. They are voluntarily members of these churches, are not hesitant to ask questions, and are bold to challenge things they feel do not count for the greater good.

Teacher-Learner: Who Is Who?
Irene Weaver with interviewer Lynda Hollinger-Janzen

At age one hundred, Irene Weaver was still peeved that editors rejected her proposed book title, *Teacher-Learner, Who Is Who?* in favor of a blander one, *The Uyo Story*. "The teacher-learner approach to indigenous churches in West Africa is essential," Irene said.

In Africa, we do well to forget who we think we are and recognize our need to learn before trying to teach others. Jesus spoke so frequently about humility with reference to God's kingdom. As Westerners, we often go to Africa to teach and give, not knowing that Africans have so much to teach us if we are humble enough to learn, and so much they would gladly share with us if we could only open our hands to receive.

Take Janet who sold vegetables and oranges under a tree in Ghana. She taught Irene that the most effective way to share the good news of Jesus is to tell everyone she meets about the great things God has done in her life. Janet had been healed in an AIC and became an enthusiastic follower of Jesus. She couldn't stop talking about what Jesus had done for her.

Photo 46: Studying the Gospel of Mark with the Church of the Messiah, Ghana

Irene felt she should train Janet to lead Bible classes so the classes could continue after Irene left the country. After working together on some Bible study outlines, Irene felt Janet was ready to lead the next class on God's promises to Abraham. The women's group met outside the church under the stars with only a candle to light the pages of their Bibles. "I was one of the students," Irene said. "Janet was the leader."

All of a sudden, I realized she was not following the outline we had made. She led the women in a discussion about Abraham and Hagar. I thought, "Shall I step in and bring us back to the subject of the lesson?" Then I thought, "No, the biblical story is about polygamy, and this discussion is relevant to their lives."

At the end of the lesson, Janet simply looked up at the stars and said, "God's promises to us are like those stars. We can't begin to count them, and we can't begin to realize what God's promises are to us. We'll never understand all about God. But he is great, and he is good, and he is the author of this word we are studying. We have to study the Bible together, and someday we'll know."

"And I was happy to leave it at that," Irene said. "It was a great lesson for me too, learning that the study didn't have to be my way because I didn't understand the culture as I should have understood it at that time. I thank God for the wisdom to let Janet do it in her way."

What Are We to Do with the Healing Stories of Jesus in the Gospels?
Stan Friesen

Christopher Agbalenyo was an elder at Ghana's Ridge International Church where Delores and I and other Mennonite colleagues frequently attended. The congregation was a member of the United Church of Ghana. Of its three pastors, one was a Twi-language speaker, one Fanti, and one a Dutch missionary.

The English service in the evening served the more professional and international communities. Christopher was a building contractor who had come to Accra from the Ewe-speaking eastern region of Ghana. The southeastern region of the country had been introduced to Christianity by the German Bremen Mission beginning in the mid 1850s. Christopher learned of the Good News Bible classes that the Mennonite missionaries were holding, first at the Church of the Lord (Aladura), Nima Temple, and later at the YMCA for leaders of the African Independent Churches in the Accra area. Christopher was intrigued by the Good News classes because, like many West African Christians, he was duly committed to the long-established Evangelical

Presbyterian Church (EPC) while at the same time finding spiritual vitality and passion in an AIC faith community, the White Cross Society established by Prophet Doh.

African traditional religious traditions have a large place for health and healing. This healing focus has also been a prominent feature of most AICs. Prophet Doh – though raised as a faithful member in the Evangelical Presbyterian Church – was eager to exercise his healing and prophetic gifts within the life of his Evangelical Presbyterian congregation. Thus he referred to his prayer and healing ministry as the White Cross Society rather than calling it a "church." For many within the EPC, however, the healing practices of Prophet Doh and the White Cross Society had a larger emphasis on Pentecostal practice and traditional religious beliefs than they were willing to absorb, so the two religious bodies diverged.[1]

In December of 1973, when Dr. Howard Charles was on a sabbatical leave in Accra from the Associated Mennonite Biblical Seminary,[2] he taught several courses at the Good News Bible Institute on his favorite subject, the Gospel of Luke. Charles encountered some of the same questions we other Mennonite teachers in Ghana had faced from our AIC students. How can Westerners read on virtually every page of the Gospels of Jesus healing or casting out spirits, yet find the center of religious faith and experience in Romans and Galatians where Paul teaches justification by faith alone? How central is the life and ministry of Jesus to our understanding of the gospel? What are we to do with these healing stories in the Gospels?

As one of our students at Good News, Christopher was eager to take me, Howard Charles, and Dr. Mary Oyer – a Mennonite music professor from Goshen College in Goshen, Indiana, at that moment studying African music at the University of Ghana in Legon – to meet Prophet Doh in his healing village and witness one of the community's biweekly Friday afternoon healing services. Christopher traveled a day earlier to make the preparations for our visit. On Friday morning, the three of us and several of our students drove a hundred miles east of Accra to Prophet Doh's healing village.

When we arrived, we were stopped about a mile from the village and told that we would wait until the village was prepared to receive us as their guests.

---

1. For a fuller description of the history and religious practices of Prophet Doh and the White Cross Society, see the work by Christian G. Baëta, *Prophetism in Ghana: A Study of Some "Spiritual" Churches* (Achimota, Ghana: African Christian Press, 1962; 2nd ed, 2004), 89–106. Baëta, a Ghanaian church historian and pro-vice chancellor of the University of Ghana/Legon, was himself a member of Ghana's Evangelical Presbyterian Church.

2. Now Anabaptist Mennonite Biblical Seminary, Elkhart, Indiana.

When a shotgun was fired at the village, we were permitted to proceed. As we approached the village, Prophet Doh and about twelve of his seers came out to welcome us. Prophet Doh was dressed very simply in white with a colorful stole and no head gear. His twelve seers were each dressed in a simple white robe with red collar, similar to those worn by Catholic fathers in Ghana and in some AICs to remind the wearer that it is costly to be a disciple of Jesus.

Photo 47: Prophet Doh (center) with other leaders of the White Cross Society

We were accompanied by our hosts past the thirty to forty simple, neat, small homes where people who had come for healing were living and waiting for the Friday healing service. At the center of the healing village was a modest white chapel building similar to what the early Bremen missionaries would have built in a village setting such as this. Some of the people in their huts that we passed on our way to the chapel gave us the appearance of suffering from forms of mental illness. Upon reaching the chapel, we were offered – in typical Ghanaian custom for guests and strangers – a drink of water to cool our hearts. We sat in the shade of the chapel, but no food was offered since fasting and prayer were essential spiritual preparation expected of all participants for the afternoon healing service.

As the three o'clock hour approached, the seers began to sit among the grove of trees on the south side of the chapel. We noticed people coming from the small houses to meet one on one with the seers. Christopher informed us that those who were prepared to go forward seeking healing would first confess their sins, their evil intentions and bitter feelings toward others in the family and community, and receive the pardon offered by the seer in the name of the Lord to whom their confession had been made.

As individuals concluded their confessions, they entered the chapel where we and others – presumably family members who were caring for the ill and troubled persons in the healing village – had assembled for worship. At the front of the chapel stood Prophet Doh behind a pulpit, and to his right were about eight anointers dressed in simple white robes and holding saucer-shaped seashells filled with olive oil in their palms. On the far right side stood two seers. Because the worship service would be conducted in the Ewe language, Christopher sat with us to interpret.

As the congregation gathered, an organist began to play hymns on a reed organ likely similar to the way that German Bremen missionaries would have conducted worship in the early twentieth century. Following an invocation prayer by Prophet Doh, a series of hymns were sung with enthusiasm and familiarity. The musical selections had hints of German Lutheran melodies and words translated from German. Prophet Doh offered a very brief homily followed by an invitation and a welcome to the healing service.

From this point onward, Prophet Doh read extensive passages of healing accounts from the Gospels, recounting the compassion of Jesus on the blind, the deaf, and people suffering from leprosy – stories of how Jesus welcomed and shared hospitality with the outcasts of society. Intermixed with these Gospel accounts were long passages of comfort and healing from Isaiah 40–66, speaking of God's comfort and healing for his people Israel in captivity. After a brief prayer that concluded the forty minutes of Scripture reading, Prophet Doh invited those seeking healing to come to the front of the chapel and kneel before one of the anointers to be individually prayed for and anointed with oil.

At the conclusion of each prayer and at the moment of anointing, the seeker appeared to receive what looked like a serious electrical shock that caused them to fall on the floor. I assumed this was interpreted as being slain in the Spirit. A group of young men entered through a side door and carried the anointed person to the shade of the grove of trees near the chapel to recover. Each time one of the officiants anointed with oil, the same reaction occurred.

Simultaneously while people came forward for anointing, other individuals approached for consultation with the two seers. One young woman, desirous of opening a business stall at the market, inquired if it would it be more profitable for her to sell cloth or pots and pans. The seer listened intently, prayed, and reported to the young woman that he had not received a clear sign from God. Another woman inquired if she should take her sick child to Accra to the University Children's Hospital at Kole Bu.

When all those seeking healing had been anointed and taken to the shade of the grove of trees to recover, the congregation left the chapel and moved to a large open space beyond the grove and near to the modest homes of the prophet, his family, and associates. As drums began throbbing, the congregation surrounded those who had been anointed, entered the encircled open space, and began to dance. No longer singing hymns, the worshippers now clapped and swayed with joyful enthusiasm to contemporary Scripture songs and melodies with indigenous tunes. Those who had been anointed began to dance in an individual manner, some more vigorously than others, to the complex rhythms of the drums. Christopher leaned over to us and said that the congregation – but especially the prophet and seers – are able to discern what kind of spirit is troubling and disturbing a particular person by the manner in which he or she is dancing.

After the group had been dancing for about an hour, the prophet and the seers began slowly moving among the dancers. When one would be overcome with exhaustion and would sit or lie down, the prophet and the anointers would encircle the individual and again anoint them with a prayer of healing blessing, then offer their right hand to raise the person to their feet. At times, the individual would offer a testimony of thanksgiving for healing. Other individuals would stand and confess that they were still awaiting healing. The prophet would then respond that the person should stay in the healing village, worship morning and evening with the congregation in the chapel, and live a life of prayer until the next healing service two weeks hence.

We did not learn much about the relationships of the prophet and his seers and anointers, or how they spiritually and psychologically nurture the people in the healing village during the two weeks between healing Fridays. Nor did we learn how long individuals and families seeking healing normally stay at the healing village. But I was encouraged, nonetheless, in this encounter with Prophet Doh to see the many ways in which this healing event resonated both with the biblical world and with an African cultural perspective in which health and healing are viewed as a communal concern and journey.

African friends have told us, "I *am* because I *belong* to a community." West African traditional healers often see the patient as part of a collective and the individual as the symptom of the disease inflicting itself upon the family unit or village. While Prophet Doh was clearly the inspiring leader at this healing event, healing gifts were also shared by others in the church community. There was humble modesty and sensitivity in the nonverbal forms of communication, in dance, and in the discernment of the spirits at work.

It was great to see the centrality and thorough grounding in the Scriptures about healing. There were no demands for instant healing, but rather patience to let God's grace work through the community like leavening of yeast in the healing and restorative journey. This ministry was a powerful and creative blending of the biblical view of healing coupled with the centrality of healing and health in a traditional African view of life lived in its fullness.

GUEST REFLECTIONS

Todd M. Johnson, Center for the Study of Global Christianity, Gordon-Conwell Theological Seminary
In this remarkable story of friendship and cooperation between Mennonites and AICs, the editors portray the single most important issue for Western churches in this postcolonial age: to address racism and conquest while encouraging the emergence of a truly indigenous Christianity in every country of the world. In a poignant echo of Christian history, an independent and "separatist" group of churches that were forged in persecution five hundred years ago in Europe is deferentially supporting churches in Africa that have faced similar opposition in the past century. Today Africans are 17 percent of the world's population, 26.5 percent of all Christians, 33 percent of all Independents, and 44 percent of all Protestants. With the future of the global Christian movement shifting steadily to the Global South, this collection of stories is a testament to how African churches are transforming the Christian movement and subverting centuries of colonial

Christianity with behind-the-scenes assistance from a now global Mennonite church that is looking beyond their own agenda and finding commonality in a shared gospel.

Todd M. Johnson *is codirector of the Center for the Study of Global Christianity at Gordon-Conwell Theological Seminary, South Hamilton, Massachusetts.*

Casely Essamuah, *Global Christian Forum*
In an increasingly polarized world, missionary activities from the Western world are usually either uncritically celebrated or unfairly vilified. Here in these pages, we have accounts of missionary engagement between the North American Mennonites and AICs that are truly other-centered and grassroots initiated. If the aim of missionaries is to bring all of Christ to bear on any given culture and worldview, while making themselves irrelevant in the long run, then these stories start from that paradigm and are thus so enriching to read. The global church has not yet plumbed the depths of the profundity of the words of our Lord and Savior Jesus Christ, that the "Son of Man came not to be served but to serve, and to give his life as a ransom for many" (Matt 20:28 ESV). In the same vein, we have this splendid promise from Jesus that "The thief comes only to steal and kill and destroy. I came that they may have life and have it abundantly" (John 10:10 ESV). *Unless a Grain of Wheat* stands as a testimony to the admirable attempts at living out these verses from our Lord. To him alone be glory for ever and ever.

Casely B. Essamuah *is secretary of the Global Christian Forum and author of* Genuinely Ghanaian: History of the Methodist Church Ghana, 1960–2000 *(Africa World Press, 2010).*

7

Watering

Vast swathes of Africa from the Sahel to the Kalahari are prone to scant rains, even droughts, as are the prairies of North America, home to many Mennonite settlements. The farmer's success often depends on the capacity to irrigate or water gardens and fields. In the field of friendship, demands are never far away. Parched inner life finds not only relief but wherewithal for life in streams of prayer, visiting, prophetic dreams and encouragement, and spontaneous anthems of promise and hope.

Sounds of Singing Soaked the Wooden Ceiling Beams, Wafting a Sweet Aroma
Nathan Dirks

The sound of singing fills the small room, rising with the joy of the choir in Setswana hymns glorifying God. The familiar rhythms of the African choral arrangements pulse through the air. A leader amidst the group has ventured a familiar line in alto or tenor. A momentary pause makes it seem almost as if the group will not catch on, leaving the lone singer to awkwardly fade out. But the pause is part of the buildup, and the entire group, all of them youth, relishes the chance to jump in. When they do, the collective sound is powerful. Neighbors across courtyards and fences are struck by the beauty of the arrangement. The voices know their parts, and each section respectfully pulls back as the others lead before chiming in when the time is right.

The vibes translate into motion, and the room sways with the bodies, each with their own movement in touch with the rhythm. In each part of the room and spilling into the adjoining ones, the youth consume the space. As they spontaneously sing, each individual claims their unique voice among the group. A surprising, confident bass to the left is the slim right defenseman from the youth football team. A few of the young women, gathered toward the dining room, send up an alto chorus with raised, clapping hands, their eyes shining. One of the elder statesmen of the group in his mid-thirties, known for his singing voice, carries freestyle duty, his own lines weaving in and out of the drift of the chorus. The tenors, a few chancing to find themselves in a group near the couches in front of a deep red wall, bend in toward each other and meld their voices, a song within a song, now in a soft cadence, now bursting out in loud exclamation.

Photo 48: The night when sounds of Setswana singing soaked the wooden ceiling beams

The music is impromptu, following an evening of sharing hopes for the future and seeking to learn more of the Scriptures and to serve in the community. A small invitation had turned into a gathering of twenty-five in the small, well-known Mennonite house in the middle of Gaborone. Food, a must in any good Setswana or Mennonite gathering, is shared freely throughout the evening, and tea is poured for everyone who desires it. In the social aftermath of the gathering, as clusters of conversation continue here and there, some of the young men wash dishes, quietly, so as to be a blessing to their hosts without needing thanks. Some, gentlemanly in demeanor, had brought a beverage for the hostess as a token of appreciation.

The conversation is the very model of respect for one another, as everyone is given a chance to speak. Setswana tradition holds that every word spoken in the *kgotla*, the community gathering, is golden. These representatives of a young generation show their deference by modeling the same attitude in this meeting of friends. Some had grown up together in the church and been companions for decades. Others found themselves here as they moved from their home village to the city, looking for a congregation with which to fellowship. The soccer team had drawn in a few who otherwise would not necessarily have found themselves in such a gathering on a Friday night, but who now took part in these less familiar circumstances with familiar and trusted comrades. A few spoke of the acceptance that they had found despite their differences in background, a sentiment with which we as alien Mennonites in Botswana could identify.

Now the room – indeed the rooms, the yard, the street – echoes with the singing of this diverse group. The sounds fill the space, enthusiasm increasing the volume. The music, a blessing, floods upwards, soaking, soaking into the wooden beams of the ceiling. Such songs, as well as prayers, conversation, and laughter, have been pooling in this habitation for decades. The saturated beams will waft a sweet aroma on future inhabitants of the house.

Those Mennonites Who Came to Find Us Here Surprised Us

Mokweni Thusang, Mashobo Baitsemole, Raletebele Kgangetsile, Kgosietsile Balefile, Raseleng Phalalo, Raditshipa Pope, Rasumako Dipapiso, Kegopotseng Thusang, Keganne Gabanatlhong, and Mosuwadibo Pope, with interviewer Jonathan P. Larson

Our encounter with Mennonites began in 1979 when we met with Larry Fischer, the Mennonite Central Committee (MCC) Botswana director, as representatives of the only two churches in our settlement of Pitseng. The two congregations were the Unity Church and the Nazareth Church. It was agreed that these two congregations would lead the way in laying plans for improving conditions in our community. We began to meet in the interest of finding water. Also, we had no nearby medical help. A well was successfully drilled, and a clinic, school, and rainwater collection system followed. This was the way things started.

It was then that we turned to studying the Bible. Our bishops, Bethuel Bolokwe and Isaac Seasole, gathered us together with Mennonite workers like Fremont Regier, *Rra Diane* (Jonathan P. Larson) and *Mothusi* (Don Boschman). We had previously been at odds with each other in our settlement, but this group caused us to work in harmony. As a result of these conversations, our churches even held monthly joint worship services for the first time. We continue even now to visit and pray for each other when sick and share in seeking Pitseng's welfare.

Before that time, we had been considered by the "white" churches – mainline denominations – as useless. They said we didn't know how to pray. So those Mennonites who came to find us here surprised us. We found them to be like us. And they treated us the same way, not as other outsiders. They could see that we were real people, that we had worthy thoughts. They knew us as friends. We shared in seeking and finding the truth together.

The studies we undertook with our Mennonite friends helped us to believe that there was a future for us. Those conversations also helped us to give substance to our preaching based on the Bible. In that teaching and in that experience, something happened that permitted us to leave behind suspicion of each other and find togetherness.

Normally for our weekend sessions, we gathered at *mokgatlo* – the program office – for two days, first reading the Bible and then seeking answers to our questions about funerals, disease, and the problems of our village. In our readings we encountered stories of poverty, illness, and cruel kings, things that we have also experienced. The events of the crucifixion of Jesus were of special interest to us, even how the Jews treated the dead by bringing spices.

In these weekend days of learning and reflection, our Mennonite friends learned how our lives were different from their own, but also that we were the same. Like them, we have our families, our children, and we often suffer.

But the great thing was to focus on God. We learned that the gifts of God are many. Some play instruments, some clap hands, some sing, but all the gifts are used in praise of God. There is no need to turn to the right and left of that goal.

We also recall that the two MCC workers who lived with us both received baptism here in our midst, though if they returned now, we would be ashamed for them to see that the service center buildings have since fallen into disrepair. But in these lessons, and in this partnership, we discerned a light – how to be a community around the Scriptures. This means learning to love one another despite differences. It was that understanding that we gathered to find together. Reading the Scriptures on our own failed to produce full understanding. As leaders, we had only partial sight. Preaching and leading of that kind is just shouting. Now that has changed.

Standin' in the Need of Prayer
James R. Krabill

In early 1980, our Mennonite team in Côte d'Ivoire conducted a survey in Abidjan to discover how many and what kind of African Independent Churches were in this city of over two million inhabitants. Our research in popular neighborhoods, back alleys, and ocean-front immigrant fishing villages yielded a plethora of struggling but vibrant faith communities, some indigenously rooted and others imported from neighboring Liberia, Ghana, Benin, and Nigeria.

Our intent was to do more than tally statistics. We wanted to know if any of these churches might be interested in partnering with us to share faith stories, to study the Bible together, and to work at preparing the next generation of church leaders for better equipped ministries. When we happened upon Apostle Manasse Adedokun of the Nigerian-based Sacred Cherubim and Seraphim Society in the bamboo shelters of his wind-swept seaside healing community, his response was immediate and enthusiastic. "*Of course*, we are interested," he exclaimed. "Can we start this coming Saturday?" As it turns out – much to our own amazement and most likely to the apostle's as well – we ended up doing just *that*!

Worshiping with the Cherubim and Seraphim required a few adjustments on our part – to eight-hour services, the oral nature of worship, strict rules of conduct in God's "holy place," the interpretation of dreams, the "descent of the Spirit" upon messengers who in turn ministered in unknown tongues, polygamous marriage arrangements, prayers to angels, repetitive chants, holy water – but most memorable of all to the unconditional embrace of a community who took us in and loved us as if we had known them forever.

My parents, Russell and Martha Krabill, came to visit us that summer to spend time with their first grandchild, our six-month-old son Matthew. In an era that predated cyberspace communication, round-trip overseas mail service took up to thirty days, and phone calls to the United States from the local hotel emptied our meager coffers at the rate of seventeen dollars a minute. So it was a marvelous experience to spend an extended period of time together as a family and to introduce our loved ones to new friends and Christian sisters and brothers who were becoming a part of our lives. The time flew by quickly, and before we knew it, we were waving goodbye to our parents as they boarded a plane at Abidjan's international airport for their return flight home.

Imagine our shock when three weeks later, we received our monthly package from Prairie Street Mennonite Church, our home congregation in Elkhart, Indiana, that contained a bulletin blurb announcing the news:

"Russell Krabill suffered a slight heart attack last Sunday" and "will probably be hospitalized ten days." We were stunned. The church bulletin had managed to get through to us before our family, despite their best efforts, could reach us.

Photo 49: Prayers, praise, and fellowship with the Abidjan chapter of the Sacred Cherubim & Seraphim Society

No words can describe the deep sense of helplessness and loneliness we felt at that moment. A myriad of questions tumbled through our minds: How had this happened to a sixty-four-year-old man in apparent good health? How serious was the attack? What were my responsibilities as the only son in a small family of two siblings? How might this impact our long-term presence in Côte d'Ivoire?

We carried our questions and burdens to the Cherubim and Seraphim church that weekend. They listened with care to our concerns. Then Apostle Manasse invited us to kneel on the cement floor in the middle of the worshiping community and lifted his voice in fervent prayer, pleading for God's healing hand to rest on my father and for our hearts and minds to be at peace in the assurance that God was in control.

I was brought to tears in that sacred circle, surrounded by God's people half-way around the world, and hearing in a new way Jesus's comforting words of promise to his disciples, "Truly I tell you . . . no one who has left home or brothers or sisters or mother or father or children or fields for me and the gospel will fail to receive *a hundred times as much* in this present age: homes, brothers, sisters, mothers, children, fields . . . and in the age to come, eternal life" (Mark 10:29–30, italics added).

Bible Study Has Increased Our Confidence and Our Standing with Other Christian Churches
Reuben Mgodeli

There has been a big change since the Mennonites came to South Africa. As my colleague Bishop Wilton of the Holy Banner of Ethiopian Apostolic Church in Zion has said, we earlier knew very little about the Bible. And we were not taken seriously by the other churches. When we went to community gatherings, we would never be asked to speak or pray. Now it is completely different. Our leaders are frequently asked to help, even to hold office in councils of churches and other organizations. Others now seek our collaboration. All of this could never have happened without partnership with the Mennonites.

The Bethany Bible School (BBS) established in partnership with Mennonites is not only for Zionists and Mennonites. It includes Methodists and charismatics as well. Its purpose is not only to help us preach, but also in our homes to be good fathers and mothers. BBS holds workshops on church organization where we learn that it is best to include single mothers and youth for the good of the whole church. We learn that we must manage money well and use good farming practices as stewards of creation.

God loves us to love others. God forgives us when we forgive others. So our personal lives are changed. We learn at BBS how to raise our children and to counsel victims of HIV. The teaching of this school applies also to us personally to be salt and light in the world. What attracts students to our school now is word of mouth about changed lives.

In the course of our study, we tell our own stories, stories of the heart. For example, I used to lead a church of three thousand members. But jealousy caused others to seek to harm me. Even the police had to patrol my house at night. In time, those who hated me came to me wanting reconciliation. But how can you restore a person's dignity when it has been marred? So now I don't have such a large church, but we are at peace.

I have completed the full cycle of twenty-four courses here in BBS. But this school is much more than study. It is a church, a family. When we stay away from BBS, we feel an emptiness. But being together makes us strong and allows us to be used in the larger community for good. In fact, I have also studied by correspondence. But being at BBS is more rewarding than studying on your own.

Now we feel free to share with other pastors, to seek their counsel, because we want to be good leaders, not just knowledgeable students. So for example at funerals, we no longer fear each other. Now we can console each other and help one another in times of difficulty. What has been born here is the same unity and togetherness told of in Acts 2.

Photo 50: Reuben Mgodeli (right) chatting with Wiseman S. Gumenke and Joe and Anna Sawatzky at Bethany Bible School

Even difficult topics like baptism are discussed at BBS humbly as learners. In such a setting, no one need take offense. One bishop who had never taught about baptism in his church said, "I can't wait to teach these things in my church." There is also the topic of ancestors. Do we "respect" them or "worship" them? Discussing this matter enlightened us. We agreed that it is good to honor our forebears, though worshiping God. When these discussions with our Mennonite friends are over, we say, "I can't wait until next time."

Of course, we are also taking thought for the future. In our Bible school we have nominated five people to be trained as teachers. In time, that fruit will appear. For now, we offer a four-year program leading to a graduation certificate. But even our graduates keep coming back because they experience growth and improvement here. When repeating material, we learn new things and go deeper.

When we meet with other [non-Mennonite] teachers, as they talk about South Africa, it's as if they are talking about some other country. They seem not to know about our life here. But Joe and Anna Sawatzky seem to understand our life and circumstances which helps us come to grips with the practical needs of our lives, how to deal with conflicts, and how to address those who are wounded and in need of healing.

Leaning on the Cross
Steve Wiebe-Johnson

Our family arrived in Côte d'Ivoire in August 1999. The country was in turmoil due to a number of factors. There were demonstrations in the streets on a regular basis. Students would take to the streets one day, opposition party supporters another. Main highways were often blocked by demonstrators on their way to or from a rally. By late November the country seemed to be walking on a very thin line as the president was losing his grip on power and social order was breaking down.

Tensions came to a peak just before Christmas as the military took over the airport and main radio station. The usual social conventions broke down completely. Looters took over any business with a connection to the president. Military personnel stopped vehicles in the streets, told the drivers to get out, and took over the vehicle for military use. Gunfire could be heard throughout the city as the military tried to bring order by scaring people into their homes.

In the two years that followed, however, calm returned to Côte d'Ivoire. Life was basically peaceful in the capital city of Abidjan, although there were occasional outbursts. Most fighting took place in the north of the country as the nation became increasingly divided.

Mennonite workers serving with the Mennonite Board of Missions had a long history of relationships with Côte d'Ivoire's Harrist Church dating back to the early 1970s. In 1999, we no longer had a formal relationship with the church, but we did maintain informal personal relationships with a number of their leaders. One of the primary people that I regularly related to was Richard Djorogo from the Anono Harrist congregation. Anono is a traditional village that has over the years been surrounded and engulfed by the city of Abidjan and yet retains the feel, identity, and social structure of a village. Harrists parade in the streets escorting the preachers to and from Sunday worship, and these services look and feel very much like they do in other parts of the country.

Richard had introduced me to the head preacher and some of the other leadership, and I was invited to lead occasional courses for a group of youth leaders. This was not a formally recognized program, however, and I did not have a relationship with the national leadership of the church.

On 11 September 2001, the day started as any other day with getting our sons to school and having some time for prayer and reading on the back porch, followed by working on various projects in the office. Then in the afternoon, we received a call from an expatriate friend asking if we had the television on. She went on to say that the Twin Towers in New York City were on fire. Airline jets had flown into them, and the images were currently being shown on Cable News Network international broadcasting (CNN). We went online to see what we could learn, but the system was overcrowded and slow on a good day. On *this* day – what came to be referred to as 9/11 – the system was completely overloaded. Our sons returned home from school with images of the Towers on fire, and by evening we were able to learn more of what was going on.

In the days to follow we spoke with family members in Pennsylvania and New York and heard stories of the rising fears in the United States. One of my sisters taught in Manhattan and told us that Muslim students were being harassed and that the conflict seemed to be growing. Our friends in Côte d'Ivoire would stop us and talk to us about the situation, and I would let them know what my family members were saying. I was invited by a cell group from a local church to come for prayer. I used the opportunity to try to put the situation into context and to ask how we as people of Christ's peace should respond to rising tensions.

The following week, Richard invited me to a Wednesday evening Harrist worship service in Anono. I attended the service, and afterward he told me that the preacher wanted to speak with me. I was taken to a room in the church compound. The preacher did not speak French, so Richard explained that he had invited me to come to pray with him. The preacher asked me a few questions, and I told him that my mother lived near a location in Pennsylvania where one of the planes had crashed, that my sister was in New York City where the major attack had occurred, and that some of the students she was teaching were being harassed.

After listening to me talk about my fears for my country and the fact that it seemed that hatred was taking over, the preacher instructed Richard and me to kneel down. He held his full-length staff-cross in his hands, placed the bottom of the staff just in front of me and Richard on the ground, and instructed us to grab hold of it. Then the preacher began to pray, and as he did, he gently swayed. Richard and I held tightly to the cross as it kept us from falling forward.

Photo 51: Richard Djorogo (center), Head Preacher and Cross-Staff Carrier in the Abidjan Anono Harrist congregation

The preacher prayed for my family, for the United States, for Côte d'Ivoire, and for peace in the world. As we knelt there clutching the cross, I felt God's Spirit pouring down over us, washing us with healing power. Leaning on the cross and depending on God – our only hope and security – took on new meaning that night as mediated by this brother in Christ in Côte d'Ivoire, West Africa.

I Shared a Long Journey of Discovery with Rev. Philip Mothetho, Friend and Brother
Tim Bertsche

On Easter Monday of 2010, Rev. Philip Mothetho, Bishop of the New Morian Apostolic Church in Zion of Botswana, died in a car accident. He was on his way home after leading the Easter celebrations at his church. I was a good friend of *Moruti* (pastor) Mothetho. My wife and I first met him in 1989 as we began our ministry in Botswana under AIMM. Pastor Mothetho was just one of many AIC leaders whom we came to know during fifteen years of working in Bible teaching, leadership training, and health education.

Pastor Mothetho was part of a second generation of Batswana church leaders to befriend Mennonite workers. Jim Juhnke and Ed Weaver, some of our early predecessors, had made contact and built friendships with the elder leaders of the AICs. Because of the warmth and humility of the first generation of leaders, those of us who followed were granted many opportunities to worship in the AIC churches as brothers and sisters and to teach their younger men and women the word of God.

Early on, Pastor Mothetho expressed a desire to learn the Bible. He attended our evening Bible study course designed to give church leaders an overview of biblical knowledge, doctrine, and practice. He participated in our weekend Bible teaching conferences which brought various church leaders together. These were always enriching days as we studied Scripture together and made application in our Setswana environment. Pastor Mothetho had a favorite phrase which I always enjoyed hearing: "I get your point. No, I really get your point." This usually meant he had discovered some insight that connected a biblical principle with an important point of faith and practice within his own culture.

During one regional conference, we were tackling the subject of inner and outer purity. We asked the question, "What is it that really makes us clean or unclean in God's eyes?" Various speakers addressed the question from a cultural and biblical point of view. I led the final discussion from Mark 7 where Jesus teaches it is not what goes into a person's mouth that makes a person unclean, but what comes out of the mouth from the heart. An animated discussion followed about the validity of the dietary laws of Moses, the Tswana totem animals that must not be eaten, certain foods which were considered "dirty," and the consumption of alcoholic beverages. Toward the end of our discussion, Pastor Mothetho stood up and said in his way, "No, I really get the point." He then gave a good summary of the resolution we had tried to bring to the tension between the law and regulations of the Old Testament and the freedom, grace, and responsibility found in the New Testament through Christ Jesus. I am thankful to have known a man like Philip Mothetho. He became a brother to me. He helped me understand the ways and values of the Batswana people. I shared a long journey of discovery with him as we sought to grasp the meaning of God's word and how it might connect to the cultural setting of the Kalanga and Tswana people. I am thankful that he embraced the importance of understanding and applying God's word.

Photo 52: Prayer and Bible study in the New Morian Apostolic Church in Zion of Rev. Philip Mothetho, Botswana

This picture captures the essence of my experience in Botswana. It portrays the power of the word of God and the light that it brings to those who read it. It is on the front cover of a book entitled *Mission in an African Way*. The picture shows a young girl kneeling on the floor in front of an open Bible. She is reading intently by the sunlight streaming through an open door. This picture was taken in Pastor Mothetho's church. It captures the heart of what took place during our wonderful years in Botswana – examining God's word together and letting its truth break into our hearts.

I was able to visit briefly with Rev. Mothetho in January of 2009. Five years after "immigrating" to North America, our family had the privilege of returning to Francistown to reconnect with many wonderful friends. When we last parted, he said, "Goodbye, brother, until next time. We will see each other again, either here or in heaven." It will be in heaven.

There Was Nothing That Separated Our Spirits
Albert Maphasa Setumo

Ntate (my father) Isaac Moshoeshoe (mo-SHWAY-shway) and I met the Mennonites later than *Ntate* Samuel Mohono who began that friendship. My first experience was having Bible studies with Brian Reimer. The Reimers came to Lesotho as a young couple. We gave them names in the Sesotho language. A child of theirs was born here and was also given a Sesotho name.

We did frequent Bible studies with the Mennonites. But in addition to these studies, the Mennonites also occasionally helped us in finishing or equipping our church buildings. That sharing was formalized by our council. We found the Mennonites to be our brothers. In my time working with Brian Reimer, there was nothing that separated our spirits. I confess it was a surprise to see these whites who wanted to work alongside the Basotho people, as though they were the same as us. This was not what we had experienced during the years of apartheid.

The Mennonites told us that they were also learning from us. For example, Bill Ens said that he was learning to sing and dance in worship. It seems this is not the custom of Mennonites back in America. At one point, we had a study conference. Bill told us that his daughter in America was giving birth, and that baby girl was gravely ill, not expected to survive. We who were together that day agreed we must pray for this infant. That child is alive and well today. We were told that she is even at university. And Bill added, "That child sings like you!" We take this to be an answer to our prayers, a gift from God.

Lately, we have been asking ourselves what made the Mennonites leave Lesotho. It seems there was some mishandling of money intended to subsidize the cost of Bibles for our members. This unfortunate turn of events caused bad feelings among the churches and blaming of one another. The mistake stemmed from failure to entrust the subsidy to the entire African Federal Church Council rather than to an individual. The Mennonites were generous in renewing the subsidy, so the Bibles were bought and distributed to the people. But soon after that, the Mennonite workers withdrew.

During our years of partnership, I was trained to be a leader for the Maseru study group. I also assisted with groups in Leribe. We had a cycle of ten study booklets. But when the supply of booklets ended, the studies also could not continue, though I would be willing today to call the study group together again. Our council also is in need of renewal, of new leaders. At last report, there were ten member churches.

GUEST REFLECTIONS

Daniel Okoh, Organization of African Instituted Churches
An African proverb says that "one does not learn how to use the left hand when one is old in age." This means that it is not easy to change the old ways of doing things. But the Mennonites who came in contact with the African Independent Churches in 1959 humbled themselves to listen to the Holy Spirit and to adopt the new mission strategy that God had for them in Africa. This humility led them to see the uniqueness of African cultures and the genuine desire of the local people to know Christ more and to make him known to other Africans, rather than seeing the AICs as people who were confused and who resisted the gospel.

Once the Mennonites received this new strategy, they persevered in teaching the Holy Bible by improvising training programs for church leaders to meet their immediate needs and to further the ministry of reconciliation among church leaders of AICs and mainline denominations. The approach of the Mennonites to missions was really refreshing to the AICs. In my opinion, this refreshing formed the basis for an enduring partnership between the AICs and the Mennonites that has lasted for over sixty years.

In this partnership and over many years, Mennonites have remained humble, focused, resolute, authentic, determined, committed, and generous. In our collaboration together, there is no question of who is superior or inferior. Resources have been shared, and learning has been two way. There is openness on both sides, and there is sincerity of purpose. This partnership has yielded much fruit in the areas of theological education and community health among the AICs, especially in West Africa, and has enriched the understanding of missions and evangelism among the Mennonites.

One of the major products of our collaborative endeavors was the 1971 establishment of Good News Theological Seminary (GNTS) in Accra, Ghana. It is important to note that although the Mennonites played a major role in establishing this seminary, they do not claim ownership of the institution. This institution remains the only known seminary in English-speaking West Africa that serves the peculiar needs of African Independent Churches. Each year, the AICs from across the subregion send their members and church leaders to the seminary for formal training in theological education. GNTS is today located on vast acres of its own land and has received accreditation from the Ghanaian government as a degree awarding institution. It is on record that the Mennonites continue to support the seminary with both financial and human resources.

Therefore, I see many more years of collaboration with the Mennonites, even as we discover more and more that we share common values, all to the glory of Jesus Christ, our Lord.

Daniel Okoh *is general superintendent of Christ Holy Church International, international chairman of the Organization of African Instituted Churches (OAIC), and chairperson of the governing council of Good News Theological Seminary (GNTS), Accra, Ghana.*

James Kwesi Anquandah, *University of Ghana, Legon, Accra, Ghana*
I was involved from the very beginning of the Mennonite/AIC initiated Good News Training Institute in Accra, Ghana. From 1969–1971, Ed and Irene Weaver were like "public relations" people, going from church to church to build interest. I remember that they often visited the Eden Revival Church.

Ed was a statesman who knew exactly what he wanted working with AICs. He was clear that he was a Mennonite, but that he had not come to plant Mennonite churches. His vision was to train AIC leaders and ground them in the word and to get AICs in conversation with each other. His connections with the Ghana Christian Council of Churches also connected AICs with the mainline denominations.

The Mennonite ministry with AICs has lasted because it was based on authenticity and honesty. Church leaders today have become politicians; they will say anything to gain power and make money. But only ministries with transparency can stand the test of time. Weaver's ministry was genuine and truthful, and here we are many decades hence.

The Good News Training Institute was launched in 1971. Prophet Mills, an AIC leader, organized "praise circles," and Solomon Krow, a young leader in the Church of the Lord (Aladura) movement, attended Good News classes at Nima Temple. The school began at the YMCA, then moved to a larger facility at Hour of Visitation.

A younger Mennonite pioneer-worker, Willard Roth, served with Ed in launching Good News in 1970–1973. I remember that in 1972, Willard drove with me to Abetifi for a weeklong seminar led by the renowned Ghanaian professor Kwabena Nketia on the topic of "The African Church and Culture."

Unfortunately, an African colleague during this period took offense at Willard's careful management of the financial records and is reported to have cast a spell on Willard. This same man had been dismissed by his own church for inappropriate financial dealings, and Willard had indication that the same was happening again at Good News. In any case, Willard fell ill for no apparent reason, and it was always somewhat of a mystery what actually happened here.

Working with spiritual churches was not easy in those early days. They had many strange practices that were a mixture of Old Testament customs, Western Christian practices, and African traditions. Still, mission-founded church members were enormously attracted to the African-initiated "spiritual churches." Many people attended Sunday services in their own Roman Catholic, Anglican, or Presbyterian churches and then went during the week to the "spiritual churches" for spiritual healing and other experiences.

I was raised in the Roman Catholic Church, but began frequenting AICs such as Eden Revival Church and many other churches. At Eden, I was "ushered into the realm of spiritual reality." Many professionals from various mainline churches – professors, doctors, intellectuals, and others – were also present. In the late 1960s, I attended Eden for one year, then went to Oxford University in England for two years of study. When I returned, Eden's spiritual leader asked me to head up their educational program. I abandoned my studies and accepted the offer. Eventually, Eden's attraction of mainline professionals pushed the Ghana Council of Churches to invite Eden to officially join the Council, the only African Independent Church ever to do so.

It is not clear to me that AIC folk were "born again" in the sense of any kind of personal faith, but they were sincere and seeking God in their faith and worship. Many, though not all, were open to studying the Scriptures and eager to learn more. I told the early students: "You will have your eyes opened by studying the Scripture. What you learn won't square with what you've been taught in your churches, because when you study the Scriptures, you will learn the truth of the gospel. Some of you will break away and start your own churches because of the new insights you receive." This is of course what happened in some cases.

Mennonites made a contribution to AIC training at a number of levels:

- They covered expenses for the training, including some transport money for students who couldn't afford it.
- They facilitated study times that fit people's schedules. Classes were held for regular students during daytime hours, and one evening session per week was offered for ten to twelve churches focusing on leaders.
- They encouraged periodic programs with church choirs and sharing the word – activities which fit the Mennonite goals of focusing on Scripture study,

training leaders, and bringing AICs churches and leaders together for study and worship.

There have been many challenges for AICs both then and now – problems of literacy, authenticity, and funding. Would Good News Training Institute have ever gotten started, and would Good News Theological Seminary continue today without outside resources? Probably not. The AICs appreciate the Bible and theology study programs. But are they committed to them enough, and do they have enough resources to do these programs on their own? Probably not. But walking with them has been an important endeavor and has strengthened them immensely on their spiritual journey.

James Kwesi Anquandah is a researcher and professor of archeology at the University of Ghana, Legon, Accra, Ghana, and the first West African to gain a postgraduate qualification at a West African university.

8

Harvest

Harvest entails unimaginable toil. Fields and gardens having reached maturity then require back-breaking effort to redeem the promise that has appeared. But it is exertion that few dwell on or notice much, because the community is besotted with reward. The season is drenched in blessing and dance and song as the cadence of joy takes hold even through darkness and weariness. It is the season of festival, wedding, christening and lavish sharing, a portent of celestial joy.

Rejoicing that a Ghanaian Praise Song is Blessing North American Mennonites
Alice Roth

When Ed and Irene Weaver came to Ghana in 1969, my husband Willard and I traveled with them to visit a Church of the Lord (Aladura) congregation in Kumasi, seat of the head of the church in Ghana. Because of the Weavers' relationships with Church of the Lord in Nigeria, they were welcomed as dear friends. I wrote to my parents of this experience, "These independent churches get a lot of criticism, both from Ghanaians who think they are too 'African' and from many missionaries. Ed and Irene are working with them to set up Bible training for the leaders. People immediately sense their love and acceptance, and respond to it. We learned a lot this weekend about the eagerness of the leaders for more Bible training, their great evangelistic fervor, and their independence from foreign money and domination."

But what I wrote is not the whole story of my experience that Sunday in Kumasi. We had been in Ghana less than a year, and this was one of our first times to worship with an AIC congregation. We four guests were welcomed warmly and presented with gifts after Ed's sermon. For Ed and Willard there were colorful shirts and sandals, for Irene and me, ivory bracelets and necklaces.

Photo 53: "I grew in appreciation of worship springing from everyday triumphs and tragedies, victories and defeats, ever praising and petitioning God all encompassing." Alice Roth

Then Irene reached for my hand and whispered, "Now it's our turn to dance around to the front to say thank you." My heart sank; my spirit rebelled. I don't dance in church. I can enjoy watching and hearing the lively music, but I'll stay seated. I had already removed my shoes at the door and covered my head with a white scarf, reminiscent of the white net "covering" of my childhood. Was that not enough?

This response in my head and heart was of course not an option that Irene was considering. Seeing no alternative, I took her hand and shuffled forward beside her. As I told Irene at her one hundredth birthday celebration in 2010, she led me that day in the first steps of a journey of growing, learning, and loving.

In the three years that followed, we worshiped often with AIC congregations. Many hands reached out to me in friendship and love, especially the hands of women. A sister beside me might lean over and whisper, "You are not used to such long services. You can step out for a walk." Or, "Let the children walk to the corner shop to buy a Coke." I grew into the realization that entering wholeheartedly into worship quite different from my previous thirty-five years of experience did not mean that I was rejecting what I valued – four-part acapella singing and quiet, orderly worship for only one hour. Truly I experienced the meaning of the lyrics of Frederick Faber's 1854 hymn (v. 1), "There's a wideness in God's mercy, like the wideness of the sea."

As I relaxed into that understanding, I grew in appreciation of worship springing from everyday triumphs and tragedies, victories and defeats, ever praising and petitioning God all encompassing. God's presence and power guarded and guided every hour of the week. The stories, the thanks, and the needs for the week ahead – all were brought to the gathering of God's people in worship.

"In your sickness, your suff'rings, your trials and pains, he is with you all the time." This lively Ghanaian song was to some AIC congregations what the hymn "Praise God from whom all blessings flow" is to many North American Mennonites. These many decades later, finding the Ghanaian song "In your sickness" in the Mennonite and Church of the Brethren *Hymnal: A Worship Book* (No. 585) reminds me that the fruit of AIC worship blesses not just the few of us who were privileged to share it first hand during our time in Africa. But today, it blesses the broader North American Anabaptist-Mennonite community in our worship as well.

Like in Marriage, There Is a Profound Mystery That You Can't Explain
Modeste Lévry Beugré

The invitation made to the Mennonites by the Dida Harrist leadership from the village of Yocoboué originated with me when I was a school teacher in the Abidjan neighborhood of Abobo-Doumé, Côte d'Ivoire. The fortunate encounter I had with David and Wilma Shank and James and Jeanette Krabill happened during a mealtime following the Sunday morning Harrist worship service in May 1979.

I was impressed with the serious study Dr. Shank had done of our Prophet William Wadé Harris, and I knew we needed that information for training our young preachers among the Dida people. Our people were also in dire need of Bible instruction for the next generation of leaders, so we planned a trip for the Mennonites to visit our region following the rainy season in July of that year. On the day of our arrival from Abidjan in the village of Yocoboué, the entire church community met us on the outskirts of town with a fraternal welcome of song, dance, drums, and calabash shakers.

Photo 54: Modeste Lévry Beugré (left) was the first Harrist Church leader to invite Mennonites to live among the Dida people of southcentral Côte d'Ivoire

In 1982, James and Jeanette Krabill with their two small children moved to Yocoboué. James, along with his local collaborator Harrist preacher Alphonse

Kobli Beugré, visited all the surrounding villages and determined with church leaders and student candidates what kind of Bible teaching would be most suitable for each locality. After three and a half years of Bible classes in six areas of southern Dida territory, we made a request to the Mennonite mission director to allow the Krabills to move north to the city of Divo for another contract of three years. There, the Bible teaching program spread out to another six localities and strengthened the young Harrist leadership in training for preaching ministry.

As I reflect on our many years of friendship with the Mennonites, I would say that our relationship is like a husband and wife in a marriage situation. In such a case, one doesn't ask who is giving and who is receiving. In marriage, there is a profound mystery that you can't explain. And that is the kind of relationship that exists between us. I am happy to say that the Mennonite presence among us is a story rich in meaning that the Dida Harrist Christians will never forget.

Spirit-Filled Faith . . . Where the Rubber Hits the Road
Rene Hostetter

After spending eleven years as a missionary kid relating to the Zionists – an African Independent Church grouping in Swaziland – I returned there in 2004 as an adult to work with those infected and affected by HIV/AIDS. For one year of my assignment, I served with an HIV/AIDS team connected to the AIC Faith Bible School (FBS).

Our work as a team focused in three areas – abstinence promotion, faithfulness in marriage promotion, and home-based care. Abstinence promotion included monthly presentations with our team of twenty-five youth forming church-based abstinence clubs where we trained two youth from each of the thirty AIC churches on "True Love Waits." Faithfulness promotion was done through marriage enrichment retreats. We also trained thirty home-based care workers within the thirty churches and provided medical supplies through the Mennonite Central Committee (MCC) and follow-up retreats for them.

What most excited me about working with FBS was the youth – the group of twenty-five volunteers on our HIV/AIDS team – who were so passionate for Christ and for serving him. What brought me hope was the enthusiasm of the youth who developed increased self-esteem and confidence as they realized God could use them to minister and teach. I was also very encouraged by the youth from our thirty churches who were trained to start abstinence clubs in their home congregations. I was amazed at their creativity and innovative ideas and confidence to stand in front of their peers and teach on abstinence, a stance that was not at all popular in Swaziland at that time. The team gave me hope that change could happen in Swaziland.

Within the home-based care worker group, I saw not only the victims of HIV/AIDS receiving grace, but also transformation in the volunteers themselves as they began to understand and embrace their capacity to be agents of God's love and grace. I often became very discouraged and depressed when I read newspaper reports describing the high HIV/AIDS rate that kept increasing; the growth in numbers of brutal murders, rapes, and suicides; and the low status of women. Just when I began to feel like I was emotionally unable to cope with the intense suffering all around me, however, one of the Zionist young people would initiate a weekly two-hour intercessory prayer meeting.

I love the way the Zionists pray, raising their voices out loud all at the same time. It creates a great deal of noise, but people really pray from their hearts. They are not worried about how their prayers might sound to others or think about what they are going to pray after the next person is finished. I always went away blessed after every prayer meeting. Worship in this way was definitely hard work, and I was exhausted after two hours of intense prayer. But it was worth it as I started to notice changes, not so much across the country of Swaziland, but within our team.

Photo 55: Vibrant, Spirit-filled prayer and song among the Zionists in Swaziland

What amazed me about the Zionists was their incredible faith. While I as an American became angry, discouraged, pessimistic, and depressed at the intense suffering all around me, my Zionist colleagues were able to face death day in and day out and still worship and pray with so much hope and passion. I observed how their faith mattered in life where rubber really hit the road. It was truly humbling to work with them. With 42.6 percent of the total population being HIV positive in Swaziland, my colleagues would recognize people in the obituaries on a regular basis, attend funerals every other weekend, spend their paychecks on funerals for their relatives, and visit one dying person after another. Yet they continued to attend prayer meetings, sing about God's goodness, and live with steadfast faith and enduring hope. In my work with the Zionists, I was the one most blessed and challenged by interacting with amazing faith-grounded, Spirit-filled people who were dedicated to prayer and living out their faith on a daily basis.

It Was Hard for the Mennonites We Met to Do the Dance Moves, but They Wanted to Try
Hlobisile Nxumalo

It was in 1986 that I attended a Swaziland youth camp organized by Faith Bible School (FBS), which was partnering with Mennonites through the Eastern Mennonite Mission. This was the first youth camp FBS had done, so the leader at the camp was Mennonite mission worker Rev. Darrel Hostetter. Since then, I have related with so many Mennonites which has been good to me as a Zionist because it has boosted my self-esteem, since Zionists are looked down upon in Swaziland.

One of the great things I have enjoyed working with Mennonites is that they didn't start their own churches, and they never tried to convert us to be Mennonites. Instead, they have learned to fellowship with us and accept us even though our fellow Swazi were despising us. Their willingness to learn and participate in what we were doing was great, and it made the relationship very strong. Darrel worked with the Zionist pastors and introduced Bible teaching which most took very seriously. Those who were carrying on with ungodly activities repented and continue even today to live holy lives.

As a young person studying at the university where I was rejected by other Christians because I was a Zionist, the youth camps were such a blessing because I found a sense of belonging. I also enjoyed that most of those coming to camps were Zionist youth like me. I am glad Mennonites came to partner with us, and they didn't change our identity. One of the exciting moments was attending night vigil services with the Mennonites and doing the dancing at night. Although it was hard to stay awake the whole night, they persevered and also tried to do the dancing. It was difficult for them to do the moves as we do them, but they wanted to try. This dancing would often make us realize that we are created by the same God and that one day we will be together in heaven dancing to the same music.

I was also empowered through attending a discipleship training course run by Darrel and Sherill Hostetter at their home during their time in Swaziland. I was able to transfer my skills learned there to the youth in my church and also at FBS youth camps. Most Zionist pastors are not paid a salary; therefore, working with the Mennonites who were volunteers was encouraging to some church leaders – that there are people who traveled all the way from the United States of America to be servants of Christ in Swaziland and did not get a salary either.

As I further worked with the Mennonite Central Committee, I have been encouraged to serve God through touching people's lives not only in preaching the gospel and evangelism but also by responding to people's basic needs, such as for food and home-based care.

Sacred Oil, Rustle of Robes
Jonathan P. Larson

Hanging in my closet in Atlanta is a one-of-a-kind green and blue preaching stole. Its distinctive features are two African kudu horns of a kind traditionally blown to summon Tswana communities of the Kalahari to red-letter occasions. The stole is an artifact marking a rare moment in modern Anabaptist mission history when African Independent Churches gathered in Gaborone, Botswana, to ordain a North American Mennonite to Christian ministry. I was the one anointed that day, 29 May 1994, by the laying on of African hands and by the entreaties of African tongues in prayer invoking the Holy Spirit, even as uniformed choirs danced to the rhythm of African hymns.

It was more than a little odd, perhaps even deviant, that for years I had traveled the length and breadth of Botswana to assist in the ordination of others and had officiated at the installation of evangelists, bishops, and archbishops, but had never myself been formally ordained. The reason for this was simple. It had long been my conviction that ordination at its best is initiated by the community in claiming the gifts of individuals for the strengthening of the people. That private conviction meant that my churchly rite of passage silently slipped away unnoticed in the passing years. This strange anomaly arose one day in conversation during a long trip with my Canadian coworker Don Boschman. And he mentioned it in turn to African colleagues, even as Mary Kay and I were preparing to conclude our years of service in Southern Africa.

Before long, a circle of African church leaders gathered to take up and own this loose thread. The upshot of their prayers and deliberation was a determination that I should not depart from those years of friendship and shared work in Africa without that sacred gesture of affirmation, blessing, and apostolic sending. Such an ordination council, the likes of which no Anabaptist has ever faced before, brought together churches with all the glories of a biblical name: The Head Mountain of God Holy Apostolic Church in Zion, The Spiritual Healing Church, The Holy Banner Mission Church of Africa, The Eleven Apostles Healing Spirit Church, and the St. Michael's Apostolic Church, to name but a few.

A date was set, a community hall reserved, assignments made, and invitations scattered to the far corners. Archbishop Israel Motswaosele, a longtime friend of Mennonites in Southern Africa, consented to preside. I was summoned to appear at an examining council of senior church leaders. Truth be told, they seemed not even faintly interested in my view of the Holy Spirit, of the inspiration of the canon, or of eschatology. But they did ask me how it would be known in my ministry that I had spent so many years with them in Africa. I replied that I could not help myself from telling the stories of their faith and their witness even in the face of local social scorn and government opposition. Would I continue to pray for the sick, the bewildered, the forgotten, and the oppressed? they asked. And finally, would I agree to be available to all, without confining myself to churchly boundaries, just as I had been with them? they wanted to know. Such was their charge to me.

When the day arrived, there gathered a company of brilliantly robed preachers of apocalyptic drama. Choirs of women, young people, and children garbed in every imaginable hue formed up in the hall, some having traveled hundreds of miles to be in attendance. A young woman from the distant village of Serowe came to recite a traditional Tswana praise poem. The platform of dignitaries including Mennonite colleagues became so crowded that one bishop in his exuberance slipped off the edge of the stage and toppled over backward into the arms of bystanders. There was such a clamor of people desiring to speak that the master of ceremonies, Rev. Otsile Ditsheko, regional coordinator for AICs, lost control of the proceedings, as often happens in inspired events.

There followed many niches in this cathedral-like event – a ceremonial washing of hands with exhortation to live henceforth as an innocent; a formal endowing of a Tswana version of the Scriptures;[1] a shrouding of the head

---

1. The 1857 translation of the Bible into Setswana by Robert Moffat, father-in-law to David Livingstone, was the first complete Bible rendered in a sub-Saharan language.

and shoulders while sonorous prayers called the florid names of God; a rustling scrum of the robed elect surrounding me as though in some womb of transformation and prayer; and then, at the hands of Archbishop Israel Motswaosele of the Spiritual Healing Church, such a lush anointing that I can still feel it on my forehead many decades later. There followed what can only be described as a love feast prepared by Kathy Fast and a bevy of cherished Mennonite fellow workers and friends.

Photo 56: Ritual cleansing before ordination

Don Boschman had reassured anxious North American senior church leaders that this ordination would cut no corners. The irony of this exchange was lost on none of us. So it was agreed that the action taken by the African churches at the edge of the Kalahari Desert would be duly honored by North American church authorities. The bizarre – but perhaps telling – epilogue to this story is that the paperwork formally documenting this event has since disappeared from the archives of the Mennonite Church USA. What does remain is the clinching memory of a moment when we witnessed a shift in the global wind. And it is that living memory of which the oral church, the church of the Global South, is champion.

Studying the History of the Church Opened My Eyes
Michel Alokpo

I have had two training experiences in my life which have shaped me more than any others. The first was a leadership formation course I took in Nairobi, Kenya. The second was the training I received at CEFCA, the Evangelical Center of Formation in Communications for Africa, located in Abidjan, Côte d'Ivoire.

Here, the most significant course I took was the "History of the Church in West Africa," under the direction of Mennonite worker Professor James Krabill. My project was to compile and record the histories of the more than thirty African Independent and mission-founded denominations existing at that time in the country of Benin. It was a huge project that involved interviewing dozens of peoples and writing up their stories for publication in a collection called *Nos racines racontées*.[2] This project is what put me on the road to understanding my AIC family roots and doing research on the important history and role of the church in my region of West Africa.

Photo 57: "The Benin Bible Institute [is] a remarkable model for how different religious communities can peaceably live and work together." Michel Alokpo

---

2. See James R. Krabill, ed., *Nos racines racontées: Récits historiques sur l'Eglise en Afrique de l'Ouest* (Abidjan: Presses Bibliques Africaines, 1996).

In more recent years, I have served the Beninese government in the "religious affairs" department, working more broadly with Muslim, Christian, and traditionalist religious communities. The model of the Benin Bible Institute, supported by Mennonites and now over sixty denominations here in Benin, has proved to be a remarkable witness for how different religious communities can peaceably live and work together. My faith in Jesus remains central, but I have learned how to live alongside and build a nation with people of very different backgrounds and perspectives. All this has helped me in the work I do for my country.

The Silent, Invisible, and Mysterious Ways That God's Kingdom Grows
Sharon Dirks

It is important to look back on our lives at significant events and pick out defining moments, watershed experiences which forever changed our lives. Sometimes we recognize such moments immediately and know that we will probably remember them for the rest of our lives. I was having one of those days as I sat in my doctor's office in Gaborone, Botswana, while my housekeeper, Matshediso, was being attended to by my own doctor. As I absent mindedly leafed through a magazine, I wondered how my life and the life of my family would be forever changed by whatever we would find out that day.

Matshediso came into our lives after a series of other workers did not work out. We liked her immediately. She was desperately poor, and this job gave her a chance to improve her situation in life a little, including providing for her tiny and sickly four-year-old son, David. Matshediso was eager to work and really loved being in the hustle and bustle of our home, singing happily away. She loved to watch the Bible teaching preparations for the various classes my husband, Rudy, was teaching with church leaders and AIC lay people in Gaborone and eventually joined one of the evening Bible studies. When I prepared the Bible lessons for a school of disadvantaged children, Matshediso loved recalling the Bible stories she had learned as a child. The "Jesus Mafa" pictures of Bible stories in a Cameroonian West African setting were particularly fascinating for her.

One day I found a dusty old trunk in the shed of our Africa Inter-Mennonite Mission home that had been inhabited by previous mission workers. In it were stacks of Bible study books which Matshediso was thrilled to be able to use. She studied them and took the tests at the end of each chapter. Sometimes she preferred to work on her Bible studies and also to "preach" to our gardener than to actually do the housekeeping!

Then Matshediso got sick. Even though my doctor advised her to get an HIV test, her fears of facing it were too great. She never did find out the truth; although in reality, she had enough qualifying symptoms that we all understood the gravity of the situation. The tragedy of illness and death that we saw all around us had entered our own home. We were no longer mere on-lookers to the suffering that the people of Botswana are facing in huge numbers. Walking this painful experience with Matshediso was to be a catalyst for future AIDS ministries of Mennonite Ministries in Botswana.

In the meantime, we had to learn how to protect ourselves and Matshediso, who was vulnerable to other infections. Our family, including our children who were ages fourteen, twelve, and nine at the time, discussed how we felt about having someone working in our home who was likely HIV positive. We knew that it was common to dismiss a worker when such a diagnosis was suspected. Rudy and I explained to the children that the risk of contracting the virus through casual human contact was minimal, but that we would take some precautions, particularly to protect ourselves from other related infections. We wanted to be sure that the decision we made to help people in the name of Jesus no matter what their HIV status would be one that we came to together as a whole family. Obviously, we were committed to our relationship with Matshediso, which meant keeping her as a worker as long as she was able. Eventually we knew that we would be continuing to provide financial assistance and care to her even though she was no longer able to work.

This period was not easy for us. Many times when I counted on having Matshediso there to do the cleaning or laundry, she was actually too sick to work. Even though I had other ministry and family obligations, care for her became part of my ministry. I remember reminding myself that it is often the interruptions that come our way which are the real ministry that God is calling us to, though raising three children should already have taught me that! Matshediso hated staying away from work. She loved our family, our home, and our food. And she clearly needed the work to be able to provide for her sick little boy, even though we reassured her that we would continue to help her. Many days we delivered a meal and her pay for the week, whether she had earned it or not.

Eventually Matshediso died, and sadly two weeks later, her very sick David died as well. But her passing would reveal the incredible way that God uses these kinds of circumstances to further his kingdom. At Matshediso's funeral, speaker after speaker mentioned her diligence in teaching the word of God. This was really fascinating and exciting to us. How humble this was of her! She had never told us about this! Then after the funeral, a small group of people approached Rudy. They represented a small branch of an obscure African Independent Church which had been meeting faithfully in a small room near Matshediso's home in her squatter settlement neighborhood. Almost every evening they got together to worship, pray, and study the Bible studies which Matshediso brought to them using the materials that Mennonite Bible teachers had prepared and taught for several years and which she studied one night and shared with her friends the next. Now that Matshediso was gone, they really missed the teaching, but they weren't sure how they could receive some of it themselves. They were too shy to come to the existing classes in the city. Would Rudy help them?

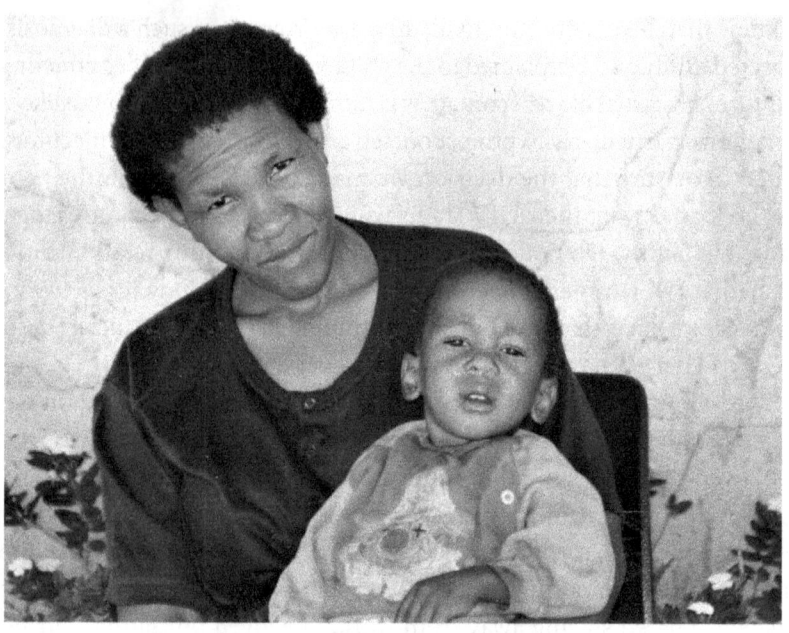

Photo 58: Matshedisco's life demonstrated the silent and mysterious ways God's kingdom grows

So it was that a new Bible study began in Bontleng. Rudy met the small group of believers in a crowded little room that was lit with only one candle. The room was cold in the winter and stifling hot in the summer, but their enthusiasm was inspiring. For the next four years, Rudy led this group along until several of them were prepared to graduate with an Inter-Church Ministries Botswana Bible certificate! Even after all the expatriate Mennonite Ministries teachers left Botswana, one of the eager students named Gaborone continued to be a key leader in the Bible teaching program.

I look back on this whole experience now, so many years later, with gratitude to God for having brought such a significant person in his kingdom into our lives. I am humbled by that. As a mission worker, I have received a lot of recognition for the work that I participated in on the field, more than I rightly deserve. In God's economy, it is really such a person as Matshediso who will be honored for her humble faithfulness.

It Takes a Village to Bless a Child
Jeanette Krabill

At 7:30 a.m. on Sunday, 20 July 1986, our family climbed into the car to travel thirty minutes east of our home in Divo, Côte d'Ivoire, to the Dida Harrist village of Tata where James gave Bible studies every Friday. Today, however, we were going to attend the Sunday morning worship service for a special presentation of our two-month-old daughter, Marie-Laure.

The ride on the hardtop road went smoothly, and the baby slept peacefully until we hit the last stretch of three kilometers of bumpy dirt road – just long enough to rudely awaken a baby. We wound our way through the village stopping at the home of the head preacher. There we parked, piled out of the car, and greeted everyone – an old man with an injured leg, a second man shaving his chin, a young mother washing her baby, and yet another man finishing up his breakfast of broiled plantain banana dipped in hot pepper.

Straight-backed chairs were quickly assembled under a mango tree, and as we sat down an elderly grandmother took Marie-Laure. The "news" – a formalized protocol of greetings for new arrivals in the village – was exchanged by the two oldest men present, and then following a round of handshakes, we were escorted to the courtyard of one of the Bible students – a dynamic youth leader named Lazare – who would be our host for the day. After the usual greetings we were led into the bedroom to change into our white church clothes. Meanwhile, the choir began assembling outside to accompany us on foot across the village to the church. The shaking of beaded-gourd calabashes rang in our ears.

James and I led the procession down the winding path through the village to the Harrist Church. The men filed into the sanctuary, sitting on backless benches on the right side, while women took their places on the left. Songs were sung and formal prayers offered, and it was time for our family to take our places in the center aisle of the church where we knelt on the hard cement floor. Since Marie-Laure is a girl, I held her during the prayer. Had she been a boy, the honor would have gone to James.

One of the church apostles questioned James concerning our request for the child blessing. James replied, "There is nothing serious" – in French, *Il n'y a rien de grave* – a standard formulaic opener indicating one is not bringing some kind of tragic news of crisis proportion. "God has blessed us with a healthy baby, and we have come to give thanks." With that, he placed our gift of candles on the front table. The apostle nodded to the head preacher who came out from behind the altar. He propped his wooden cross-cane in front of us, and we clasped it with our right hands.

Then after placing the open Bible on top of our heads – including Marie-Laure's, he began a long and fervent prayer of thanks. Upon uttering his final "Amen," he quietly asked us the baby's name and solemnly pronounced it to the congregation: "Marie-Laure." The congregation responded by repeating the name again: "Marie-Laure." Then shaking our hands, the preacher returned to his official chair, and as the choir broke forth into joyous song, we too returned to our respective places. Marie-Laure, frightened by the excessive noise, screamed. I finally got her quieted by the end of the song. Nursing an infant for a full hour does wonders to calm crying!

The sermon, taken from Psalms 127:1 and 128:1–3, reminded the congregation that "unless our houses are built on the Lord, our work is in vain. If we put our confidence in the Lord and obey his commandments, then our work will prosper. Our wives will be like fruitful vines and our sons like young olive trees around the table. We look to God who sent us these gifts – babies – to now protect them and care for them. Amen." Following the sermon came two offerings, and we were once again outside.

Tradition has it that the entire congregation must accompany the mother and child to their home courtyard. I took the place of honor between the preachers for the procession. The noon day sun was hot, and a guard-usher was summoned to hold an umbrella above my head. The *femmes d'honneur*, "honor women," who led the procession danced and scattered leaves and flower petals on the path, carrying handkerchiefs to periodically wipe the perspiration from the preachers' faces. Today I was also one of the honored guests whose face got wiped!

Back at Lazare's house, a table was set outside underneath a bamboo *apatam* structure covered with palm branches. I was led to the table with the preachers, and after a short prayer, we shared a ceremonial drink with choices of warm beer, orange pop, or wine. From there, everyone dispersed to change clothes, eat, and rest. We were served a copious meal of some ten different dishes, including newly harvested rice with grilled snails. Indeed, one *did need* a rest after such a feast!

**Photo 59: Baby Dedication Day in the
Dida Harrist Church of Tata, Côte d'Ivoire**

While most people stretched out on benches or relaxed on chairs, the older women led me inside a nearby house to begin "decorating" me for the afternoon activities. The decoration is a process in which colorful designs are painted on one's shoulders and upper arms with indigenous perfume of crushed sandalwood bark mixed with various berries and kaolin to produce the color. For my white skin, the women chose rust, blue, white, and tan colors which they paint-printed on my body with their fingertips creating a polka-dot effect. To top off the design, a blue line was traced across each of my cheeks. When the decoration process was completed, I was draped in colorful traditional cloth and bedecked with gold earrings, necklaces, and bracelets. I have never received as many compliments in my life as I did on that day.

By 2:00 p.m., the church choir had once again assembled for the afternoon festivities. I was positioned along with James – by now also draped in colorful cloth and wearing a golden necklace – in Lazare's courtyard in front of the mud kitchen on stuffed chairs covered with golden cloth. The choir danced and sang while drinks were served to all.

About every thirty minutes, Lazare and his wife, Odette, took us inside a neighboring house to exchange our garments for different colored cloths.

Each time, another necklace was added, so that by the end of the afternoon, my neck was heavy laden! We would then be returned to our places of honor as "king and queen," only interrupted from time to time by invitations to join the dancers for a few rounds as beckoned and led by an old man and woman. One particularly wiry old fellow led James in a "whooped-up" dance in which he half-squatted while still rapidly shuffling his feet. When James imitated him in the dance, the crowd went wild.

The singing, dancing, and general amusement went on until 6:00 p.m., by which time we were quite exhausted. Our babies, unlike their Dida counterparts, have always remained sensitive to noise, and by this late hour, Marie-Laure was screaming uncontrollably. A final procession through the village to the head preacher's house for a closing prayer of blessing brought the day to a close. Night had fallen by the time our car was loaded, and we were heading home to Divo. On this day, it took an entire village to bless our child!

GUEST REFLECTIONS

Nicta Lubaale, Organization of African Instituted Churches
The Organization of African Instituted Churches (OAIC) Secretariat has not had a structured partnership with Mennonite missionaries, yet there are two areas that reflect their important role in the work of the OAIC and the AICs. These are the HIV and AIDS response in the Southern Africa region and the establishment of the Good News Theological Seminary (GNTS) in Accra, Ghana. Many stories could be told that relate to the work of these missionaries and the life of AICs, but I choose to focus on just these two areas as we celebrate the great contribution made.

It was 1998 when I was sent by the OAIC Secretariat to the Southern Africa region to work at setting up the HIV and AIDS program in the region for the purpose of enabling the OAIC member churches there to deepen their response to the crisis. Archbishop Njeru Wambugu, who was the general secretary at the time, was giving leadership to the building of a response that would enable the AICs to use their resourcefulness in dealing the challenge. It was a time when the impact of the HIV and AIDS crisis was being felt across the continent, particularly in Eastern and Southern Africa. The rate of infection was high, and the impact of the epidemic was felt across the spectrum of family, congregational, community, and national levels.

On this trip I visited Swaziland, Botswana, Zimbabwe, and South Africa. One of the very first people I met on my arrival in Gaborone was Bishop Otsile Ditsheko, the chairman of the OAIC Southern Region. There were several Mennonite missionaries in the country working with the AICs, notably Rudy Dirks who was among the first people I met in the initial meeting with the leaders of AICs around Gaborone, the capital city of Botswana.

Rudy was gracious as he provided transportation to take me to the outskirts of the city to meet the AIC leaders. As we moved around the city, our conversation focused on mobilizing the AICs to play a role in responding to HIV and AIDS. The crisis was emerging as a major challenge, yet the AICs were still struggling to find their place in building a cohesive response. Rudy became a key person in this work by playing a major role in encouraging leaders of AICs to be part of a process that resulted in the eventual establishment of the Tshepong Counselling Center in Gaborone.

"Tshepong" means a place of hope. And consistent with its name, the center provided mobilization and training of churches, community education, counseling, and home-based care. This effort was a joint initiative with the Botswana Christian Aids Project (BOCAIP) – one of the largest NGOs in the country responding to HIV and AIDS. We had a lengthy discussion on the role of the church in response to the crisis and how AICs could be encouraged to play a major role in prevention and provision of care for people living with HIV and AIDS. This discussion helped to break the stigma and release AICs to provide care and support at a time when people had little or no access to antiretroviral drugs.

In Francistown, Tim Bertsche was an encouragement to young people from the AICs as they worked to respond to HIV and AIDS. One the initiatives there was setting up a youth center which later became a major point for the mobilization of AICs and the wider community. Taboka Rosti and Clive Maluke went through the OAIC training and were among the initiators of the center.

In 2001, a regional meeting for AIC leaders was organized in Botswana. Representatives from Zimbabwe, Botswana, Lesotho, South Africa, and Swaziland – now the Kingdom of Eswatini – participated. This meeting was followed by the training of community facilitators. A team from South Africa's Eastern Cape later established several community level initiatives.

When I visited the Eastern Cape, I was warmly received by the local AIC leaders and a missionary couple, Bryan Dyck and Lynell Bergen, who were serving in the area. This couple played a major role in working with the local leadership to organize the AICs in building a strong community response to the HIV and AIDS crisis. Bryan and Lynell threw their hearts into the work and even participated in mobilizing the resources that were needed to support the families impacted by the crisis. We organized the training sessions together. And Bryan and Lynell worked with the local leadership, especially Ms Mavis Tshandu, to provide ongoing support to the community facilitators and pastors. This partnership resulted in the following:

- the reduction of the stigma based largely on misreading the Scriptures;
- the growth in overall impact by joining the efforts of other churches and agencies;
- the establishment of community support systems for prevention, care, and support.

These initiatives became a highlight of our OAIC and AIC work on HIV and AIDS in Southern Africa. The Mennonite missionaries played a major role in making this happen, and the OAIC looks back at this period with deep appreciation for the meaningful partnership that resulted in such an effective response to regional crises.

In West Africa, one of the legacies of the Mennonite missionaries is the establishment of Ghana's Good News Theological Seminary (GNTS). This training institution is a point of excellence in the formation of AIC pastors. It has the potential to grow into both a center for pastoral training and a place of research and production of appropriate training materials for AICs. GNTS has well-trained lecturers who have been educated in reputable universities and seminaries – a factor that gives the seminary credibility and witnesses to the fact that AICs are capable of academic excellence. For these reasons, the OAIC highly values the seminary and is committed to playing a role in securing its future as a training hub for West Africa and beyond. GNTS is an important resource available to AIC leaders today because of the significant role Mennonite missionaries played in establishing it and handing it over to the African Independent Churches.

Nicta Lubaale *is general secretary of the Organization of African Instituted Churches (OAIC), with headquarters in Nairobi, Kenya.*

Partnerships Map

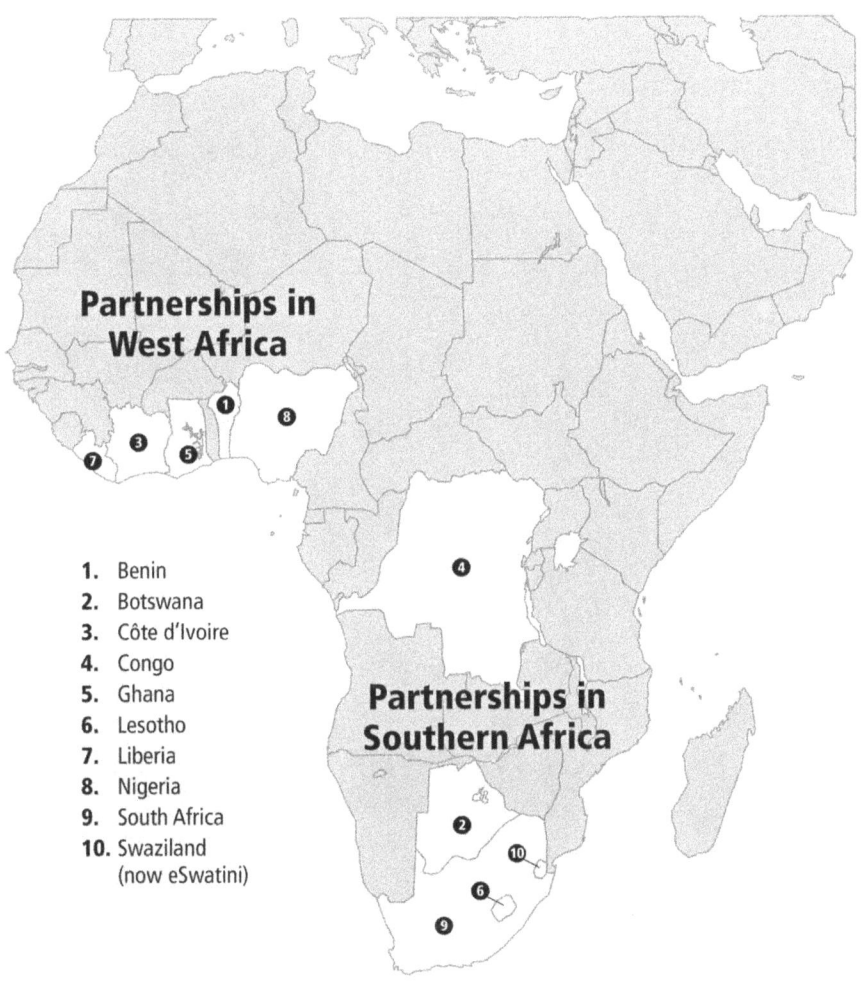

Partnerships in West Africa

Partnerships in Southern Africa

1. Benin
2. Botswana
3. Côte d'Ivoire
4. Congo
5. Ghana
6. Lesotho
7. Liberia
8. Nigeria
9. South Africa
10. Swaziland (now eSwatini)

Additional Resources

The following resources, both published and unpublished, are written by Mennonites and African Independent Church colleagues. Many focus specifically on relationships as they developed between Mennonites and AICs over the years. Others are studies and academic research carried out on AIC histories and trends emerging from the Mennonite-AIC partnerships described in this volume. The vast literature on African Independent Churches by non-Mennonites and other AIC scholars far exceeds the limited list assembled here.

Afaton, Saturnin D., and Marianne Goldschmidt-Nussbaumer. "Activités Sanitaires du Conseil Interconfessionnel des Eglises Protestantes en République Populaire du Bénin." In *Ministry in Partnership with African Independent Churches*, edited by David A. Shank, 381–94. English summary, "Health Activities of the Interconfessional Protestant Council in the Popular Republic of Benin," 395–97. Elkhart, IN: Mennonite Board of Missions, 1991.

"African Independent Churches." *Southern African Regional Newsletter 11*, featuring reports by Tina Bohn, Harry Dyck, Jim Egli, Irvin Friesen, Stan Nussbaum, Jonathan P. Larson, and Judy Zimmerman-Herr. Akron, PA: Mennonite Central Committee (June 1983): 10 pages. Available: @ MCC-USA, Akron, PA, USA.

AIMM Messenger and *Africa Journal*, two publications of Africa Inter-Mennonite Mission – "An evangelical Anabaptist 'family gathering' in which African, North American and European members are working together to become an answer to Jesus' prayer: 'Your kingdom come, Your will be done, on earth as it is in heaven.'" See: the AIMM website (www.aimmint.org) and the Mennonite Church Archives (https://archives.mhsc.ca/index.php/informationobject/browse?repos=938698&topLod=0&sort=relevance&query=AIMM&sq0=AIMM&sortDir=desc).

Akogyeram, Humphrey. "African Indigenous Church and the Ministry of the Holy Spirit." *Journal of Theology and Religion* 1, no. 1 (Spring 2000): 73–83.

Assani, Samson, "Historique du Conseil Interconfessionnel Protestant du Bénin." In *Ministry in Partnership with African Independent Churches*, edited by David A. Shank, 371–78. English summary, "Development within the Interconfessional Protestant Council of Benin," 379–80. Elkhart, IN: Mennonite Board of Missions, 1991.

Bertsche, James E. "Kimbanguism: A Challenge to Missionary Statesmanship." *Practical Anthropology* 13, no. 1 (Jan.–Feb. 1966): 13–33.

———. "Kimbanguism: A Separatist Movement." Master's thesis, Graduate School of Northwestern University, Evanston, IL, 1963. https://archives.mhsc.ca/index.

php/informationobject/browse?repos=938698&topLod=0&sort=relevance&query=AIMM&sq0=AIMM&sortDir=desc.

———. "Report on Gaborone Consultation on Bible Teaching Among AIC." Unpublished report submitted to the Africa Inter-Mennonite Mission (July 1981), 15 pages. Available at the Mennonite Archives, 3145 Benham Ave, Suite 1, Elkhart, IN 46517; ph. (574) 523-3080.

———. "Some Key AIMM Decisions of the Past." *Mission Focus Annual Review* 12 (2004): 6–8.

———. "Venturing into the South." In *CIM/AIMM: A Story of Vision, Commitment and Grace*, 443–590. Elkhart, IN: AIMM, 1998.

Born, J. Bryan. "A Personal Look at African Spiritual Churches: Reflections, Challenges, Hopes." *Mission Focus Annual Review* 12 (2004): 47–55.

———. "Promise of Power: An Analysis of Bible Life Ministries in Botswana." Unpublished Masters in Theology Dissertation, University of South Africa, Pretoria, 2002.

Born, Bryan, Stan Nussbaum, Thomas A. Oduro, and Hennie Pretorius. *Mission in an African Way: A Practical Introduction to African Instituted Churches and Their Sense of Mission*. Wellington, West Coast, South Africa: Christian Literature Fund, 2008.

Boschman, Don. "The Conflict Between the New Religious Movements and the State in the Bechuanaland Protectorate Prior to 1945." Unpublished Masters in Theology Dissertation, Harvard Divinity School, Boston, 1989.

———. "Some Theories about the Causes of Independency: The Case of Botswana." In *Ministry in Partnership with African Independent Churches*, edited by David A. Shank, 40–55. Elkhart, IN: Mennonite Board of Missions, 1991.

Clarke, Clifton, "African Indigenous Churches in Ghana: Past, Present and Future." *Journal of African Instituted Church Theology* 2, no. 1 (September 2006): 5–30.

———. "A Quest for an African Christology Among African Instituted Churches." *Journal of Theology and Religion* 1, no. 1 (Spring 2000): 2–9.

Clarke, Clifton, gen. ed. *Journal of Theology and Religion*, a journal launched in 2000 focused on AICs and produced by the Good News Theological College and Seminary, PO Box AN 6484, Accra-North, Ghana.

Ditsheko, Enole. *Dipolelo tsa Semoya: The Parched Voice of the African Church*. Gaborone: Yearbook, 2021.

Egli, Jim. "Consultation of Southern African Mennonite Personnel Working with AICs." Unpublished report submitted to the Africa Inter-Mennonite Mission (February 1983), 15 pages. Available at the Mennonite Archives, 3145 Benham Ave, Suite 1, Elkhart, IN 46517; ph. (574) 523-3080.

Famiyeh, Frank. "Stewardship of Money in African Independent Churches in Ghana." *Journal of Theology and Religion* 1, no. 1 (Spring 2000): 28–31.

Fehderau, Harold. "Concerning a Culturally Relevant Witness in Congo." *Practical Anthropology* 8, no. 2 (March–April 1961): 71–76.

———. "Enthusiastic Christianity in an African Church." *Practical Anthropology* 8, no. 6 (November–December 1961): 279–80, 282.

———. "Kimbanguism: Prophetic Christianity in Congo." *Practical Anthropology* 9, no. 4 (July–August 1962): 156–78.

Frey, Nancy, and Lynda Hollinger-Janzen. *3-D Gospel in Benin: Beninese Churches Invite Mennonites to Holistic Partnership*. Missio Dei series, vol. 23, edited by James R. Krabill. Elkhart, IN: Mennonite Mission Network, 2015.

Friesen, Delores H. "The Healing Fields: Five Lenten Lessons from Liberia." *The Christian Leader* (24 March 1992): 3–11.

———. *Let Love Be Your Greatest: A Study Guide to a Happy Marriage*. Kehl, Germany: Editions Trobisch, 1979.

———. "Peace Education and Conflict Resolution." In *Healing the Children of War*, edited by Phyllis Kilbourn, 251–66. Monrovia, CA: MARC, 1995.

———. "Worship – Important and Real." In *A Kingdom of Priests*, edited by Wilbert R. Shenk, 52–56. Newton: Faith and Life, 1967.

Friesen, J. Stanley. "African Christian Witnesses to Peacemaking." In *Violence and Peace: Creating a Culture of Peace in the Contemporary Context of Violence*, 276–99. Pune, India: Union Biblical Seminary, 2010.

———. "The Significance of Indigenous Movements for the Study of Church Growth." In *The Challenge of Church Growth: A Symposium*, edited by Wilbert R. Shenk, 79–106. Elkhart, IN: Institute of Mennonite Studies, 1973.

Friesen, J. Stanley, and Delores Friesen. "Anthropology, Anabaptists and Mission." *Mission Focus Annual Review* 8 (2000): 55–62.

———. "Educating for Global Ministry." *Mission Focus* 17, no. 4 (December 1989): 81–84.

———. "A Survey of HIV/AIDS Initiatives in Eight African Countries." Unpublished Report Commissioned by the Mennonite Central Committee, Akron, PA, March–May 2001.

Friesen, Rachel Hilty. *Ditso tsa Spiritual Healing Church mo Botswana*. Botswana: Mennonite Ministries, 1992. For use by congregations and members of the church, written to mark a quarter century of fruitful relationships between Mennonites and the Spiritual Healing Church in Botswana.

Gbedo, Victor. *Histoire des pères fondateurs de l'organisation non-gouvernementale Bethesda en République du Bénin*. Cotonou: ONG Bethesda, 2016.

Hollinger-Janzen, Rodney. "A Biblical Teaching Program by the Interconfessional Protestant Council of Benin with Mennonite Cooperation." In *Ministry in Partnership with African Independent Churches*, edited by David A. Shank, 161–70. Elkhart, IN: Mennonite Board of Missions, 1991.

Hostetter, Darrel M. "Bible Training Among Zionists in Swaziland." In *Ministry of Mission to African Independent Churches*, edited by David A. Shank, 190–96. Elkhart, IN: Mennonite Board of Missions, 1987.

———. "Disarming the Emadloti, the Ancestors." In *Ministry in Partnership with African Independent Churches*, edited by David A. Shank, 354–70. Elkhart, IN: Mennonite Board of Missions, 1991.

Jacobs, Donald. "Sunday in Africa . . . Let's Go to Church." *And Some Fell on Good Ground: RISK Journal* 7, no. 3. Geneva: World Council of Churches (1974): 36–39.

Jacobs, Don, and James Bertsche. *Southern Africa Study*. Unpublished manuscript. Available: https://archives.mhsc.ca/index.php/informationobject/browse?repos= 938698&topLod=0&sort=relevance&query=AIMM&sq0=AIMM&sortDir=desc.

Janzen, John M. "Deep Thought: Structure and Intention in Kongo Prophetism, 1910–1921." *Social Research* 49, no. 1 (Spring 1979): 106–139.

———. "Kongo Religious Renewal: Iconoclastic and Iconorthostic." *Canadian Journal of African Studies* 5, no. 2 (Spring 1971): 135–43.

———. "Renewal and Reinterpretation in Kongo Religion." In *Kongo Across the Waters*, edited by Susan Cooksey, Robin Poynor, and Hein Vanhee, 132–42. Tervuren, Belgium: Central Africa Museum, 2013.

Juhnke, James. *A Collection of Writings by Mennonites on Southern Africa*. Reproduced and edited by Vern Preheim, n. p., 1972, 53 pages. Available: https://archives.mhsc.ca/index.php/informationobject/browse?repos=938698&topLod=0&sort=relevance&query=AIMM&sq0=AIMM&sortDir=desc.

Kaethler, Andrew Brubacher. "Christology in African Independent Churches: Theological Reflections in Mennonite Missions Perspective." Unpublished Masters thesis, Emmanuel College, Toronto School of Theology, University of Toronto, 1999. Copy available in the Anabaptist Mennonite Biblical Seminary library, Elkhart, Indiana. https://cdm15705.contentdm.oclc.org/digital/collection/p15705coll31/id/297/rec/53.

———. "Church of Moshoeshoe (Lesotho)." In *Religions of the World: A Comprehensive Encyclopedia of Beliefs and Practices*, vol. 1, edited by J. Gordon Melton and Martin Baumann, 325–26. Santa Barbara, CA: ABC Clio, 2002.

———. "Spiritual Healing Church (Botswana)." In *Religions of the World: A Comprehensive Encyclopedia of Beliefs and Practices*, vol. 4, edited by J. Gordon Melton and Martin Baumann, 1211–12. Santa Barbara, CA: ABC Clio, 2002.

Krabill, James R. "Evangelical and Ecumenical Dimensions of Walking with AICs." In *Evangelical, Ecumenical, and Anabaptist Missiologies in Conversation*, edited by James R. Krabill, Walter Sawatsky, and Charles E. Van Engen, 240–47. Maryknoll, NY: Orbis, 2006.

———. "Hymn Collecting among the Dida Harrists." In *Ministry in Partnership with African Independent Churches*, edited by David A. Shank, 220–38. Elkhart, IN: Mennonite Board of Missions, 1991.

———. *The Hymnody of the Harrist Church among the Dida of South-Central Ivory Coast (1913–1949)*. Frankfurt am Main: Peter Lang, 1995.

———. "Ministry among the Dida Harrists of Côte d'Ivoire: A Case Study." In *Ministry of Mission to African Independent Churches*, edited by David A. Shank, 33–55. Elkhart, IN: Mennonite Board of Missions, 1987.

———. "Neither 'Reached' nor 'Unreached': The Response of One Mission Agency to Independent Churches of West Africa." *Mission Focus Annual Review* 6 (1998): 97–112.

———. "Scripture Use in AIC Hymnody: Fourteen Fields of Investigation." In *Afro-Christian Religion at the Grassroots in Southern Africa*, edited by G. C. Oosthuizen and Irving Hexham, 293–331. African Studies, vol. 19. Lewiston, NY: Edwin Mellen, 1991.

———. "Six Decades in the Making: A Story of Friendship and Ministry Partnership between African-Initiated Churches and North American Mennonites." *Anabaptist Witness* 5, no. 2 (October 2018): 85–104.

———. "Where Teachers Become Learners and Learners, Teachers." A booklet in Mission Insight series, vol. 23, edited by James R. Krabill. Elkhart, IN: Mennonite Board of Mission, 2001.

———. "William Wadé Harris (1860–1929): African Evangelist and Ethnohymnologist." *Mission Focus* 18, no. 4 (1990): 56–59.

Krabill, James R., and Jeanette Krabill. "Scriptural Impact through a Dramatic Reenactment." *Orality Journal: The Word Became Fresh* 5, no. 1, (2016): 83–86.

Larson, Jonathan P. "Reflections on a Four-Day Mule Ride or The Encounter of Literate and Nonliterate in Independent Churches of Rural Botswana." In *Ministry of Missions to African Independent Churches*, edited by David A. Shank, 172–79. Elkhart, IN: Mennonite Board of Missions, 1987.

———. Collection of unpublished articles and essays by Larson available at the Mennonite Archives, 3145 Benham Ave, Suite 1, Elkhart, IN 46517; ph. (574) 523-3080. These include "New Star in the Mennonite Mission Constellation: Faith Mission in Southern Africa," Mennonite Ministries Botswana, undated; "Pitseng Study Group: Worship," Mennonite Ministries Botswana, undated; "Occasional Paper," No. 1, Mennonite Ministries Botswana (August 1984), 18 pages; "Tenth Anniversary Reflections on Our Work with AICs in Botswana," Mennonite Ministries Botswana (20 January 1986); "Double Dip Day at Spiritual Healing Church," Mennonite Ministries Botswana (18 March 1987); "In the Night Also My Heart Instructs Me: A Case Study in Dream Revelation Among AICs," Mennonite Ministries Botswana (April 1987); "Trailmarker #4," Mennonite Ministries Botswana (10 April 1987); and "A Bell Rings In Kobajango," Mennonite Central Committee, Akron, PA (13 November 1987).

Loewen, Jacob A. "Mission Churches, Independent Churches, and Felt Needs in Africa." *Missiology: An International Review* 4, no. 4 (1976): 405–25.

Martey, Emmanuel. "Prophetic Movements in The Congo: The Life and Work of Simon Kimbangu and How His Followers Saw Him." *Journal of Theology and Religion* 1, no. 1 (Spring 2000): 45–58.

Nussbaum, Stan W. "African Independent Churches and a Call for a New Three-Self Formula for Mission." In *Freedom and Interdependence*, 1–8. Nairobi, Kenya: Organization of African Instituted Churches, 1994.

———. "A Biblical Narrative Approach to Strengthening the Christology of Independent Churches in Lesotho." In *Ministry of Missions to African Independent Churches*, edited by David A. Shank, 180–89. Elkhart, IN: Mennonite Board of Missions, 1987.

———. "Liturgical Innovation in the Nazarite Association of Lesotho." In *Afro-Christian Religion at the Grassroots in Southern Africa*, edited by G. C. Oosthuizen and Irving Hexham, 216–26. African Studies, vol. 19. Lewiston, NY: Edwin Mellen, 1991.

———. "New Religious Movements: Contextualization and Church Growth." *Mission Focus* 17, no. 1 (March 1989): 11–14.

———. "New Religious Movements and Missiological Surprises." *Mission Focus* 17, no. 2 (June 1989): 30–34.

———. "New Religious Movements: The Neglected Component of Missionary Preparation." *Mission Focus* 16, no. 2 (June 1988): 29–32.

———. "New Religious Movements: Partnership and Dialogue." *Mission Focus* 16, no. 3 (September 1988): 58–61.

———. "Proposal: African Bible Guides Project." In *Ministry in Partnership with African Independent Churches*, edited by David A. Shank, 275–91. Elkhart, IN: Mennonite Board of Missions, 1991.

———. "Rethinking Animal Sacrifice: A Response to Some Sotho Independent Churches." *Missionalia* 12, no. 2 (1983): 49–63.

———. "Toward a Theological Dialogue with African Independent Churches: A Study of Five Congregations in Lesotho." Unpublished DTh Dissertation, University of South Africa, Pretoria, South Africa, 1986.

Nussbaum, Stan, gen. ed. *The Review of AICs*. An occasional newsletter of wide-ranging materials by and about AICs, Mennonites, and a few other Western expatriate missionaries and scholars compiled by Stan Nussbaum, Mennonite mission worker, scholar, and erstwhile director of the Centre for New Religious Movements at Selly Oak Colleges, Birmingham B29 6LQ, United Kingdom. Features of the newsletter included book reviews, teaching curricula, ministry accounts, obituaries, project proposals, requests for assistance, trip reports, new resources and opportunities, AIC histories and trends, prayer requests, network news, conference announcements and reports, thematic bibliographies and reading lists, "half-baked" ideas, "Nussbaum Awards," and updates on the African Bible Guide Project. *The Review* launched its first issue in January 1990 and ceased publication in September-December 2004. Avaliable: https://archives.mhsc.ca/index.php/informationobject/browse?repos=938698&topLod=0&sort=relevance&query=AIMM&sq0=AIMM&sortDir=desc.

Nussbaum, Stan, ed. *Freedom and Interdependence: Papers presented at the Conference on Ministry in Partnership with African Independent Churches, Johannesburg, South Africa, April 1993*. Nairobi, Kenya: Organization of African Instituted Churches, 1994.

Oduro, Thomas A. "African Christian Theology: The Contributions of African Instituted Churches." *Ogbomoso Journal of Theology* 13, no. 1 (2008): 58–74.

———. "The African Independent Churches in Ghana." In *Christianity in Ghana: A Post-Colonial History*, vol. 1, 114–35. Legon, Accra: Sub-Saharan Publishers, 2018.

———. "Agnes Okoh: An African Prophetess, Missionary, Pastoral Trainer and Mother." *Journal of African Christian Biography* 2, no. 3 (July 2017): 5–17.

———. "'Arise, Walk through the Length and Breadth of the Land:' Missionary Concepts and Strategies of African Independent Churches." *International Bulletin of Missionary Research* 38, no. 2 (April 2014): 86–89.

———. "Challenges, Heartbreaks and Successes of Contextualized Mission: The Story of African Independent Churches in Ghana." In *Rethinking the Great Commission: Emerging African Perspectives*, edited by Emmanuel K. Asante and David N. A. Kpobi, 93–112. Accra: Type, 2018.

———. "Charles Yaw Yeboa-Korie, 1932–2000." *Journal of African Christian Biography* 4, no. 3 (July 2019): 31–48.

———. "Christ Holy Church International: An African Independent Church in Transition." *Trinity Journal of Church and Theology* 15, no. 2 (July 2005): 26–51.

———. "Christ Holy Church International (1947–2002): The Challenges of Christian Proclamation in a Nigerian Context." Doctoral Dissertation, Luther Seminary, St. Paul, MN, 2004. Available at the Luther Seminary library, St. Paul, MN.

———. *Christ Holy Church International: The Story of an African Independent Church*. Minneapolis: Lutheran University Press, 2007.

———. *Church of the Lord (Brotherhood): History, Challenges and Growth*. Kumasi: Jerusalem Press, 2012; 2nd ed, Accra, Ghana: SonLife, 2016.

———. "Contributions and Challenges of the African Instituted Churches in Developing African Theology." In *African Theology on the Way: Current Conversations*, edited by Diane B. Stinton, 46–55. London: SPCK, 2010.

———. "Healing a Strained Relationship between African Independent Churches and Western Mission-Founded Churches in Ghana, 1967–2017: The Role of Good News Theological Seminary, Accra, Ghana." In *African Instituted Christianity and the Decolonization of Development*, edited by Phillipp Öhlmann, Wilhelm Gräb, Marie-Luise Frost, 227–39. Abingdon: Routledge, 2020.

———. "The History and Pedagogy of the Good News Training Institute in Accra." In *Ministry in Partnership with African Independent Churches*, edited by David A. Shank, 132–60. Elkhart, IN: Mennonite Board of Missions, 1991.

———. "Independent Churches in Africa." In *Anthology of African Christianity*, edited by Isabel Apawo Phiri and Dietrich Werner, 431–40. Oxford: Regnum Books International, 2016.

———. "Symbolism in African Independent Churches: Aides to Spirituality and Spiritual Formation." *Ogbomoso Journal of Theology* 15, no. 1 (2011): 67–84.

———. "Theological Education in African Independent Churches: A Plethora of Pedagogies." In *Handbook of Theological Education in Africa*, edited by Isabel Apawo Phiri and Dietrich Werner, 423–32. Oxford: Regnum Books International, 2013.

———. "Theological Education and Training: Challenges of African Independent Churches in Ghana." *Journal of African Instituted Church Theology* 2, no. 1 (September 2006): 31–44.

———. "Water Baptism in African Independent Churches: The Paradigm of Christ Holy Church International." In *Baptism Today: Understanding, Practice, Ecumenical Implications*, edited by Thomas F. Best, 181–91. Collegeville, MN: Liturgical, 2008.

Oduro, Thomas, Hennie Pretorius, Stan Nussbaum, and Bryan Born. *Mission in an African Way: A Practical Introduction to African Instituted Churches and Their Sense of Mission*. Wellington, South Africa: Christian Literature Fund, 2008.

Prieb, Garry. "Ten Years with AIMM, 1994–2004: Reflections on Trends and Possibilities." *Mission Focus Annual Review* 12 (2004): 9–20.

Sawatzky, Joseph C. L. "Toward an Anabaptist-Pentecostal Vision: Exploring Ecclesial Identities in North America Mennonite Mission with Pentecostal-Type Churches in Southern Africa." Unpublished Doctoral Dissertation, University of KwaZulu-Natal, Pietermaritzburg, South Africa, 2021.

Schrag, Rhoda M. "Kimbanguist Beliefs Taught in Zambia – Law, Jesus Christ, Simon Kimbangu: A Study of the Lusaka Congregation." *Mission Focus Annual Review* 2 (1994): 105–122.

Shank, David A. "African Independent Churches, African Theology, and Western Co-Workers in the Missio Dei." In *Ministry in Partnership with African Independent Churches*, edited by David A. Shank, 3–21. Elkhart, IN: Mennonite Board of Missions, 1991.

———. "A Decade with God's Mission among African-Initiated Churches in West Africa." In *Mission Focus Annual Review* 11 (2003): 85–104.

———. "The Legacy of William Wadé Harris." *International Bulletin of Missionary Research* 10, no. 4 (October 1986): 170–76.

———. *Mission from the Margins*. Edited by James R. Krabill. Important and relevant chapters written by David Shank are "The Legacy of William Wadé Harris," 201–17; "What Western Christians Can Learn from African-Initiated Churches," 219–30; "A Religious Itinerary from African Traditional Religion to New Testament Faith," 249–65; "Reflections on Relating Long Term to Messianic Communities," 295–309; "John Howard Yoder, Strategist for Mission with African-Initiated Churches," 311–36; and "Qualities That Enable Mennonites to Relate to African-Initiated Churches," 337–38. Elkhart, IN: Institute of Mennonite Studies, 2010.

———. "Mission Relations with the Independent Churches in Africa." *Missiology: An International Review* 13, no. 1 (1985): 23–44.

———. *Prophet Harris: The "Black Elijah" of West Africa*, abridged by Jocelyn Murray. Leiden: Brill, 1994.

———. "A Prophet of Modern Times: The Thought of William Wadé Harris, West African Precursor of the Reign of Christ." Unpublished Doctoral Dissertation, University of Aberdeen, Aberdeen, Scotland, 1980.

———. "What Western Christians Can Learn from African-Initiated Churches." A booklet in the Mission Insight series, vol. 10, edited by James R. Krabill. Elkhart, IN: Mennonite Board of Mission, 2000.

———. "The Work of the Group for Religious and Biblical Studies in West Africa (GERB)." In *Ministry of Missions to African Independent Churches*, edited by David A. Shank, 13–32. Elkhart, IN: Mennonite Board of Missions, 1987.

Shank, David A., ed. *Ministry of Missions to African Independent Churches: Papers presented at the Conference on Ministry to African Independent Churches, Abidjan, Côte d'Ivoire, July 1986*. Elkhart, IN: Mennonite Board of Missions, 1987.

———, ed. *Ministry in Partnership with African Independent Churches: Papers presented at the Conference on Ministry in Partnership with African Independent Churches, Kinshasa, Zaire, July 1989*. Elkhart, IN: Mennonite Board of Missions, 1991.

Shenk, Wilbert R. "The Contribution of the Study of New Religious Movements to Missiology." In *Exploring New Religious Movements*, edited by Andrew F. Walls and Wilbert R. Shenk, 179–205. Elkhart, IN: Mission Focus, 1990.

———. "Go Slow Through Uyo." In *Fullness of Life for All*, edited by I. Daneel, C. Van Engen, and H. Vroom, 329–40. Amsterdam, New York: Rodopi, 2008.

———. "Mission Agency and African Independent Churches." *International Review of Missions* 63, no. 251 (October 1974): 475–91.

Spruth, Erwin L. Kwajo. "African Instituted Churches in the 21st Century: Education and Training of AIC Leaders." *Journal of Theology and Religion* 1, no. 1 (Spring 2000): 10–27.

Wambugu, Njeru, and John Padwick. "Globalization: A Perspective from the African Independent Churches." *Journal of Theology and Religion* 1, no. 1 (Spring 2000): 59–72.

Weaver, Edwin, and Irene Weaver. *From Kuku Hill: Among Indigenous Churches in West Africa*. Elkhart, IN: Institute of Mennonite Studies, 1975.

———. *The Uyo Story*. Elkhart, IN: Mennonite Board of Missions, 1970.

Wiebe-Johnson, Stephen. "Background to Mennonite Board of Missions Involvement in Liberia." In *Ministry in Partnership with African Independent Churches*, edited by David A. Shank, 106–11. Elkhart, IN: Mennonite Board of Missions, 1991.

Yoder, R. Bruce. "Mennonite Missionaries and African Independent Churches: The Development of an Anabaptist Missiology in West Africa: 1958–1967." Unpublished Doctoral Dissertation, Boston University, Boston, MA, 2016.

———. "Mennonite Mission Theorists and Practitioners in Southeastern Nigeria: Changing Contexts and Strategy at the Dawn of the Postcolonial Era." *International Bulletin of Missionary Research* 37, no. 3 (2013): 138–44.

Editors Biographies

THOMAS A. ODURO

Thomas A. Oduro is the president of Good News Theological Seminary, Accra, Ghana – a theological institution founded initially to train leaders and members of African Independent Churches (AICs). He received his PhD in History of Christianity (Distinction) in 2004 from Luther Seminary, St. Paul, MN, USA. An Associate Professor of African Christianity and History of Christianity, Oduro has been a teacher of AIC leaders and members for over three decades and currently serves as an Adjunct Lecturer at Akrofi-Christaller Institute Theology, Mission and Culture, Akropong-Akuapem, Ghana. Author of many published books and articles on AICs, Oduro also serves as a member of the Executive Committee of the Organization of African Instituted Churches (OAIC), an ecumenical body of AICs, and a pastor of Christ Holy Church International, an AIC.

JONATHAN P. LARSON

Jonathan P. Larson was raised in post-colonial India where he attended Woodstock School in the Himalayan foothills. He went on to Asian studies (BA) at the University of Minnesota in Minneapolis having edited a campus newspaper during the Vietnam war. As a conscientious objector, he together with his wife, Mary Kay, served in a teacher-training institute in Zaire (now, DRC) in Africa's Great Lakes region where he had early contact with the Kimbanguist church. Subsequent training in theology (MDiv, Bethel Seminary, St. Paul, MN, and independent study at Selly Oak Colleges, Birmingham, UK, and Columbia Theological Seminary, Atlanta, GA) led to a Mennonite assignment in Botswana during the HIV/AIDS epidemic and the waning days of apartheid South Africa. Grassroots engagement with the movement of African Independent Churches awakened his interest in oral cultures. Ordained by the AICs of the Kalahari, now a Mennonite minister, he has pastored congregations both in Africa and America while continuing to travel, speak and write with a global horizon. He has since published a book set amidst the strife of Afghanistan, *Making Friends Among the Taliban*, together with a 60-minute documentary aired on ABC television. He keeps a story blog, "Traipse," at jonathanlarsonblog.com.

JAMES R. KRABILL

James R. Krabill is retired from full employment, having served for forty-two years as a mission worker and administrator with Mennonite Mission Network, 1976–2018. For fourteen of those years Krabill lived and worked with his family in West Africa as a Bible and Church History teacher among African Independent Churches (AICs) in various village settings, Bible institutes and theological faculties, including eight years with members of the Harrist Church among Côte d'Ivoire's Dida people, collecting, recording, transcribing, and publishing over 500 original Harrist hymns for use in literacy and music training. Many of these hymns appeared in Krabill's published PhD thesis, *The Hymnody of the Harrist Church* (Frankfurt: Peter Lang, 1995). Dr. Krabill has been a frequent speaker in various church and academic settings across the United States and has lectured or taught courses in over twenty countries, currently serving as an adjunct professor at Eastern Mennonite Seminary, Anabaptist Mennonite Biblical Seminary, and Dallas International University. He has authored or edited/co-edited numerous other books and articles, including, "Scripture Use in AIC Hymnody," in *Afro-Christian Religion at the Grassroots in Southern Africa* (1991), 293–331; *Nos Racines Racontées* (1996); *Evangelical, Ecumenical and Anabaptist Missiologies in Conversation* (2006); *Music in the Life of the African Church* (2008); and *Worship and Mission for the Global Church* (2013).

Subject Index

A

AACCC. *See* All-Africa Council of Christian Churches
Abetifi 165
Abidjan 17, 41, 59, 69, 102, 153, 157, 171, 179
Abobo-Doumé 171
abstinence 139, 173
Accra 16, 23, 24, 35, 61, 62, 78, 93–95, 121, 135, 142, 146, 164, 186
Accra Community Center 24
Adedokun, Manasse 154
administration (church) 119, 120, 155
Africa Inter-Mennonite Mission 33, 180
Africa Inter-Mennonite Mission (AIMM) 19
African Federal Church Council 115, 162
African Independent Church. *See* also Turner, Harold W.
African Spiritual Churches (ASCs) 49
AIMM 34, 67, 108, 109, 117, 160
Aladura. *See* Church of the Lord (Aladura)
All-Africa Conference of Churches 17. *See* All-Africa Council of Christian Churches (AACCC)
All-Africa Council of Christian Churches (AACCC) 41
all-night (service) 26, 93, 98, 107, 113, 135, 175
Amasaman 95
Anabaptist 28, 98, 171, 176, 177
ancestors 157
angels 153
animal sacrifice 111. *See* also burnt offerings
anointers 145, 146
anointing 93, 125, 145, 146, 176, 178
Anono 158
apartheid 19, 116, 162
Apostolic, Cherubim and Seraphim 42
apostolic sending 177
ASCs 51. *See* African Spiritual Churches (ASCs)
Associated Mennonite Biblical Seminary 95, 143
Association Evangélique Universelle. *See* Eglise Evangélique Universelle
Attié 61

B

Bakongo 14
Bantu Prophets 10. *See* also Sundkler, Bengt
baptism 82, 152, 157
Baptist Mission 14
Basotho 162
Batswana 52, 76, 78, 160, 161
BBI 31
Belgian colonial government 14
Belgian Fellowship of Reconciliation 15
Belgium 15
Benin 16, 24, 30, 41, 74, 153, 179
Benin Bible Institute (BBI) 17, 30, 43, 180
Benin Inter-Confessional Council of Protestant Churches 41, 43, 133
Bethany Bible School (BBS) 81, 129, 155
Bethesda Hospital 17, 43
Bible school 13, 87, 105, 121
Bible seminars 42. *See* also Bible teaching

Bible studies 40, 78, 97, 142, 151, 162, 180, 182, 183
Bible study 12, 16, 23, 122, 153, 160, 166, 182
Bible teaching 18, 26, 41, 59, 67, 108, 117, 133, 160, 163, 172, 173, 175, 180, 183
Bible training 70, 81, 131, 169
Birmingham (England) 28
blessing 84, 107, 120, 125, 146, 150, 177, 184
Bloemfontein 82
Bodawa 42
Bontleng 182
Book of God 109
Bopaganang 118, 119
Bopaganang Basha ba Semoya 117
born again 166
botho 111
Botswana 19, 33, 49, 52, 56, 71, 76, 83, 90, 92, 102, 108, 110, 117, 119, 124, 138, 139, 151, 160, 176, 180, 181, 187, 188
Botswana Christian Aids Project (BOCAIP) 187
Breakthru Church International 31
British Wesleyan Methodist Mission 41
burnt offerings 111

C
Cairo 101
Canada 117
CEFCA. *See* Evangelical Center of Formation in Communications for Africa
Celestial Christianity 42
Centre for New Religious Movements (Birmingham, England) 28
chants 153
Cherubim and Seraphim Church 42, 154
children 26, 35, 44, 70, 99, 110, 125, 127, 155, 177

choirs 71, 111, 118, 119, 125, 149, 166, 176, 177, 183–185. *See* also singing
Christian Catholic Apostolic Holy Spirit Church in Zion 26
Christian education (children) 125
Christian Service College 94
Church as a Community of Healing and Peacemaking (ECGAP) 104
Church Mother 123
Church of God in Zion 81
Church of the Lord (Aladura) 12, 13, 23, 78, 93, 96, 105, 107, 121, 142, 165, 169
church planting 41, 86, 110, 128, 165
circumcision 88
clapping 106, 111, 125, 134, 138, 146, 150
colonial 14, 64, 101, 130, 137, 147
coming-out ceremony 27
Commission on World Mission and Evangelism 12. *See* also World Council of Churches
community 29, 42, 49, 51, 83, 98, 103, 104, 120, 147, 152, 153, 176
community facilitators 188
community health 164
confession 93, 145
conflict 11, 51, 95, 96, 99, 103, 157, 158
Congo (Democratic Republic of) 15, 19, 29
Congo Inland Mission 14
Congolese Mennonites 15
Conseil Interconfessionnel Protestant du Benin. *See* Benin Inter-Confessional Council of Protestant Churches
context 33, 34, 42, 50, 54, 64, 76, 101, 137, 158
contextualization 33, 64
contextualizing 86
contextually appropriate 15
Côte d'Ivoire 16, 59, 60, 69, 153, 154, 157, 158, 159, 171, 179
Cotonou 24, 74, 133

Subject Index   207

Cotonou Methodist Church 43
Council for African Instituted
    Churches (CAIC) 39
counseling 39, 95, 104, 123, 155
cross 33, 81, 94, 107, 157, 159, 184

D
Dahomean Methodist Church 41
Dahomey 41. *See* Benin
dance 29, 64, 81, 88, 112, 134, 146, 147, 162, 170, 172, 176, 184, 186
dancing 26, 106, 111, 119, 125, 175, 186
Daystar University 40
deliverance 14, 98, 113
demons 81, 113
Denmark 15
development projects 86
Dida 59, 61, 70, 171, 173, 183, 186
Diphapo Christian Church 117, 119
disabled people 75
discipleship 139, 140
discipleship training program 99, 176
divisions 24, 37
Divo 173, 183, 186
drama 71, 72, 100
dream 42, 50, 54, 55, 106, 112, 153
drums 28, 106, 134, 146, 172

E
Eastern Mennonite Board of Missions 100
Eastern Mennonite Missions 19, 80, 175
economics 33
Eden Revival Church 164, 166
Efik-Ibibio 98
Eglise Christique Primitive 42
Eglise Evangélique Universelle 133
Eledja 42
Eleven Apostles Healing Spirit Church 33, 138, 177
Elkhart 153
England 28, 166
equipping church leaders 20

Evangelical Center of Formation in
    Communications for Africa 179
Evangelical Lutheran Church in Ghana 23, 24
Evangelical Presbyterian Church of Ghana 143
evangelism 164, 176
evangelist 71, 110, 113, 176
evil spirit 42, 50, 122
Ewe 142, 145

F
Faith Bible School 99, 113, 173, 175
Fanti 142
fasting 50, 54, 94, 105, 123, 144
FATEAC (Faculté de Théologie Evangélique de l'Alliance Chrétienne) 103
femmes d'honneur 184
fire churches 121. *See* also Pentecostal
forgiven 93, 123, 155
Fourah Bay College 11
France 17
Francistown 56, 84, 117, 138, 139, 162, 187
Free State 116
friendship 12, 65, 70, 71, 74, 87, 94, 95, 101, 117, 119, 139, 147, 149, 160, 162, 171, 173, 177
funding 24, 75, 101, 167

G
Gaborone 20, 76, 90, 108, 119, 150, 176, 180, 187
garbage collection 43
German Bremen Mission 142, 145
Germany 107
Ghana 16, 23, 35, 46, 58, 61, 62, 78, 93, 94, 95, 102, 105, 121, 135, 141, 144, 153, 164, 169, 186, 188
Ghana Christian Council (GCC) 46, 165
Ghana Council of Churches 166
Ghanaian Presbyterian Church 38
Ghana Mennonite Church 95

gifts (spiritual) 78, 82, 89, 111, 143, 147, 176
Gilgal 26
Good News Theological Seminary (GNTS) 17, 25, 35, 38, 40, 47, 59, 62, 121, 142, 164, 167, 186, 188
Good News Training Institute (GNTI) 17, 35, 46, 58, 62, 79, 94, 143, 164, 165, 167. *See* Good News Theological Seminary (GNTS)
Goshen College 143
gospel 15, 31, 33, 42, 64, 68, 76, 143, 148, 163, 166, 176
grace 51, 91, 104, 123, 147, 161, 174
guiding principles 20

H

Harrist 18, 158, 171, 173, 183
Harrist Church 18, 59, 60, 158, 183
Harrist National Committee 59, 60
heal 14, 24
healer 64, 88
healing 14, 26, 37, 49, 50, 52, 55, 80, 83, 88, 90, 93, 104, 106, 111, 113, 124, 134, 143, 144, 146, 147, 154, 157, 159, 166
healing community 153
Healing Home 123
healing village 143, 145, 146
healthcare 17
health education 160
heaven 51, 72, 123, 162, 176
heretical 63
hermeneutics 49, 52
Hermon Church 50
hierarchy 117
HIV/AIDS 173–175, 181, 186, 187
  counseling 111, 187
  counsling 155
  education 76, 187
  ministry 87
  prevention 76, 100, 187, 188
  response 187, 188
  testing program 99

Holy Banner Mission Church of Africa 177
Holy Banner of Ethiopian Apostolic Church in Zion 155
holy city 15, 106
Holy Face Church 98
Holy Land 120
Holy Spirit 11, 30, 42, 49, 51, 52, 55, 74, 82, 90, 107, 117, 119, 125, 153, 159, 163, 176
holy water 84, 120, 153
home-based care 173, 174, 176, 187
honor 78, 108, 111, 115, 117, 184, 186
hospitality 44, 46, 145
Hoy Spirit 125
hymns 71, 145, 146, 149, 171, 176

I

Ibadan 124
Ibibio 73
Immanuel Believers Ministry 39
immigrants 28, 124, 153
independency 11
independent 11
independent churches 19
Indiana 153
indigenous 10, 40, 42, 47, 49, 64, 78, 83, 85, 130, 141, 146, 147, 153, 185
INTERACT Research Centre 102
intercession 93, 98
Inter-Church Ministries Botswana 182
interchurch relations 20
Inter-Church Study Group 12, 37
Interconfessional Protestant Council (ICPC) 17
International Fellowship of Reconciliation 15
International Review of Missions 10
interpretation (biblical) 50, 63, 119
interpretation (of dream) 42, 153

J

Jesus 19, 20, 49, 50, 55, 64, 68, 76, 82, 88, 91, 92, 94, 98, 100, 103, 107,

113, 123, 141, 143, 144, 148, 154, 160, 164, 180, 181

K
Kalahari 176, 178
Kalanga 161
Kenya 12, 40, 76, 120, 179
Kimbanguism 9
  A Challenge to Missionary Statesmanship 15
  A Separatist Movement. *See* also Bertsche, James E.
Kimbanguist Church 15
Kimbanguists 15
King of Swaziland 113
Kingdom of Eswatini. *See* also Swaziland
kingdom of God 19, 42, 55, 65, 69, 92, 100, 107, 141, 181, 183
Kinshasa 102
kneel 123, 145, 154, 159, 183
Kolojane Ha Thuhloane 67
Kumasi 93, 94, 169

L
Lagos 11, 13
language study 26
laying on of hands 93, 123, 138, 176
leadership training 18, 119, 140, 153, 160
League of African Churches 113, 115
legalistic interpretation 51
Leribe 163
Lesotho 19, 67, 102, 115, 128, 162, 188
Letlhakane 117, 119
Liberia 16, 17, 105, 153
listen 16, 55, 146, 154, 159
listening 12, 23, 47, 58, 138
loan investment program 43
Lutheran Theological Seminary at Philadelphia 95

M
Mahalapye 110, 121

mainline churches 24, 25, 37, 41, 82, 110, 117, 120, 127, 128, 152, 163, 165, 166
Mandela Park 54, 87, 88
Manzini 139
marginalized 50, 85, 101
marriage 76, 111, 173
marriage, Christian 36
marriage officers 110, 119
marriage retreats 173
marriage teaching 76
married couples' fellowship 76, 110
Maseru 128, 163
Maseru Consultation 19
Matatiele 54, 55
Matsiloje 90, 110
Maun 138
medical supplies 173
Mennonite Board of Missions 18, 28, 41, 105, 158
Mennonite Central Committee (MCC) 15, 80, 100, 140, 151, 173, 176
Mennonite Church Nigeria 37, 136, 137
Mennonite Church USA 178
Mennonite Ministries in Botswana 92, 181
Mennonite Mission Network (MMN) 103, 104
Messianic Popular Movements in the Lower Congo. *See* also Andersson, Efraim
migration 130
Mindolo 12
miracle 53, 54, 90
missiological anthropologist 63, 65
missiology 86
mission-founded churches (MICs) 11, 46, 49, 165, 179
Mission in an African Way 161
Misty Mount 128
Mmadinare 117
Mochudi 124, 127

money 31, 35, 37, 42, 51, 54, 55, 62, 99, 106, 134, 155, 162, 165, 166, 169, 176
moruti (minister, teacher) 90, 91, 140, 160
Mosaic law 51, 97
Mthatha 54, 55, 87
Muslim 75, 103, 121, 158, 180

N
Nairobi 12, 40, 102, 179
Nazareth Church 151
Network on AICs and Missions 102
New Morian Apostolic Church in Zion 160
Nigeria 11, 16, 25, 37, 41, 72, 78, 96, 98, 105, 107, 136, 137, 153, 169
Nigerian Civil War 13
Nima Temple 23, 79, 93, 96, 121, 142, 165. See Church of the Lord (Aladura)
Nkamba 15
North America 130, 140
Nxumalo family 80

O
offering 31, 89, 106, 134, 184. See also burnt offerings
Ohio 125
Old Testament 30, 73, 97, 98, 127, 160, 165
Order of Preachers 60
ordination 14, 140, 176, 177, 178
Organization of African Instituted Churches (OAIC) 101, 120, 186–189
Oxford University 166

P
PAG. See Pentecostal Association of Ghana
Parana Apostolic Church 53, 54
Paris 18

partnership 17, 25, 86, 110, 111, 116, 117, 120, 121, 128, 139, 140, 152, 155, 163, 186
pastoral training 17
peace 49, 56, 72, 94, 103, 104, 131, 154, 155, 158, 159
peacemaking 104
Pentecostal 112, 143
Pentecostal Association of Ghana (PAG) 25, 38, 78
perspective 35, 65, 146
Petit Bassam 60
Pietermaritzburg 33, 82
Pitseng 151, 152
polygamist 105
polygamous 35, 153
polygamy 42, 142
pork 126
Porto Novo 42
power 29, 49, 51, 55, 68, 72, 76, 81, 84, 88, 91, 111, 119, 123, 159, 161, 165, 171
Prairie Street Mennonite Church 153
praise 28, 42, 109, 110, 152, 169
praise circles 165
praise poem 177
pray 52, 54, 55, 74, 75, 88, 93, 96, 106, 152, 159, 162, 174, 177, 182. See also praying
prayer 42, 45, 52, 54, 71, 78, 81, 90, 92–94, 98, 106, 109, 120, 122, 134, 143, 145, 153, 154, 158, 162, 174–176, 183, 184, 186. See also pray
prayer ground 106
praying 50, 52, 80, 84, 88, 105. See also prayer
preach 14, 55, 112, 155
preaching 14, 26, 34, 53, 71, 95, 121, 128, 139, 152, 173, 176
pregnant 74, 98, 106
presence (ministry) 51, 102, 131, 171, 173
primate 105, 106, 108
prison 14

Subject Index

procession 71, 72, 125, 183, 184, 186
prophecy 106, 110, 111, 143
prophesy 138
prophet 9, 59, 60, 64, 69, 105, 111, 124, 125, 172
prophetess 106
prophetic word 55, 71. *See also* prophecy
prosperity 32
Protestant Methodist Church of Benin 24

R
racism 56, 130, 147
reconcile 50
reconciliation 94, 100, 137, 155, 163
relationship(s) 12, 18, 20, 26, 27, 34, 36, 39, 47, 50, 57, 59, 75–77, 92, 103, 127, 130, 131, 136, 146, 158, 173, 175
respect 12, 20, 57, 58, 110, 111, 113, 115, 139, 151, 157
retreat 76, 139, 173
Review of AICs: A Practitioners Journal 102
Ridge International Church 142

S
Sacred Cherubim and Seraphim Society 153
salvation 32, 51, 56, 61, 71
Salvation Army 99
sangoma 112
Schism and Renewal in Africa. *See also* Barrett, David B.
scholarships 13, 25
sectarians 15
sects 64
seers 146. *See also* prophet
Sefophe 50
Selly Oak Colleges 28, 102
seminars 17, 24, 95, 113, 165
separatist 64, 147
separatist churches 9, 10
Serowe 125, 177

Sesotho 162
Setswana 76, 77, 84, 110, 117, 139, 149–151, 160
sexuality 77, 97
Sierra Leone 11, 105
sin 123, 145
sing 53, 64, 88, 149, 162
singing 71, 106, 119, 125, 134, 138, 149, 151, 171, 186. *See also* song
Sitegi 114
song 88, 125, 134, 146, 150, 169, 172, 183, 184. *See also* hymns
South Africa 19, 31, 33, 54, 81, 87, 98, 108, 112, 115, 127, 155, 157, 187, 188
spell 165
spirits 79, 81, 113, 123, 143, 146, 147, 162
spiritual 81
Spiritual Churches 165. *See* African Spiritual Churches (ASC)
Spiritual Healing Church 33, 71, 90, 92, 108, 110, 119, 124, 125, 127, 138, 177, 178
spoken word 84
St. John's Apostolic Faith Mission 83
St. John's Healing Church 33
St. Michael's Apostolic Church 76, 177
stomping 138
student center 18
study guides 67, 82, 110, 163
Sudan Interior Mission 107
Swahili 98
Swaziland 19, 26, 44, 72, 76, 80, 98, 112, 139, 173–176, 187, 188
syncretistic 9, 46, 64

T
Tata 183
teaching 35, 95, 97, 125. *See also* Bible teaching
testimonies 26, 57, 100, 132, 146, 148
thanksgiving 39, 93, 98, 146
The Church of Jesus Christ 14
The Church of Melchizedek 78

The Council of African Indigenous
    Churches 78
The Eternal Sacred Order of the
    Cherubim and Seraphim.
    See Cherubim and Seraphim
    Church
The Head Mountain of God Holy
    Apostolic Church in Zion 33,
    177
The Holy Nazarene Church 33
theological education 86, 163, 164
theological education by extension
    (TEE) 116
Theological Education by Extension
    (TEE) College 82
Theological Education Fund 13
theological study 13, 167
theological training. See also Bible
    teaching
The Theological Education Fund (TEF)
    24
The Uyo Story 137, 141
time 68, 118, 123
tithe 32
Togo 24
tongues 153
traditional 27, 33, 42, 49, 75, 85, 86,
    103, 112, 139, 143, 147, 177, 180,
    185
training leaders 16, 59, 104, 113, 128,
    135, 163, 165, 167, 169, 172, 173
train women 40
transformation 100, 103, 174, 178
trauma healing 104
Trinity College 24
Tshepong Counselling Center 111, 187
Tswana 160, 161, 176, 177
Twi 98, 123, 142

U
UCBC. See United Churches Bible
    College
uniforms 120, 124, 125, 127
Union of Harrist Youth of Côte d'Ivoire
    59

United Churches Bible College
    (UCBC) 37
United Church of Ghana 142
United States 25, 116, 159, 176
unity 50, 156
Unity Church 151
Universal Prayer Fellowship 38
Université de l'Alliance Chrétienne
    d'Abidjan (UACA). See FATEAC
    (Faculté de Théologie
    Evangélique de l'Alliance
    Chrétienne)
University of Ghana 24, 143
University of South Africa 86
University of Swaziland 99
Uyo 37, 41

V
vision 93, 106
Volta 24

W
war 17, 104
Western-Initiated Churches (WICs)
    41, 42
Western Kenya Diocese of the Anglican
    Church 12
white churches 152
White Cross Society 143
white people 46, 56, 57, 82, 106, 109,
    110, 115, 116, 138, 162
white robe 26, 28, 42, 106, 122, 144,
    145
witness 60, 64, 72, 85, 90, 91, 94, 103,
    177, 189
women 26, 74, 77, 82, 96, 98, 99, 112,
    119, 123, 125, 142, 171, 174, 183,
    185
women's Bible studies 40
women's meetings 73, 111
word 42, 47, 55, 70, 71, 79, 81, 98, 113,
    142, 160, 161, 165, 166, 181
workshops 119, 127, 128, 155
World Council of Churches 12, 24, 107
World Evangelism Ministry 38

worldviews 33, 63, 64, 93, 124
worship 28, 29, 64, 83, 87, 88, 98, 106,
111, 119, 121, 134, 138, 145, 146,
160, 162, 167, 169, 171, 174, 182,
183

X
Xhosa 128

Y
YMCA 142, 165
Yocoboué 59, 70, 171, 172
Yoruba 124
youth 59, 76, 117, 119, 140, 149, 155,
173, 175, 176
youth camp 175
youth center 187
youth conferences 99
youth leaders 33, 70, 117, 140, 158, 183
youth ministry 99, 117, 139

Z
Zambia 12
Zimbabwe 19, 86, 187, 188
Zionist 44, 82, 99, 113, 127–129, 139,
155, 173–175

People Index

A
Aby, Raoul 61
Adedokun, Manasse 153
Adegoke, Prophetess 29
Agbalenyo, Christopher 142
Ahui, John 18, 59, 60
Akousi, Julien 60
Aldén, Karl 9
Amoah, Herbert 25
Amoah, James 25
Andersson, Efraim 14
Anin, Pierre 59, 60
Annang, E. L. 25
Anquandah 79
Anquandah, James Kwesi 24
Ansre, Gilbert 24

B
Barrett, David B. 12, 101
Bender, Philip and Julie 39, 58, 94, 95
Benoît, Papa N'Guessan 70
Bergen, Lynell 188
Bertsche, James E. 14, 19
Bertsche, Tim 120, 140, 187
Bertsche, Tim and Laura 139
Beugré Alphonse Kobli 172–73
Bohn, John and Tina 115
Bolokwe, Bethuel 52, 151
Bolokwe, Mma Tiny 52
Boschman, Don 151, 176, 178
Boschman, Kathleen 52
Boschman, Mary Kay 176

C
Célestin, Djako 133
Charles, Howard 143
Coleman, Joseph 23

D
Dagadu, Mrs. 98
Daneel, M.L. (Inus) 86
Diangienda, Kuntima 15
Diéké, Lazare 183–185
Diéké, Odette 185
Dirks, Rudy 182, 187
Dirks, Rudy and Sharon 110
Ditsheko, Otsile Osimilwe 33, 102, 124, 138, 177, 187
Djorogo, Richard 158, 159
Dlamini, Isaac 112, 113, 115
Doe, Prophet 146
Doh, Prophet 143, 144, 147
Dougall, J. W. C. 10
Dube, Musa 49
Dyck, Bryan 188
Dyck, Buddy and Lois 138, 139

E
Egli, Jim 128
Eirene 15
Ellis, K. B. 24
Ens, Bill 162

F
Fakudze, Makeh 27
Fast, Kathy 178
Fatunmbi, Femi 124
Fehderau, Harold 14, 15
Fischer, Larry 151
Freeman, S. P. 23
Frey, Nancy 75
Friesen, Stan 96
Fynn, Paul 23, 24

G
Gaborone (persons proper name) 183

Goldschmidt-Nussbaumer, Daniel and Marianne 17
Grove, Erma 24, 58, 61, 78

H
Hamm, Peter and Betty 17
Harris, William Wadé 59, 60, 64, 69, 172
Henry, Harry 17, 41
Herr, Robert 128
Hiebert, Paul 65
Hills, Larry 128
Hollinger-Janzen, Lynda 133
Hollinger-Janzen, Rodney 28
Hollinger-Janzen, Rodney and Lynda 17, 74
Hostetter, B. Charles and Grace 13
Hostetter, Charles 105, 107
Hostetter, Darrel 99, 175
Hostetter, Darrel and Sherill 176

I
Isaac, Gary 128
Isaac, Gary and Jean 128

J
Jacobs, Donald 19, 65
Janzen, Diane 117
Juhnke, James 19, 160

K
Kimbangu, Simon 14, 64
Kraay, Robert 24
Krabill, James 70, 130, 172, 179, 183–186
Krabill, James and Jeanette 18, 59, 60, 171–173
Krabill, Russell and Martha 153
Krow, Solomon 23, 121, 165

L
Larson, Jonathan P. 117, 125, 130, 140, 151. *See also* Rra Diane
Lekuta, Rachel 33, 84
Lerrigo, P. H. J. 9

Letsatse 56
Loba, Pita 60
Loewen, Jacob 65
Loram, C. T. 9

M
Madimabe, Joel 50, 51
Maka, Cornelius 54–56
Mallela, Pastor J. K. 67
Maluke, Clive 187
Mambo, Veliswa 26, 27
Mandela, Nelson 129
Markos, Antonious 101
Marumo, Lilian 91
Matakule, Peter 33
Matshediso, Ms. 180, 182, 183
McLaughlin, Sandy 120
Miller, Elinor 120
Miller, Marlin 18, 41
Mills, Frank 94, 165
Mogomela, Golwelwang Paul 117, 119
Mogomela, Onkabetse 117
Mohono, Ntate Sam 102
Mohono, Samuel 162
Moilwa, Benjamin 90, 91
Mokaleng, Prophet 91, 110. *See* Motswaosele, Jacob
Molake, T. L. 91
Morapedi, Silas 33
Moshoeshoe, Isaac 162
Moshoeshoe, Rebecca 116
Moshweshwe, Fanani 76
Mothetho, Philip 160, 161
Motibe 56
Motswaosele, Israel 71, 91, 108, 119, 125, 138, 177, 178
Motswaosele, Jacob 90
Motswaosele, Joseph 124, 125
Msibi, Makeh 44

N
Nketia, Kwabena 165
Nsiah, Emmanuel 25
Ntapo, Mthethiseni 54
Nussbaum, Stan 102

Nxumalo, Hlobisile 98

O
Oduro, Thomas 102, 130
Oyer, Mary 143

P
Pretorius, Hennie 127

Q
Quinn, Melanie 117

R
Ramseyer, Robert 65
Regier, Fremont 151
Reimer, Brian 162
Reimer, Brian and Tricia 115
Rosti, Taboka 187
Roth, Willard 165, 169, 170
Roth, Willard and Alice 24, 46
Rra Diane 151. *See* also Larson, Jonathan P.
Rudy, Carolyn 79, 80
Rueben, Freedman 33

S
Sanneh, Lamin 63
Sawatzky, Joseph and Anna 81, 157
Schloneger, Wendell 62
Seasole, Isaac 151
Shank, David A. 102, 172
Shank, David and Wilma 15, 18, 171
Shenk, Wilbert 101
Shepherd, R. H. W. 9, 10
Spruth, Ed and Lorraine 39, 58
Spruth, Erwin 24
Sundkler, Bengt 10

T
Tetteh, Emmanuel 24
Thompson, Jack 28
Tshandu, Mavis 188
Tshwene, John 121
Turner, Harold W. 11, 13, 28
Tutu, Desmond 24, 107

U
Udoh, Frank 136

W
Wambugu, Njeru 186
Weaver, Edwin 18, 23, 37, 41, 160, 165
Weaver, Edwin and Irene 11, 12, 16, 19, 24, 26, 33, 37, 78, 83, 92, 119, 121, 137, 164, 169
Weaver, Irene 141, 142, 170
Wenger, Harold and Christine 26
Wiebe-Johnson, Steve and Dorothy 17
Wilton, Bishop 155
Wontumi, Isaac 25
Wright, P. Andrew 91

Langham Literature and its imprints are a ministry of Langham Partnership.

Langham Partnership is a global fellowship working in pursuit of the vision God entrusted to its founder John Stott –

> *to facilitate the growth of the church in maturity and Christ-likeness through raising the standards of biblical preaching and teaching.*

Our vision is to see churches in the Majority World equipped for mission and growing to maturity in Christ through the ministry of pastors and leaders who believe, teach and live by the word of God.

Our mission is to strengthen the ministry of the word of God through:
- nurturing national movements for biblical preaching
- fostering the creation and distribution of evangelical literature
- enhancing evangelical theological education

especially in countries where churches are under-resourced.

Our ministry

Langham Preaching partners with national leaders to nurture indigenous biblical preaching movements for pastors and lay preachers all around the world. With the support of a team of trainers from many countries, a multi-level programme of seminars provides practical training, and is followed by a programme for training local facilitators. Local preachers' groups and national and regional networks ensure continuity and ongoing development, seeking to build vigorous movements committed to Bible exposition.

Langham Literature provides Majority World preachers, scholars and seminary libraries with evangelical books and electronic resources through publishing and distribution, grants and discounts. The programme also fosters the creation of indigenous evangelical books in many languages, through writer's grants, strengthening local evangelical publishing houses, and investment in major regional literature projects, such as one volume Bible commentaries like *The Africa Bible Commentary* and *The South Asia Bible Commentary*.

Langham Scholars provides financial support for evangelical doctoral students from the Majority World so that, when they return home, they may train pastors and other Christian leaders with sound, biblical and theological teaching. This programme equips those who equip others. Langham Scholars also works in partnership with Majority World seminaries in strengthening evangelical theological education. A growing number of Langham Scholars study in high quality doctoral programmes in the Majority World itself. As well as teaching the next generation of pastors, graduated Langham Scholars exercise significant influence through their writing and leadership.

To learn more about Langham Partnership and the work we do visit **langham.org**

www.ingramcontent.com/pod-product-compliance
Lightning Source LLC
Chambersburg PA
CBHW071434150426
43191CB00008B/1120